The Gender of Oppression

By the same author:

Birth and Afterbirth: A Materialist Account
'Sex' at 'Work': The Power and Paradox of Organisation Sexuality
(with Wendy Parkin)

The Gender of Oppression

Men, Masculinity, and the Critique of Marxism

Jeff Hearn

St. Martin's Press
New York

First published in the United States of America in 1987

Printed in Great Britain

ISBN 0–312–00962–3

Library of Congress Cataloging-in-Publication Data
Hearn, Jeff.
    The gender of oppression.
    Bibliography: p.
    Includes index.
    1. Men. 2. Masculinity (Psychology). 3. Marxian
school of sociology. 4. Patriarchy. I. Title.
HQ1090.H43   1987   305.3′1   87–9542
ISBN 0–312–00962–3

Contents

Figures

Acknowledgements

Much of the inspiration for writing this book has come from work, politics, theorising, and experience in various collective situations and struggles—in particular in men's consciousness-raising groups and men against sexism groups; the Politics of Reproduction Seminar Group, and the Men and Masculinity Study Group at Bradford University; the Bradford Under-fives Group; and the *Low Plains Drifter* newsletter collective.

In addition there are very many individuals with whom I have talked or corresponded on the questions examined; it is not possible to mention all of these by name. However, I would particularly like to acknowledge the specific assistance, be it information, conversation, or encouragement, of the following people: Bob Ashcroft, John Barker, Peter Bluckert, Gavin Bissell, David Butcher, Bill Bytheway, Bernard Campbell, Alan Carling, Kate Carr, Nicky Colston, Celia Davies, Mary Ann Elston, Harry Ferguson, David Ford, Alison Froggatt, Jean Gardiner, Hilary Graham, Julia Graham, Jacqui Halson, Kerry Hamilton, Dave Harrison, Jay Hearn, Owen Heathcote, Lesley Jenkins, Jim Kincaid, Chris Knight, Mary Locking, Mark Long, Andy Metcalf, Paul Morrison, Keith Motherson, Albert Pannell, Jan Pahl, Wendy Parkin, Christine Parton, Graham Partridge, Maggie Pearse, Val Remy, Yvonne Roberts, Satya Schofield, Margaret Stacey and Chris Tribble.

Invaluable information from Europe and North America has been provided by Eugene August, Harry Brod, Sam Femiano, Michael Kimmel, Hans-Peter Lütjen, Joseph Pleck and Frans van Velden.

I am also grateful for permission to reprint extracts from the following: the Achilles Heel Collective for chapters 2, 3, 4 of

Birth and Afterbirth: A Materialist Account, London (1983);
the British Sociological Association for 'Notes on patriarchy,
professionalisation and the semi-professions', *Sociology*, 16
(1982); Radical Community Medicine for 'Childbirth, men and
the problem of fatherhood', *Radical Community Medicine*, 15
(1984); Paul Morrison for 'Our common ground ...', *anti-sexist men's newsletter*, 10 (1980); Keith Motherson for *Sleep
Well, Father Marx* (n.d.(b)); Margaret Stacey for 'Masculine
or feminine power? Action in the public domain', (1982), and
for 'The application of feminist theory to a study of the
retention of male power: the case of researching the General
Medical Council', (1986).

Finally, I offer special thanks to Romesh Vaitilingam
formerly of Wheatsheaf Books for his encouragement and
support; to Janet Tyrrell, and to the staff of Wheatsheaf Books
Ltd for their hard work and guidance; to Sue Moody for her
superb typing; and to those I live with, Amy, Jay, Molly, and
Tom, for so much.

Foreword

Here, I write of men. I apprehend this with an intense involvement and a dread alienation. As such, this text is contradictory. It is delivered with deep pessimism and joyous optimism. The pessimism lies in men's remorseless and potential domination at almost all times and in almost all spheres; the optimism jumps out from the fact that men can be different, can be loving, sharing, caring and intimate. This is a fact from my experience with other men.

I shall consider the huge power that men have and maintain over women, and over children; and yet at the same time the ways in which that power is becoming less certain, so that and as men we become less certain of ourselves.[1] Paradoxically in that lesser certainty, and even in an increasing alienation, we may find ourselves.[2] I shall therefore write from a position of sympathy and solidarity with men, and yet also with a continuous auto-critique of men.

There are many possible ways of theorising 'men'—at least as many as there are theoretical approaches within sociology and social science. Men may be, for example, seen as 'essentially' biological substances, as receivers of sex-role socialisation, as bearers of social role, as psychologically 'masculine' essences, as productive 'labourers'. My specific task is to write in a critical relationship to the major radical and progressive tradition that men have created in this kind of society, namely marxism. This involves the production of a critique of men through the means and method of marxism, and a critique of marxism by means of a focus upon rather than the usual neglect of men. And yet straightaway there is a problem, for there is of course a mass of literature already on men within marxism as within other social theories and practices. However, most of this speaks of 'men', without attending to the social construction or determination of men. In the worst cases, men are equated with the human race of all genders, while in many works of Marx and of marxism men are equated with workers. Both of these formulations are unsatisfactory in that they fail to investigate men as 'men', socially produced, and fail to understand what men have in common with each other and what it is that distinguishes different types of men.

To pursue these questions necessitates much more specific attention to the social location and position of men; to our (that is, men's) frequent oppression and control of women; our diverse forms of alienation; and how together our power and our alienation produce, socially construct, what we recognise as 'masculinity', in its own diverse forms. These are the major themes developed throughout the text.

There are both pragmatic and strategic reasons for pursuing this task. In pragmatic terms, I have accumulated in recent years a short book, a number of completed published papers, a number of completed unpublished conference papers, and outlines of papers prepared for public lectures and seminars on the questions of gender, men and masculinity. These are necessarily scattered, but together they form a body of words on these topics as outlined. Thus this book has not been written from scratch, or from some overriding act of will; rather it has largely been written almost inadvertently. Having said that, the way in which these various papers have developed with definite interrelations means that there are some overlaps and repetitions within them. The more glaring and inconvenient have been edited out. These papers have a story of their own.[3]

The strategic reason is that as far as I can see no such book at present exists. There is of course the large amount of literature within socialist feminism or marxist feminism that implicitly at least addresses men's power. However, that remains distinct from this project in two important ways. Firstly, it usually explores the 'marxism' rather more fully than the 'feminism', so that in the final analysis the roots of oppression are usually located in economic class relations rather than gender relations. Although this is an area of great complexity and debate, there are few marxist feminist writers who would appear to see gender oppression as more fundamental. Some attempt to resolve the difficulty by adopting a dualist analysis of the two major systems of oppression.[4] Secondly, this existing body of literature is quite understandably written by women, and centrally concerned with women, women's experiences and women's economic plight.[5]

That literature that does focus in a more critical way upon men and masculinity rarely does so from a marxist or a dialectical materialist perspective. Much of this literature is American in origin and culturalist in its theoretical assumptions. It tends to be centrally concerned with such issues as men's roles at work, at home, at play; changing forms of masculinity in terms of changing values; the variety of men's 'cultures'. Important as these are (as shall be seen in chapter 1), they do not necessarily address some of the more fundamental problems of men's power, nor perhaps the lived complexities of men's experience.

In contrast to both of these approaches, marxist feminist and 'men's culturalism', the project here is to analyse and change men and men's practice through the tenets of dialectical materialism. In doing so it is intended to constitute a critique of marxism, in its usual and present malestream[6] forms at least. This is a book that is therefore about men, gender and oppression.

By 'gender' I refer to the social construction of sex and sexual division(s) to produce, however indirectly, sex-related categorisations and classifications of people.[7] The term 'oppression' is a shorthand for social practices, tendencies and relations that discriminate against, ignore, neglect, degrade or harm people, to *reduce* people to less than human.[8] It is thus both a specific term, as in the harming of another person, and global, in its implication of reaching out to a fuller humanity of greater ability, variability, flexibility, and commitment to labouring for all life. It also refers to direct actions, say of murder and torture, and less direct social relations, such as the oppression of the Third World by the neglect and the domination of the first two. Oppression thus rests on some form of unfair denial of or exclusion from a preferable alternative course of action, such as in the gender case, women's control of their own fertility or sexuality.[9]

In this context the title, *The Gender of Oppression*, is a deliberate ambiguity. First, men are the gender of oppression. We are the gender which routinely engages in the oppression of others, women, children and indeed animals. But we also oppress ourselves and each other. Part of the process of oppressing women and children is that some men oppress others. Some men, such as soldiers in war, suffer particularly and viciously. Thus oppression is more complex than simply one set of people oppressing another set. Indeed, oppression itself has a *gendered* character. In this and most other societies, oppression even when it has other bases or other visible expressions, for example, in class or race or disability, still occurs in gendered ways. In other words, even when oppression *appears* as, say, class oppression, as in the selling of wage labour, the form that it takes in actual situations involves gender. Thus we are concerned here with a second meaning of the gender of oppression, namely the gender *dimension* present within oppression. After all, bearing in mind that we live in a profoundly patriarchial society, it would be rather surprising if particular social events, and especially social oppressions, were found to be ungendered. The *genderic* nature of oppression characteristically comprises part of the other oppressions, such as those of class and age.

Finally, some brief comments are necessary on the general structure of this book. The first section, 'Problematic men, problematic masculinity', is concerned with some of the implications of feminism for an understanding of men and masculinity. Chapter 1, 'The personal is political is theoretical', considers these three reasons for a focused attention upon men and masculinity; chapter 2 presents a more detailed account of possible causes and explanations of the problematisation of men and masculinity. This involves description of relevant social forces, as well as some of the reactions of both women and men to the social changes of feminism.

The remainder of the book is divided into three main sections: on theorising patriarchy and reproduction, on the work of reproduction (or reproductive work), on politics and practice. The 'theory' section considers the concept of patriarchy, the relationship of production and reproduction, marxism and feminism, theories on and about reproduction, and the major institutions through which reproduction is controlled by men and patriarchy is maintained.

'The patriarchal organisation of reproductive work' section begins with a review of men's various involvements in and continuing domination of reproduction and reproductive work. It continues with analyses of the power of the 'professions' and 'semi-professions', and their impact upon the construction of masculinity.

The final section on 'Politics and practice' considers the implications of the previous more general analyses for re-evaluating and changing men's practice. Four particular areas are examined: fatherhood, childcare, men's anti-sexist politics, and the 'professional' work of the social sciences. These are chosen because of my own personal involvement and experience within them. This final section attempts to develop positive and specific strategies and possibilities for practice. Needless to say the ideas considered in the previous more general sections have been developed over a number of years from practice. The theory though subsequent to practice, is placed first here for convenience; in practice it has come out of practice.[10]

May 1986, Bradford

Part 1

Problematic Men, Problematic Masculinity

INTRODUCTION

One of the hardest things for men to do is to take feminism seriously. To do so can seriously change our lives. It is difficult for men to begin to appreciate the enormity of what feminists are saying, and have been saying for many years. And just as white people rarely give much attention to the effects of white domination on black people, so it is difficult for men to appreciate what it might be like for women to live in a society and a world where (almost) every sphere of life is dominated by men.

Having said that, feminism, in its multitude of forms and expressions, can certainly have immense impacts on men. These can occur in all areas of life, from the apparently most trivial to world historical events. For me, they have occurred in my 'private' and domestic life, in men's groups and similar activities, in politics and especially childcare politics, in my paid work, in writing, giving talks, and so on. Some of these were described in the short book, *Birth and Afterbirth: A Materialist Account*, published in 1983. Writing that book, over the period from 1978 to 1983, showed me that we need to be aware of a number of interrelated aspects of change: personal experience, work, politics and theory. From about 1980 it became more and more apparent to me that in addition to reacting to feminism, an urgent task was to specifically and proactively address the reformulation of men, in all of these aspects.

The impetus for clarifying these ideas initially developed with the presentation of a number of papers in academic and

3

similar contexts. These included 'Patriarchy, social policy and men's practice' at the Critical Social Policy Conference on Socialist Strategies for Welfare, Sheffield Polytechnic, April 1982 (1982b); 'Conceptualising men' in the workshop, 'Men, Sexism and Social Work', Department of Sociology and Social Administration, University of Sussex, April 1983; and 'Are men a serious issue?' at the Interdisciplinary Human Studies Forum, University of Bradford, November 1983. Giving these and other talks around this time demonstrated that putting these issues 'upfront' was not only urgent but also often emotionally and personally demanding both for myself and for others present. These first two chapters arise out of these papers, with their attempts to make sense of what feminism says of men and masculinity, and how men can look at, understand, and change ourselves. Above all taking feminism seriously has meant taking 'men' seriously, though not necessarily with seriousness.

To complete the story, parts of the first chapter have been more recently presented in papers on 'Changing men's studies: problems, possibilities and promises' at the Social Analysis Research Seminar, University of Bradford, February 1986, and the British Sociological Association Annual Conference on the Sociology of the Life Cycle, Loughborough University, March 1986 (1986a). I am grateful to all those who have participated in these various sessions, and so have become critical contributors to the next.

1 The Personal is Political is Theoretical[1]

The rise of the Women's Liberation Movement and of modern feminism have brought about a deep questioning of what it is to be a woman. An indirect, yet surely inevitable, consequence of this process has been a growing questioning of what it is to be a man. This is to be seen in a whole range of changes in men's expressed feelings, action and activities, as we attempt to redefine our masculinity. We may note, for example, the development of unisex or bisexual images, and the frequently apolitical blurring of gender roles in pop culture, as in the Boy George, Marilyn, Sigue Sigue Sputnik, and other members of the 'gender bender' phenomenon. Men also seem urged by both the leaders of pop fashion and commercial advertisers to change their clothes, wear skirts, make-up and jewellery.[2] Men's images and masculinity are fragmented, softened, subtly altered by reference and allusion.[3] Men occasionally appear in advertisements as sensual, caring, even effeminate; the 'new man' phenomenon, a true creation of the media, is promoted in magazines and television, particularly in America but now also in Britain, Australia and elsewhere;[4] and sportsmen and trade unionists weep in public in times (and perhaps as signs) of victory and defeat. Increasingly, though not for the first time, masculinity is in 'crisis' (Kimmel, 1987).

Alongside these cultural changes there are at a more general, structural level, a number of major social changes for men, such as the loss of interest in the traditional male 'breadwinner role' with increased divorce, rising unemployment and even 'men's liberation'. Perhaps most important are the various direct and indirect impacts of feminism, and men's various

5

responses to feminism—on one hand, feminist critiques of dominant masculinity,[5] male violence and patriarchal power; on the other, a variety of men's responses, from outright hostility to sympathetic stances, in the form of men's anti-sexist groups and other activities. No longer is it possible to take for granted maleness or masculinity. No longer is there one particular dominant model of masculinity. And yet while men and masculinity are problematic, men still are powerful, perhaps even more powerful. The macho backlash comes in all shapes and guises, from the Rambo and Rocky film culture to imperialist 'gunboat diplomacy' and escalating state violence. Men's power remains, while that power is becoming less certain, so that men are becoming less certain of ourselves. As men and masculinity have become more problematic, we/they have come to be seen more as 'topics' for study and observation. To pursue this dual theme I shall consider in more detail possible justifications and reasons for men turning to consider ourselves and our masculinity as problematic, through the three interrelated realms of the personal, the political and the theoretical.

THE PERSONAL

During the late sixties and early seventies I had a rather vague awareness of sexual politics. The American Civil Rights Movement, Black Power, Paris 1968, the British student 'revolts', feminism itself, the New Left, the anti-Vietnam war protests, all had in their different ways raised the radical critique of society, including, in different ways, gender roles.[6] Yet the same period was one of confidence, 'affluence', optimism, governmental reform, the further development of the 'managerial revolution'.[7] The progressivism typical of the period meant that all things were possible, including the liberal democratic rational reform of opportunities for all, all genders and all races. I lived very much at the time in this contradiction, with an unspoken pledge of support to the social changes of both types. I accepted that I had to 'knuckle down' and do a 'little better' than previous generations of men on these counts; but though my sympathy with various radical causes was considerable, my overt consciousness of what sexual politics and feminism meant to me(n) was small.

In 1972 I started buying *Spare Rib*, when it was subtitled a 'news magazine' before becoming a 'women's magazine' and then a 'women's liberation magazine', simply because it was the best magazine around. From this, one of the first concrete, or rather conscious contacts, with the possibility of questioning what men and masculinity are came in the following year. While holidaying in Tenby in South Wales I was surprised to find in a local bookshop a copy of the *SCUM Manifesto* (Solanas, 1971). This quiet Welsh coast had offered up nothing less than the document of the Society for Cutting Up Men, a text written by Valerie Solanas, famed for her shooting of Andy Warhol. She had produced a powerful and angry attack on men, the message of which has remained with me. She wrote:

Every man, deep down, knows he's a worthless piece of shit. Overwhelmed by a sense of animalism and deeply ashamed of it; wanting, not to express himself, but to hide from others his total physicality, total egocentricity, the hate and contempt he feels for other men, and to hide from himself the hate and contempt he suspects other men feel for him.   (1971, 7)

And yet hurtful as these words might appear, they slid off me because I knew them partly to be true. They even gave me a kind of reassurance in explaining that the world we lived in was at least controlled, if not subjugated, by these nasty forms of manhood. The feelings of things-not-being-quite-right could be attributed to the peculiar ways in which men and I had developed under their effects.

My personal awareness of the 'male gender role' had become a little sharper. The subsequent year, 1974, I was fortunate to get a job as a lecturer at the University in Bradford. I began to develop the practice of encouraging, where possible, student participation in the direction and content of courses. In 1977 when planning with students the detailed structure and content of a final-year course on Organisations and Groups, a great deal of interest was expressed by the predominantly female student group in issues of sexual discrimination, the sexual division of labour, and so on. I was very enthusiastic about this development, particularly in view of the gender-blindness and sexism of most organisational sociology. Accordingly, a series of seminars on these and related questions were begun, which provided me with a direct link with issues of gender in my own personal paid work. More particularly these working and academic experiences caused me to reflect more and more on the implications of the sexual division of labour, sexual oppression and so on, for me and men. Even the academic study of such issues is a personal experience, something that still remains largely unrecognised.[8]

The following year, 1978, I was involved in forming a men's group, initially within the University department where I worked. At first this was a closed group of teaching and research staff. The group developed with an understandable caution; after a number of months its composition changed and its base shifted outside work, with a broader range of members. Although that group was slow to become consciously against sexism, it provided me with a very valued experience, of getting to know a few men closely. In it I also found the relief of being able to talk of difficult areas, such as marriage, homosexuality, rape, that contributed to my masculinity.

Since then my absorption in the questions and questioning of men and masculinity has continued in all sorts of activities and experiences. Perhaps most important has been *just being with* men, and enjoying it a lot. This period has produced many experiences of friendship, intimacy and sexuality, experiences about birth, childcare and childwork, that do not fit the traditional stereotypes and models of masculinity, and do not seem to be adequately reflected in what one might call the sex differences or the sex-role socialisation literature.[9] Frequently these (my) experiences of being a man have been unclear, confused, subtle, intimate, contradictory, joyful, painful, bodily—what some would describe as not worthy of a 'real man' at all. And that may be the point, for reassessing men and masculinity necessitates a revaluation of men, and the less articulated and less familiar aspects of masculinity, to give them worth. Paradoxically, although men clearly have great power relative to and over women in certain crucial respects, such as through the control of public positions, men, and especially certain qualities of men's lives, are at the same time not given much worth and value.

This perspective is elaborated in the Preliminary Report to the International Women's Conference of the Re-evaluation Counselling Communities in 1984, as follows:

Within the society there is a general and almost universal anti-male conditioning as part of the oppression of men. These anti-male attitudes consist of seeing men as mean, more powerful than they actually are, 'innately' rapists, sexually compulsive, 'out to get women', dumb and brutal.

(*Women*, 1985, 49)

The realisation of personal discrepancies with such 'anti-maleness' may lead on to political motivations for change and motivations for political change.

THE POLITICAL

The recognition and appreciation of men's *value* leads quickly to political, and not just personal, considerations. A concern with men, including this project of writing this book, is a political point of prime importance. It is politically necessary for me to turn to men, to what I know about and to what I am. To face other men is to face myself, and vice versa; to face the violence and greet the love of other men is to see myself, and so realise more clearly what makes me personally and men collectively. This is the political inspiration for focusing on (the question of) men and masculinity, both here in writing and elsewhere in life. I emphasise this as there is sometimes a tendency for men concerned about sexism to assume that they should (a) see themselves as feminists and (b) focus politically on women and 'women's issues'. I see these political positions as misguided, a form of 'false consciousness' in the sense that *men cannot be feminists* (Hearn, 1983). Men can clearly be interested in and instructed by feminism—but if feminism is to be theory and practice by women for women, then political participation by men in the women's movement will be likely to interfere with and reduce its autonomy, if only indirectly. A man may well use feminism as a *reference*, as a source of information and insight, as a context, and though this may appear a fine line from *interference* it is still a line all the same; it still leaves men's main problem as ourselves, not women.

Even having said this, to justify a focus on men and masculinity on political grounds in this way is still, I would guess, to invite other misunderstandings. It has to be said bluntly that to advocate a focus on men by men arises out of support for women's liberation and women's action, and not any form of competition, as is sometimes supposed. A political focus on men is intended as complementary, not antagonistic or competitive; support for women's liberation is essential for men. Thus though this may raise practical contradictions in specific situations, men's respect of the autonomy of women and the women's movement can continue alongside men's support of women's liberation, at both an individual and collective level.

An additional problem raised in referring to political justifications, including men's focus on men, stems simply from the historical legacy of men's domination of politics. To justify in terms of the development of 'men's politics' is immediately to bring into vision the already rather well established set of activities and institutions called 'politics'. These comprise the mainstream or malestream political organisations, the political parties, the trade unions, and so on (see Lamm, 1977), based predominantly in the politics of production rather than the politics of reproduction. And it is for this reason that the politics of peace, of food, of water, of freedom from murder, slavery and oppression, are so fundamentally important, being the struggles around the possibility of reproduction at all.[10]

Inextricably linked to these institutional forms of politics are the dominant models of what political practice means to men. Political performance has been one of the most obvious ways for men to show masculinity, and 'machismo', that it is as if this whole human activity has become corrupted. In electioneering, public speaking, 'politicking', the very exercise of power, men have repeatedly shown themselves as visible men. And even though these practices may apply to only a minority, a relative elite, their influence on models of masculinity, in stressing particular kinds of leadership, strength, coercion is considerable and widespread (Parkin and Hearn, 1987; Hearn and Parkin, 1986–87).

Accordingly, a rather cautious approach to politics is appropriate for men concerned to change political relationships with women and other men. Politics with other men thus becomes not just a matter of fighting for 'the cause' in as aggressive and uncompromising manner as possible but in engaging in collective and sometimes public action with men on a quite different basis. This means seeking out and building political initiatives that include changing ourselves and each other, not just opposing some external threat from 'other men'.

THE THEORETICAL

I have already mentioned my increasing frustration with the way much academic writing has seemed at odds with the messy and confusing patterns and experiences of men. Typically the personal and political issues just referred to have not been seen as of importance in the development of most academic and theoretical work. The reasons for this are complex, but they include not only the personal and political orientation of such work, but also the way the 'personal' and the 'political' themselves are analysed. In other words, the recognition of the facts of the existence of the 'personal' and the 'political' is a necessary part of theory. Academic theory that 'chooses' to ignore half of the 'facts' of existence is simply poor theory. While this is not the place to develop a wholesale theory of practice and politics, it is important to recognise that both are apparent *generic* categories, in reality socially produced. Briefly that which we call 'practice' coincides closely with what is deemed personal to people, what is done privately, and what is done in connecting the private towards the public. Practice is a series of attempts to act privately in public, to insert what may be called a private morality into the public realm. Politics appears to derive in the opposite way, from a series of impositions of public standards and styles of life, the application of public over private morality.

Politics thus tends to coincide with what is 'not personal' to people, what is done publicly, and what is done in connecting the public towards the private. These relationships of 'practice', 'politics', private, public do not just occur; they need to be theorised especially in relation to relations between women and men.[11] The very slogan 'the personal is political' problematises these relationships, in crossing the public–private division, and so itself begins theory.

This line of argument is, however, almost unnecessarily sophisticated, or at least several stages on on a path of theoretical development. There are indeed much more basic issues that need attention in theory, of which perhaps the most basic is the still frequent conflation of 'humans' and 'man'/'men'.[12] This is not merely a matter of arbitrary language; it recurs in the sets of assumptions that may be used about what it is to be human. For example, much social theory, including much marxist theory, begins with analysing what people *do* rather than what people *are*. More to the point, social theory analyses what *men do*, particularly what *work* they do, and all the more so what *public, paid, productive work* they do, and then equating all that with 'economic relations', 'economy' or '(economic) classes'. Sometimes the equation is made, less satisfactorily still, with 'humans' or 'society', though Marx himself warned against 'above all ... establishing "society" as an abstraction over against the individual' (Marx, 1975, 350). Following such conflations it may or may not be pointed out that women sometimes do different things, that is, are 'non-men'.

A slightly more complicated interpretation of this kind of theorising is that the doing, the work, public work and so on, are equated not so much with abstractions like 'society' as with the people themselves. Thus the individual, person, woman, man, in this formulation is made equivalent to their labour. Throughout most of his writing, Marx emphasises the prime force of labour in determining social, societal and human development,[13] yet the question remains of how far can people be reduced to their labour. The equation of person and their labour only makes sense if the relevant labour can (a) be performed under a social compulsion and (b) be performed voluntarily, as would be the case with prison 'hard labour' or wage labour respectively. Much reproductive labour, of which 'being in labour' and breast feeding are good examples, is not, or not necessarily, of this sort. With productive labour, people can be socially arranged, by coercion and/or voluntary action to become what they *do*; with reproductive labour people often cannot be so directly arranged. In other words, women and men in different ways have a different *being* rather than *doing* in relation to reproductive labour.

This is not to say that such being is not socially constructed; it clearly is in all sorts of ways. But unlike productive labour women and men are not socially interchangeable, as, for example, within capitalism the capitalists care not for the gender or race or age of workers, as long as they *do* what is necessary to produce surplus value for that given wage; indeed more than that they are indifferent to the 'humanness' of commodity labour; *being in relation to labour* is of no interest. A conflation of labour and the person within capitalism, as a commodity, is not only possible but almost inevitable. Capitalism as a system of social relations in which the person *qua* worker is reduced to their labour also reproduces theorising in which the person is reduced to their labour, as in the marxist tradition. In contrast, in relation to reproductive labour such a conflation of person and labour leaves categories like 'men' and 'women' untheorised. What 'women' and 'men' historically *are* rather than what they *do* is left unsaid in most social theory.

A crucial theoretical problem here seems to be that while the feminist theorisation of the category 'women' can be conducted partly *in opposition to* such conflations and mainstream theory generally, and partly *within separate* practices and politics, this is not possible for the category 'men'. For although 'men' (and 'masculinity') are clearly problematic, this process of theorisation cannot be carried in any simple *opposition* and *separateness*. Such an attempt is likely to breed a petit bourgeois anarchism or 'anti-ism'. Critical theorising of men and masculinity has to be conducted in connection with, not antithesis to, the mass of men. This is for two main reasons. First, critique of men, at least by men, is carried out by those who are part of that 'mass' which is subject to critique. Secondly, dominant theorising, including the conflations mentioned, produced largely by men, is itself part of dominant practices and constructions of men. Critique is thus in contradictory relation to, both part of and not part of, dominant theorising.[14]

To put this 'theoretical' issue more crudely: we, as men, only know about ourselves; we know how partriarchy works in its operation, though not its effects; in particular we know how it works in terms of relations between men, including dominant theorising, which tends to leave 'men' untheorised.

We are thus brought to the question: 'Can there be a men's anti-patriarchal theory?' It is a question worth asking. Can there be a theory that would parallel but not compete with women's theory. Some would say 'no'; it is ridiculous for an oppressor class to propound theory, contradictorily in an anti-patriarchal form. For example, one could argue that it would be meaningless for bourgeois to construct bourgeois anti-capitalist theory, apart from as an extended and convoluted exercise in ideology and smoke-screening. Yet the comparison is not exact—for members of the bourgeoisie can change classes, both individually and collectively; men cannot. It is men's fix in biology that paradoxically creates the possibility of critical, anti-patriarchal theory and practice. If bourgeois are convinced that they want to oppose capitalism they can renounce their social class and change sides; men cannot do that in the same way. It is this contradiction of consciousness and biology that creates the possibility of anti-patriarchal theory—of theory against patriarchy whilst remaining a man.

One possible interpretation of these issues is that rather than (or perhaps in addition to) patriarchy serving capitalism, as suggested in the socialist feminist and marxist feminist traditions, capitalism may serve patriarchy. Capitalism in its conflations of person and labour not only dominates the day-to-day practice of commodity production and exchange, it also dominates (and is reproduced in) the theorising that develops within it. 'Capitalist' theorising thereby could be said to produce a capitalist domination of the mental environment. For if capitalism is superstructure to patriarchy's base, 'capitalist' theorising with its conflations will obscure patriarchal relations.

Patriarchy operates in a somewhat different way from capitalism, despite numerous interrelations. One way of conceptualising patriarchy is as a system of social relations in which the person *qua* woman, or indeed man, is a person solely in terms of their body—so that which is most one's own is 'taken away' (MacKinnon, 1982). This differentiation applies particularly in as much as woman can be distinguished from man, for example through reproduction, sexuality, visible appearance. Thus the conflation of labour and person may obscure, *that is force out of sight*, the conflation of bodily appearance and person under patriarchy. It is in *non-appearance* that the conflation of appearance and other is maintained. Capitalism might be the non-appearance, the obscuring, of patriarchy; patriarchy might well be the non-appearance of appearance: the process of obscuring differentiation of appearance.

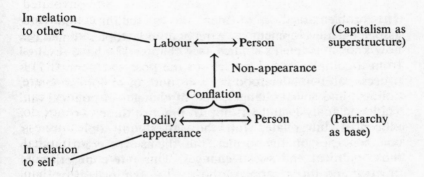

Figure 1:   Appearance and non-appearance in patriarchy and capitalism

These problematisations of men and masculinity at personal, political, and theoretical levels in turn produce the 'topic', indeed the problematic, of men and masculinity. Paradoxically, it is only in the possible disruption of a social phenomenon that it becomes apparent, just as one could argue that the very existence of feminism indicates that women's power is changing.

The doubting and questioning of men and masculinity, the possibility of men being doubted and doubting ourselves, of being questioned and questioning, creates the topic, question, indeed doubt of men and masculinity. Academic discourse, including the structure of 'sciences' and 'human sciences', is in this way a form of conversation, including the doubts and the questions, writ large.

2 Causes, Explanations and Critiques

The problematisation of men and masculinity and their associated development as a recognisable topic, sometimes now known as 'men's studies' (see chapter 12), have resulted from a complex social process in the post-war period. This process can be understood in terms both of major economic, political and social changes, and of changes in political and academic analysis and writing. In practice these two sects of influences interrelate, for the latter not only act as commentaries on the former, but themselves contribute to those political and social changes. This interconnection of practice and theory applies above all in feminist theory and practice, including feminist writing.

MILITARY AND INTERNATIONAL CHANGE

At the global level, there have been immense changes in the 'world order' which, although usually described in the genderless language of international relations, certainly have implications for the production of men and masculinity throughout the world.

Andrew Tolson (1977, 113), writing in the British context, argues for the importance of the world war experience and the subsequent post-imperialism in producing a 'crisis of masculinity'.

The first indications of a masculine emotional crisis became apparent through the experience of war. The suffering of the First World War—as new destructive machinery confronted the anachronistic strategy of trench warfare—is now part of our cultural heritage. But there was also an experience of the Second World War, less apparent in sheer human sacrifice, more a matter of temperament, which has had a 'hidden' historical significance. During the war a feeling of disbelief began to undermine the unquestioning will to fight. This war was the last moment of 'high' British imperialism.... Possibly the involvement of women in the province of men penetrated the soldier's vain-glory. But certainly, for many sections of the middle class, the Second World War shattered the prestige of an imperialist masculinity.

Men, particularly certain sections of the middle classes, have, he suggests, lost their role as confident bearers of culture throughout the Empire. Shepherd Bliss (1985, 3) in the American context presents a rather similar account of more recent events:

It is crucial that we think about our international moment; a key characteristic of our international moment as U.S. men is that the United States lost the war in Viet Nam—the first war that we lost. Then we were humiliated in Iran, and finally ... the United States went into tiny Grenada.... That's where we went to try to resurrect that soldier image, which is one of the places men have historically gone to find their masculinity.[1]

International, military and imperialist relations are of relevance to the construction of men and masculinity in a number of ways: in providing particular forms of activity and labour, in providing models of masculinity, in the expenditure of vast and increasing sums on arms, in killing, seeking to kill, harming, threatening. They are effectively the most drastic and damaging forms of men's public violence; the threat and possibility of conscription and other military involvements leaves a deep oppression on men, even with the abolition of statutory service in Britain.[2]

Changes in imperialist and post-imperialist relations have also had a profound effect on the internal workings of states, particularly in the changing development of ethnic relations. Although it would be a mistake to overstate the extent of racial interaction in Britain, the United States and similar societies, there have been significant changes in the extent to which 'race' can be understood to constitute a *non-problematic* feature of masculinity. A dominant form of imperialist masculinity includes a strict Manichean view of the world, a clear split between Black and White, a perceptual and social apartheid. In short, race has often constituted a significant part of the definition of 'men'. Accordingly, Clyde Franklin (1984, 207) comments that:

White males have generally perceived men to be dominant and decisive, and that those persons who were submissive and indecisive were not men. White males also have been taught that men are nonexpressive and nonemotional.... White males are taught traits of masculinity that are often opposite to the traits many Black males exhibit. Given increased interaction between Black males and White males, their perceptions of each other in all likelihood will be affected.

Thus the changing pattern of interaction at cultural and local levels may reflect and even oppose the changing pattern of international and imperialist relations. Cultural and racial heterogeneity, and associated change in masculinity, may stand in contradiction with attempts to reassert lost masculinist powers of the imperialist stage.

It is no wonder that the rhetoric of mainstream politics frequently makes its appeal to this unspoken knowledge. In the face of threats to imperialism and thus certain sorts of masculinity, 'President Reagan and Mrs. Thatcher sell themselves as military leaders, the leaders of fighting men, real men, not wimps and wets ...' (Metcalf, 1985, 12). The Falklands War proved to be not only a remarkable boost to the electoral fortunes of the Conservative Party, but also through the 'War Cabinet' pronouncements and media coverage in Britain to be a 'War transformed into a paean to manhood, a celebration of the phallus draped in the Union Jack. Resurgent nationalism and a refurbished manhood were fused into one ...' (ibid., 13). These ideological developments should, however, be placed alongside the material pain and damage of men fighting and killing each other.

Heaped upon these international and military matters is the impact of living in the nuclear age—that most terrible creation of men (*sic*) (Easlea, 1983) and yet that ultimate threat to our fragile social and human power. According to Christopher Lasch (1984) the awful possibility of nuclear annihilation creates a deep-seated problem for the sense of self. For men, both as creators of this terribleness and as bearers of frequently externally-directed and alienated senses of self, this may be both senseless and immobilising. Masculinity, in the face of all this, seems to be particularly worthless; any pre-existing sense of worthlessness, which remains a major element in the rearing of boys, may be exacerbated. For those men who find themselves in positions of power, with even partial access to nuclear decisions, such personal and psychological damage could produce more lasting damage. Nuclear power may be the ultimate development and destruction of men's power.[3]

EMPLOYMENT AND UNEMPLOYMENT

The realm of paid work has been and remains important for the creation of men and definitions of masculinity. It is for this reason that it is sometimes suggested that changing patterns of employment, and particularly increasing unemployment, in the capitalist economies of Europe and North America threaten masculinity. At the very least, mass unemployment among men may produce a re-evaluation of 'work'. Indeed, writing in the American context, Franklin (1984, 206) considers that '(i)n the early 1980s thousands of men have suddenly found themselves incapable of fulfilling the requirements of the male sex-role because of the society's economic crisis.'[4] On the other hand, while increases in 'unemployment' may mean that men spend more time at home, this does not necessarily mean an immediate or commensurate change in men's behaviour. Loss of job may mean loss of status, increasing frustration, domestic difficulties, and even a reassertion of a certain sort of 'masculinity' through violence.[5] Additionally, although unemployment means less income, being poor is hardly new to millions of men, especially working-class and ethnic minority men. What is perhaps new is the changing relation of people, especially some young people, to the state, as the prime provider of income support for dependants.

Changes in unemployment patterns also have to be understood in relation to changes in employment patterns, particularly through technological innovation and capital reorganisation. Ann Game and Rosemary Pringle (1983, 28–33) have discussed the numerous associations between industrial and technological divisions and gender divisions, so that 'heavy/light', 'skilled/unskilled', 'dangerous/less dangerous', 'dirty/clean', 'interesting/boring', 'mobile/immobile' are all seen as reproducing 'male/female' to some extent, especially in men's perceptions. Thus to remain in the limited number of 'less hard' jobs may produce as much questioning of masculinity as to become unemployed. Indeed some men may welcome this kind of 'release' as indeed they may welcome the entry of women into new sectors of paid work (Cockburn, 1983, 117–18, 110).[6]

CHANGE IN THE FAMILY

The changing structure of the employment and unemployment market, in size, gender division and technological structure is paralleled by changes in family and household structure. For example, between 1970 and 1980, the proportion of 'non-family' households increased from 18.8 to 26.1 per cent in the United States (Turner, 1984, 151). Not only is the mixed gender two-parent 'nuclear' family much less common than in the recent past but the *internal* workings of families are themselves subject to transformation, in terms of the declining authority of the father, men's loss of interest in the role of 'breadwinner' (for others) (Ehrenreich, 1983) and so on. On the other hand, such tendencies may not necessarily undermine associations of masculinity and money, and its control.[7]

Not only are individual fathers more problematic as fathers, but so too is any crude notion of patriarchy, as determined by the power of the family father alone. Instead the 'father figure' is becoming transubstantiated into the body of the state, the professions, and the law. These new 'fathers' are both massive material entities and symbolic of the family father (see chapters 5 and 6).

The family, the experience of women, and indeed the power of men have all been further transformed by changes in patterns of fertility, and the form, availability and use of contraception, both outside and within marriage. According to

O'Brien (1981), the development, or the possibility, of (near-) universal contraception is a major 'world historical event', shifting the relations of reproduction, promoting both the entry of women into the public sphere and the growth of modern feminism. Men are thereby and equivalently changed, perhaps even shocked, by the loss of (potential) power. Meanwhile other changes in family structure follow from population ageing, in Western societies at least. More men survive into 'old age'; more marriages include substantial non-fertile years; and more men need more caring, often in practice provided by women. Again the impact of these changes is likely to be mixed, with more visibility of older men and their images, and yet the perpetuation of pre-existing patterns, for example, between wives and husbands.[8]

As with employment patterns, men may experience, through familial changes, a release from ties and/or a sense of anomie (see Doyle, 1983). Changes in family structure and process have occurred in association with an increased sensitivity and valuation of men as persons and as *bodies*. Men may be more aware of the 'hazards of being male' (Franklin, 1984, 206; Ehrenreich, 1983; Goldberg, 1976)[9] may admit feelings, cry, at 'family crisis' of birth, divorce, death, and seek to define themselves as *being more than* familial or formal work roles. Such changes are not necessarily caused directly by changes in the family; they represent the more visible expression of uncertainties surrounding how men have and conduct private lives.

FEMINIST CRITIQUES OF MEN

These causes and explanations of the problematising of men and masculinity—international, employment, domestic—have all been the focus of attention for feminist analysis. Indeed the very separation of causes into such distinct types or levels is itself open to critique. Such apparent divisions, if viewed too rigidly, merely reproduce an ideology founded on separation, between class and gender, even between economy and ideology, so dominant in this society. Furthermore, feminist theory and practice have themselves both been a major force for social change, including the critique of men and masculinity. Before considering some of these, some initial, cautionary points need to be made. First, while there are definite dangers of men writing 'on' feminism, it would be ridiculous and uninformative for me to ignore feminist critiques of men in this text. Secondly, the prime concern of feminist theory and practice has characteristically been women, women's oppression and liberation, and women's experience. Accordingly, men are characteristically of secondary interest, and defined *implicitly*, as, say, doers of violence to women. Thirdly, it is necessary to emphasise that feminist theories/practices are immensely varied, so that men and masculinity assume different significances within different feminist approaches and analyses, even though the recognition of sisterhood and reduction of the excessive power of men are probably unifying themes of feminism.[10]

In some radical feminist theory/practice men may be literally ignored. Men may become the 'main enemy' (Delphy, 1977), to be treated accordingly. The *Redstockings Manifesto* of 1969 put this *class* analysis clearly enough:

In reality, every such relationship [between a woman and a man] is a *class* relationship, and the conflicts between individual men and women are political conflicts that can only be solved collectively. We regard our personal experience, and our feelings about that experience, as the basis for an analysis of our common situation. We cannot rely on existing ideologies as they are all products of a male supremacist culture. We question every generalization and accept none that is not confirmed by our experience. We identify with all women. We define our best interest as that of the poorest, most brutally exploited woman. In fighting for our liberation we will always take the side of women against their oppressors. We will not ask what is 'revolutionary' or 'reformist', only what is good for women.

(*Redstockings Manifesto, 1969*; emphasis in original)

In short, if women are a class, then so too must men be. Such approaches to men, however, raise, or express a contradiction. To see men as a class, to 'classify' men, as in radical feminism, means that there is both nothing to say about men and yet everything to be said about all men. Indeed paradoxically those feminists who have put forward some of the most explicit and insightful analyses of men's class position may do so in conjunction with a separation from men: a true unity of opposites.

Unfortunately the cogency of gender class analysis is all too frequently dismissed, certainly by men, and even by most women. More usual are tendencies to reincorporate feminism within existing political and academic frameworks, predominantly marxist. This possibility is considered in more detail in the following chapter, so at this stage it is enough to say that marxist feminism has much to say about the capitalist institutions of men but little about men's specific oppression of women. As already noted, within marxism men remain strangely unproblematic. Thus radical feminist analysis may see men as the 'main enemy' but often be directed at women rather than men; and marxist and socialist feminist analysis may be more concerned with men or at least men's institutions but not see men as the main problem. Lynne Segal (1983, 46) writes of such possible relations with men as follows:

Feminists who are not separatists do engage with men. We engage with men politically, in fighting the oppression of class, race and other hierarchies, because we also to a certain extent share a common fate with particular men. We engage with men because of our personal histories . . . and yes, some of us engage with men sexually, because we desire them. The prescription that women should repress heterosexual desire to further the cause of feminism is one I believe to be strategically and morally wrong.

Thus for women the problematisation of men may also apply in personal life (should men be spoken to, befriended, even loved?), in politics (can men be allies?), as well as in theory (is there a category of 'men'?). At the political level Joan Cummings (1980, 26), the Canadian feminist, has written with both optimism and an awareness of contradictions:

beyond . . . immediate vested interest, there would be those men who, despite their competitive advantage (and perhaps because of it), will have experienced an oppression different from, but analogous to our own. There is within the grasp of these men a consciousness of common interest with us—a desire to escape from social definitions that inhibit, distort, and contain individual potential. In a political struggle, these men and we could pursue common goals.

Such political alliances between feminist women and sympathetic men (see chapter 11) are probably best viewed as contradictory social practices that have to be forged by concrete actions not mere rhetoric; that take time to develop; and that are subject to frequent redefinition.

The clearest statement of the possibilities and realities of men's contribution to feminist revolution has been made by the black American feminist, bell hooks, from her experience of black and anti-racist struggles. She writes:

Bourgeois white women cannot conceptualize the bonds that develop between women and men in liberation struggle and have not had as many positive experiences working with men politically. Patriarchal white male rule has usually devalued female political input. Despite the prevalence of sexism in black communities, the role black women play in social institutions ... is recognized by everyone as significant and valuable.   (1984, 69)

She specifically resists separatist feminist ideology for neglecting the co-existence of the 'facts' that both 'men *do* oppress women', and 'people *are* hurt by rigid sex role patterns' (73). She concludes with an overwhelming optimism:

Separatist ideology encourages us to believe that women alone can make feminist revolution—we cannot. Since men are the primary agents maintaining and supporting sexism and sexist oppression, they can only be successfully eradicated if men are compelled to assume responsibility for transforming their consciousness and the consciousness of society as a whole. After hundreds of years of anti-racist struggle, more than ever before non-white people are currently calling attention to the primary role white people must play in anti-racist struggle. The same is true of the struggle to eradicate sexism—men have a primary role to play. This ... mean[s] ... they should share equally in resistance struggles. In particular, men have a tremendous contribution to make to feminist struggle in the area of exposing, confronting, opposing, and transforming the sexism of their male peers. When men show a willingness to assume equal responsibility in feminist struggle, performing whatever tasks are necessary, women should affirm their revolutionary work by acknowledging them as comrades in struggle.
(81)

Despite differences, feminism has shown men many things, including, of particular relevance for us, that it is possible to produce and re-produce critiques of men. Even where men are welcomed with optimism, or where men are confidently described as being oppressed, being 'used ... as a group ... to oppress women' (*Women*, 1985, 49), the explicit challenge to men as a *social class* remains. This social construction and therefore possible social destruction of men, as men not people, is stated with particular force by Amanda Sebestyen (1982, 229):

I've become certain, after some years of separatism and many more in my present compromise position, that I do want some relationships with men, sexual and otherwise. But I still want to transform my life in the way that separatism is aiming for. I'm a radical feminist which means I see men as my political enemies. But I don't want to kill them, that's too conservative a solution. I want them to *stop being men* any more. (emphasis is original)

More subtly, and yet perhaps more totally, Annie Leclerc (1981, 79) advises women on a similar theme: 'One must not wage war on men. That is his way of attaining value. Deny in order to affirm. Kill to love. One must simply deflate his values with the needle of ridicule.'

MEN'S CRITIQUES OF OURSELVES

The critical reactions of men to feminism, in terms of understanding the social construction of men and masculinity, have been made slowly and with obvious difficulty. If we ignore those purely hostile responses found in such texts as *In Praise of Male Chauvinism*, there are a range of more openly (self-) critical positions that attempt to learn, to some extent at least, from feminism. Their authors have often been participants in or influenced by self-proclaimed anti-sexist activities, such as men's consciousness-raising groups, as have developed in Canada, the United States, Britain, France and elsewhere since the late 1960s and early 1970s (see, for example, Bradley *et al.*, 1971). The analyses developed out of these and similar experiences may as before be both explanations of and contributions to change, often both academic and political, and sometimes personal too. It is tempting to draw broad parallels between strands of feminism and the various identifiable reactions by men. Thus radical feminism might be compared with effeminism,[11] gay liberationism, and radical anti-patriarchal men; marxist/socialist feminism with marxist/socialist anti-sexist men; and liberal feminism with men's liberationism, men's rights, and 'free men'. These pairings make some sort of sense but they suffer from several shortcomings, such as the general problems of labelling 'tendencies' (see note 10); and the fact that 'radicalism' for men in sexual politics may derive from sources, including gay sexuality and bisexuality, that do not necessarily imply support for women's liberation. Furthermore, specific labels like 'men's liberation' can actually refer to quite different positions, defined either independently without reference to feminism, or strongly pro-feminist (see chapter 11).

Critical, academic analyses of men and masculinity by men can also in broad terms be related to these kinds of political spectra. During the 1970s a dominant American tradition developed around the central theme of 'sex role socialisation', often arguing that the nurturing and gentler side of men has unfortunately been obscured by the processes of family, school, peer group and work role socialisation (Harrison, 1978). Texts like *The Liberated Man* (Farrell, 1974) and *Men's Liberation* (Nichols, 1975) espouse the need for men's liberation from these oppressive (of men) roles. Useful though this genre of men's writing is, it is typically more descriptive than explanatory, more cultural than structural. It generally fails to address the relationship of changing forms of masculinity to economic and social structure.[12] In contrast, the Jon Snodgrass (1977) collection, *For Men Against Sexism*, has drawn on and developed a more definite anti-sexist commitment, and a broader societal and structural view. This wide-ranging American series of essays is more self-consciously pro-feminist and yet is also more diverse, less predictable, so adding strength to the project. It has represented something of a landmark in going beyond the sex role approach in developing a more radical critique of men. There is as yet no single equivalent compilation text of British material; instead Tolson's (1977) *The Limits of Masculinity*, published in the same year as Snodgrass, has acted as a comparable reference point for men's anti-sexism. The major difference is that Tolson, as sole writer, is analysing masculinity, in the context of British left politics, and in particular focusing on the interplay of economic class and masculinity.

Reviewing some of this literature, the Australian

sociologists, Tim Carrigan, Bob Connell and John Lee (1985, 577), suggest that: 'the political meaning of the "men's movement" and the Books-About-Men genre ... is not, fundamentally, about uprooting sexism or transforming patriarchy, or even understanding masculinity in its various forms.... [W]hat it is about is *modernizing* hegemonic masculinity' (emphasis in original). In its place they urge that the 'question of transformation, its possibilities, sources, and strategies, should be central to the analysis of masculinity', emphasising the need for much closer attention to structural analysis, psychoanalysis (Carrigan and Connell, 1984) and gay sexuality. On this last point, they scathingly note that:

None of the 1970s Books-About-Men made a serious attempt to get to grips with gay liberation arguments, or to reckon with the fact that mainstream masculinity is heterosexual masculinity. Nor did the 'men's movement' publicists ever write about the fact that beside them was another group of men active in sexual politics; or discuss their methods, concerns or problems.
(Carrigan, *et al.*, 1985, 584)

This is a telling comment in view of the impact of gay politics and gay liberation from the late 1960s and early 1970s. The formation of the New York Gay Liberation Front in 1969 and the London GLF in 1970 represented important parts of the transformation of gay private politics to gay public politics (Weeks, 1977). Gay politics, gay scholarship, gay liberationism constitute explanations of the state of masculinity, as well as contributory challenges to and causes of change in masculinity. They have a direct relevance to the understanding of gay men, gayness and individual male psychodynamics, but they are equally significant in the analysis of men's power, 'hegemonic masculinity', heterosexuality, as well as the variety of cultural, and ideological forms that masculinity takes. Gay politics and gay scholarship have thus challenged and changed the understanding of men and masculinity at a number of levels and in a number of specific ways, for example, as a disruption of the notion of a unified, progressively evolving masculinity, as a specific historical critique through the identification of the category 'homosexual' as a late-nineteenth-century creation (Weeks, 1977), and as a demystification of heterosexual institutions. In short male heterosexuality becomes problematic.

These developments parallel to some extent shifts in emphases within the Women's Liberation Movement through the 1970s, with the recognition of the significance of lesbianism and lesbian analyses (Brackx, 1979). They also have to be understood in relation to the 'new sexual debates' of academic social science, following the work of Mitchell, Foucault, Lacan and others, often of a post-structuralist orientation, ready to reclaim the relevance of psychoanalytic discourse. Mieli's *Homosexuality and Liberation*, published in Italy in 1977 and in Britain in 1980, has proved to be a particularly influential text. He argued for 'universal homosexuality' and the revolutionary potential of homosexual consciousness and action against what he calls the (heterosexual) Norm that subjects them. In this he connects gay liberation with liberation more generally, of women, children, blacks, 'schizophrenics', old people, and indeed workers under capitalism, in moving towards a gay communism. Mieli adapts the Freudian and Marcusean concepts[13] of 'polymorphous perversity', Oedipus complex, Eros, and so on, in examining masculinity at an *intra-psychic* as well as interpersonal and structural levels.

Recent critical writing by men, such as Emmanuel Reynaud's (1983) *Holy Virility*, published in France in 1981 and in Britain in 1983 by an activist in the French 'men's movement', Bob Connell's (1983) *Which Way Is Up?*, produced in the context of Australian academic sociology and labour movement politics, and the Andy Metcalf and Martin Humphries (1985) collection *The Sexuality of Men*,[14] attempts to take account of feminism, gay liberation, psychoanalysis and marxism in focusing on the social construction of men's sexual power. The explanations that arise from such quarters are typically multi-levelled and somewhat eclectic. They take the gender of oppression, of women and indeed of gays, for granted; and they seek to explain and change that oppression by an explicit and consistent focus on (the problem of) men and masculinity. They look outwards and inwards at the same time; and they attempt to link theory and practice, the public and the private, the political and the personal. Such texts are intent on reminding their readers of the entrenched nature of men's power; the central association of (hetero)sexuality and violence; and the importance of relations *between* men, of male hierarchies, of men being 'both guarantor and victim' of patriarchy (Reynaud, 1983, 114). There is also frequently the realisation that the decline or end of patriarchy necessitates a loss of power for men, but also 'does promise a kind of liberation for men too' (Connell, 1982, 61). This current genre of men's writing could not have been written in this way in, say, the early 1970s. It reaffirms the possibility of being critical yet positive about ourselves; the social construction, and indeed variation, of men and masculinity; and the acknowledgement, yet contextualising, of personal experience.

FEMINIST CRITIQUES OF MEN'S CRITIQUES

Men's critiques, important and necessary though they are, are a continuation not the end of a story. They, in turn become available for discussion and critique by women. Although some women have welcomed or given a qualified welcome to men's self-critique (for example, Clements, 1980), there has been a range of further critiques by women of these developments. These to some extent replicate the range of feminist positions and approaches already briefly discussed. Thus some women see men's activities against sexism as a flight from the tackling of sexism in the 'mainstream men's movement', that is, political parties, trade unions and other public institutions (Campbell, 1983, 20). Others argue that these attempts against sexism are not public enough, not sufficiently clear or committed, not sufficiently accountable to feminist women, avoiding of the central issues of pornography and sexuality, and indeed a form of 'cloak and dagger chauvinism' (e.g. Hester, 1984; Bradshaw, 1983)—perhaps above all not sufficiently collective by men as men, not sufficiently confronting of masculinity, and of 'how male/men relate to other men and to the patriarchal structure we both live in' (Eberhardt, Hamilton, McKechnie, 1980, 11).[15] All these criticisms certainly apply at certain times, with certain men or certain groups. They illustrate possible illusions that may hide within liberal and libertarian approaches to changing men and masculinity. To put it simply: being nice is not enough (Hester, 1984, 36). They also demonstrate that the understanding of men and masculinity is a continuing, changing and dialectical process, between women and men.

The causes and the explanations of the problematisation of men and masculinity are many, and not mutually exclusive. In this process, men and masculinity become more liable to critique, more open to critique, and perhaps more able to respond to critique by changing. As soon as we recognise that we exist within the male problematic, men and masculinity become problematic, and may remain so.

SOME UNRESOLVED ISSUES

In charting 'causes, explanations and critiques', attention has been given to the appearances of men and masculinity. Throughout the processes and areas of change described there have been a number of recurrent, though often implicit, themes, issues and questions, which deserve statement or restatement. These include:

(1) How do we theorise men and masculinity?
(2) What are the relevance, contribution and shortcomings of the major malestream critical tradition, marxism, in this task?
(3) How useful is the maintenance and development of a concept of patriarchy?
(4) What is the nature of men's oppression, both by and of us?
(5) Are men a class? If so, in what respects?
(6) What is the significance of specific activities—sexuality, birth, childcare, violence—in understanding men and masculinity?
(7) How useful is a focus on reproduction rather than production?
(8) What implications follow for men's politics, practice and experience?
(9) What form should the academic study of men and masculinity take?

These and other questions will be addressed, to varying extents, in the following chapters. While it is not possible to suggest closed answers to them, it is hoped that what is said will contribute towards the continuation of their asking.

Part 2

Theorising Patriarchy, Theorising Reproduction

INTRODUCTION

It may seem strange to continue at this point with theory. Indeed there is something of a tradition in sexual politics, and especially amongst interested men, against theory. On the other hand, theory, or rather theorising, is an activity we all do, and that is done alongside and in relation to other activities, such as political campaigning or washing up. Theorising is important because it is a human activity, and also because it can help us understand what is going on, in politics, in work, in our own experience. More than that, theorising can also be revolutionary in leading us to consider the 'impossible', in opening up 'what we all know to be commonsense'.

The basis of these ideas was developed from the spring of 1980 in trying to write the 'theoretical chapter' for *Birth and Afterbirth*. In doing that, I was trying to make theoretical sense of personal and political issues around birth and childcare, in particular to address the question of the material base of patriarchy—in other words, was it possible that men's domination of women was not just the expression of capitalist or socialist or feudal economies but had a *material dynamic of its own*. This seemed likely from the evidence of the transcendent gender power in history to that of my own personal experience. To my surprise the theorising of patriarchy in this materialist way, and especially in relation to reproduction, did not seem to preoccupy most of those writing around gender—and certainly not most sex-role theorists or marxists. In a few places I found the glimmerings of such a theory—mainly in the work of critical anthropologists and

33

materialist feminists, particularly Mary O'Brien (1979), Maureen Mackintosh (1977), Felicity Edholm (1977), Lucy Bland *et al.* (1978b) and their co-workers—a reassurance that I was not going mad, yet.

The first draft of that 'theoretical chapter' was written over the winter of 1980–1, and rewritten over a year later in the summer of 1982, under the published title 'Theorizing on Reproduction'. The version included here as chapter 4 is edited in style rather than content. As such, 'reproduction' refers to 'the arrangements that precede birth after conception ... as well as the whole process of care and work for dependent children' (Hearn, 1983, 8). Such theorising brought the realisation that although I was writing largely in relation to marxism, or rather dialectical materialism, I had been somewhat dismissive of Karl Marx's own writing, without setting down a detailed evaluation. If life was more ordered, this might have been done earlier; but as it was during 1981–2 I set about doing my bit for marxigraphy. The result, much of which has since been revised as part of my Ph.D. thesis (Hearn, 1986b), necessarily considers various, broader meanings of reproduction, and comprises the basis of chapter 3, 'The difficult concept of patriarchy'. Chapter 5, 'Reproduction, men and the institutions of patriarchy', has been written over the period from 1983 to 1985, with the benefit of work with the Politics of Reproduction Seminar Group, University of Bradford, 1982–3; correspondence with Keith Mothersson; and discussions with many more.

3　The Difficult Concept of Patriarchy

The theory and concept of patriarchy has long been the subject of academic and political debate, a debate that with the emergence of modern feminism, has seen a considerable revival. Recent critiques of patriarchy have demonstrated its problematic nature; yet despite this the concept persists, is widely used, and particular actions, institutions and social processes are referred to as 'patriarchal', usually in derogation. Here, the variety of meanings of the concept and some of the major problems in its use are considered; some of these problems are countered through the case for the retention of the concept, and its development relative to the philosophical and political tenets of dialectical materialism. The term 'reproduction' is necessarily used here in a broad sense to refer not only to the biological reproduction of babies but also to the reproduction of social life in other respects, for example, sexuality and labour-power. A concluding section briefly examines some analytical and political implications of this analysis.

THE CONCEPT(S) OF PATRIARCHY

It is not the task here to chart the historical development, less still the historical evaluation, of the concept of patriarchy. Suffice it to say that modern usage owes much to the twin ghosts of sociology, Marx and Weber. Clearly a distinction needs to be made between the specific use of the term, 'patriarchy', and the retrospective characterisation of discourse as 'patriarchal' (O'Brien, 1981; Elshtain, 1981).

Similarly, detailed historical studies of patriarchal (and other) forms of family and political life (Stone, 1977; Schochet, 1975) may provide useful material for the analysis of patriarchy, though distinct from considerations of consciousness of patriarchy at a given historical time.

Marx's treatment of patriarchy was scant; and in many ways his legacy remains with us. He wrote of 'patriarchal' relations rather than a specific form or forms of 'patriarchy', as one might refer to 'racist' relations rather than 'racist' society or 'fascism'. In particular, he relates patriarchal relations to family relations, and uses 'the notion of the patriarchal family to refer, without exception, to the social relation of domestic production in pre-capitalist modes of production' (McDonough and Harrison, 1978, 38), which all the same survived well and performed necessary functions under capitalism. Marx did not investigate the organisation of (biological or sexual) reproduction itself. Birth, family arrangements and so on were seen as part of the means by which society produced 'labour-power', such that the family's future labourers are important rather than the production of prior organisation of reproduction.

Marx's treatment of the 'patriarchal family' should be placed in the context of his tendency towards 'naturalism'. In *The German Ideology* he and Friedrich Engels relate *the general division of labour to sexual divisions*, seen as natural

there develops the division of labour, which was originally nothing but the division of labour in the sexual act, then that division of labour which develops spontaneously or 'naturally' by virtue of natural predisposition....
(Marx and Engels, 1970, 51)

This is part of a general discussion of the materialist theory of history, not a specific discussion of 'patriarchy' or the 'patriarchal family' (which it could have been). They go on to assert that the division of labour:

is based on to the natural division of labour in the family and the separation of society into individual families opposed to one another. ... This latent slavery (of wife and children) in the family, though still very crude, is the first property.... 						(ibid., 52–3)[2]

The analysis and interpretation of the development of the

patriarchal family is given closer attention by Engels (1972) in *The Origin of the Family, Private Property and the State*. His general position is that

> [t]he determining factor in history ... is the production and reproduction of immediate life. This ... is of a twofold character: on the one side, the production of the means of existence ... on the other ... the production of human beings. (Engels, 1972, 71)

More specifically, he suggests '[t]he establishment of the exclusive supremacy of the man shows its effects first in the patriarchal family ...' (121). This Engels holds as an (the!) essential part of the 'overthrow of mother right' and his rather notorious assertion of the 'world historical defeat of the female sex'.[3] The exact nature of historical change from the matriarchal, communistic family to the modern, isolated family is uncertain—or as he puts it: 'these questions will be in dispute for a long time to come' (201). He refers to the work of Kovalesky (1890), as suggesting the patriarchal household community, consisting of 'several generations or several single families, and often includ[ing] unfree persons as well' (123) was 'a very common, if not universal, intermediate form' (201), as opposed to the 'most natural transition' described by Marx (quoted, p. 120) himself. Like Marx, Engels emphasises the enslavement embodied in the family, noting that the word 'family' (*familia*) originally referred to the total number of slaves belonging to one man (Engels, 1972, 121). Ironically, the Latin word, 'proletariat', meaning he who has no wealth but his children, was rather closer to the modern meaning of 'family' or rather 'head' of the family, i.e. father.

Despite the frequent contrasts made between Marx (and Engels), and Max Weber's theorising, the latter's consideration of patriarchy follows rather similar lines of argument. He considers first, patriarchalism, with authority invested in the master over his household, and secondly, patrimonialism, with 'domestic authority decentralised through assignment of land and sometimes of equipment to sons of the house and other dependants' (Weber, 1968, 1011). Perhaps the most relevant theme for present purposes within Weber's writing is his treatment of the patrimonial state, 'when the prince organizes his political power over extrapatrimonial areas and political subjects—which is not discretionary and not enforced by physical coercion—just like the exercise of his patriarchal power' (ibid., 1013). Thus we have a progression of dominance within Weber's text from the household to political institutions and the state (rather than the economy). Both Marx and Weber saw 'patriarchy' in its literal meaning of power of the father. However, perhaps surprisingly, Weber goes further than Marx in analysing the societal implications of that particular social relation.

Reliance on the centrality of the family remains strong within many feminist analyses of patriarchy. As Annette Kuhn (1978, 44) puts it:

> The family ... is constantly referred to, or deferred to, as the crucial site of the subordination of women, and its absence or dissolution, it is implied, would pose a threat to property relations both patriarchal and capitalist and even to the psychic relations through which ... social relations are mapped onto relations of subjectivity. In this sense, the family is very often invoked as a final, catch-all explanation of the various characteristics of women's position in different societies and at different times, ...

This statement also highlights a further major approach to the analysis of patriarchy, namely the investigation of those 'relations of subjectivity'. Thus we have the conjunction of psychoanalysis and feminism, promoted by Juliet Mitchell (1975) and others, itself closely paralleling the general interrelation of freudianism and marxism, within the work of the Frankfurt School and other Critical Theorists. This broadly psychoanalytic approach has been continued through the use of object-relations theory to elucidate reproduction, mothering, and gender identities (for example, Chodorow, 1978); the investigation of the symbolising use of language, and construction of sexuality through such symbols (for example, Coward, Lipshitz and Cowie, 1976); and the growth of feminist therapy, as both practice and theory (for example, Eichenbaum and Orbach, 1982). The result of these and similar developments is both an increased sophistication and a serious problematising, even undermining, of the concept of patriarchy.

In contrast, approaches to patriarchy through biological functioning and political power appear broad brush. The best-referenced text that gives primacy to biological divisions as the basis of patriarchy is Shulamith Firestone's *The Dialectic of Sex*. It is also much criticised, on grounds of reductionism, biologism, historical inaccuracy and general crudity (for example, O'Brien, 1981). Firestone (1971, 8) writes:

Unlike economic class, sex class sprang directly from a biological reality: men and women were created differently, and not equally privileged ... this difference of itself did not necessitate the development of a class system ...— the reproductive *functions* of these differences did.

Although she goes on to link this viewpoint with the unequal power relations of the family, her perspective is probably of more lasting significance in reviving interest in the control of biological reproduction, fertility or even sexuality as possible bases of patriarchy.

Interestingly, Kate Millett's (1971), *Sexual Politics*, one of the most widely read and influential texts that focuses on political power as the driving force of patriarchy, also pays considerable attention to the family as a microcosm of societal power relations. However, Millett goes far beyond attention to the family to address other sources and arenas of men's power over women—including the historical, 'political', social, psychological. Impressive as *Sexual Politics* is, the concept of patriarchy in use is ultimately a catch-all to include in effect all of men's power over women. There is little indication of social structure or the processes of social change, let alone dialectical change. Millett is not a 'social scientist' and admits here greater comfort in the world of literature and her difficulties with socio-political analysis.

PROBLEMS WITH THE CONCEPT

Apart from the question of definition, perhaps the major problem in the use of the concept of patriarchy is its analytical, empirical and indeed political status. More precisely, this involves its relation to the totality of this or any other society, and the problematic of the implied separation of patriarchal and any other social relations. The most usual way in which this problem is posed is in terms of the relationship of patriarchy and capitalism (Eisenstein, 1979; Hartmann, 1979; Barrett, 1980; Phillips, 1980–1)—their separability, their interrelation, their supposed or possible supremacy one over the other. These sub-problems are neatly summed up in what Veronica Beechey (1979) has referred to as 'dualism', that is the unwarranted and false separation of production and reproduction, mode of production and ideology, the economic and the political, even base and superstructure (cf. Burnham and Louie, 1985).

A further set of problems arises from the argument that conceptualisations of patriarchy tend to be inherently restricted and thereby restricting, even disempowering to women. Sheila Rowbotham (1979) in her admittedly highly concentrated account of 'the trouble with patriarchy' conveniently sums up some of these and the associated links between analytical and historical judgements, and political statements and programmes. She writes:

the word 'patriarchy' ... implies a universal and historical [*sic*] form of oppression which returns us to biology—and thus it obscures the need to recognise not only biological difference, but also the multiplicity of ways in which societies have defined gender. By focusing upon the bearing and rearing of children ... it suggests there is a single determining cause of women's subordination. ... Moreover, the word leaves us with two separate systems in which a male/female split is implied. We have patriarchy oppressing women and capitalism oppressing male workers. ... It does not carry any notion of how women might act to transform their situation as a sex. ... 'Patriarchy' suggests a fatalistic submission which allows no space for the complexities of women's defiance.

These points can be responded to in a variety of ways. Working backwards, it can be argued firstly that 'patriarchy' is no more fixed than feudalism or capitalism; secondly, that there is no reason why patriarchy should imply that capitalism oppresses male workers only, for it is quite possible for women to be oppressed (at least) twice over; thirdly, there is no reason why the relationship of class relations and gender relations should be one-way; and fourthly, the use of the concept of 'patriarchy' does not necessarily imply that its sole or even fundamental basis should be biological reproduction.

Of these sub-debates around patriarchy, perhaps the most important is the question of historical specificity. For as patriarchal domination is usually accepted as preceding capitalist domination, it is unlikely that the former would take the same form in, say, feudal and capitalist societies. There is a serious danger of neglecting such historical specificities in using the concept of patriarchy without qualification in terms of the precise societal form under consideration.

MOVEMENTS TOWARD THE CONCEPT

In the face of these and no doubt other difficulties in the use of the concept of patriarchy, there have been a variety of attempts to move on to some other formulation of men's oppression of women. Many of these come from marxists or marxist feminists, and represent in some way or other a reassertion of the supremacy of the capitalist mode, albeit usually in an advanced and complex form. Thus, for example, we have a retreat towards marxist orthodoxy in the domestic labour debate, whether 'orthodox' or 'unorthodox' (Smith, 1978), as well as more specific analyses of the role of 'new' technology (Barker and Downing, 1980) and the re-evaluation of sex and skill (Phillips and Taylor, 1980). Other responses include the return of the ideas of the young Marx and the investigation of alienation (Atkinson, 1979) or less charitably the 'capitulation to indeterminacy' (Phillips, 1980–1, 134).

Arising out of the difficulties and complexities described are more thorough reformulations of what is understood by patriarchy. Thus, for example, Roisin McDonough and Rachel Harrison (1978) see patriarchy in terms of the control of fertility *together with* the sexual division of labour; while Heidi Hartmann (1979) in her classic discussion of 'The unhappy marriage of Marxism and Feminism ...' moves to definition around men's restrictions on women's sexuality *and* access to economically productive resources. At first sight these sorts of approaches to patriarchy seem more satisfactory in that they attempt to bridge the 'dualist' divide between economy and ideology. Yet ultimately they remain unsatisfactory as they retain within their own definition of patriarchy the very dualism they seek to transcend. Both McDonough and Harrison's, and Hartmann's formulations are themselves 'dualist' in placing fertility or sexuality alongside a neo-Weberian view of economic class.

In these approaches to patriarchy as well as those described earlier there is a resilient tension between the tendency to *over-particularise* the basis of patriarchy, for example, in the family or certain family forms, and the tendency to *over-generalise* it, for example, in biology.[4] On the first count, analysis can fall into a false reductionist scientism; on the second, it can lean on the assertion of a crude, imprecise politicism and essentialism. There remains a need for an understanding of women's oppression by and *social relation* to men, and men's oppression of and *social relation* to women, that is total yet neither reductionist nor imprecise.

THE CASE FOR THE CONCEPT: PATRIARCHY IS REALISM NOT ESSENTIALISM

The viability of counter claims against the need for a concept of patriarchy depends to a large extent on what is meant by the term. If patriarchy refers to the direct, autonomous power, *the rule*, of the father or the fathers then it cannot be said to exist now in any simple form. As Jean Bethke Elshtain (1981, 214–5) discusses, Sir Robert Filmer's description of patriarchial familial relations is historically no longer accurate. The power of the father can of course be still employed in other senses, including as an element in psychoanalytic explanations, whether people have known a father or not. For men, at least the father, including the powerful, violent, incestuous father, may often persist, as part of a (Jungian) shadow.

Even if fathers do not literally rule, men clearly do continue *de facto*, if not *de jure*, rule. The particularised, traditional power of the father or the fathers or elders may have been overtaken by history but men, if not every man, do collectively hold power, and effectively rule (*pace* the Queen and Margaret Thatcher). It is also clear that not all of men's power is *directly* connected to their being fathers, for some are not fathers. On the other hand, resort to a generalised power of men, whether as a class of all men or even an aggregation of individual powers, raises further difficulties. Principally, it is relatively easy to find analytical and empirical *exceptions*, either in terms of the socially powerless, or the biologically unusual or problematic. To the great relief of men, social scientists and others, it becomes possible to say again, 'There never really was such a thing as patriarchy, after all'.[5]

However, just as within capitalism, *certain* capitalists will be powerless, may be 'killed off' in the struggle of competition, so too are *certain* men within patriarchy. Indeed more than that, it is essential for both social forms that certain of the powerful are killed off, metaphorically or literally. No, just as capitalism is founded on, in fact *is*, the social relation of capital and labour, so too is patriarchy a social relation, in this case of men and women. And just as capitalism does not depend upon all capitalists being more powerful than all labourers, similarly the persistence of patriarchy does not depend upon all men or even all fathers being specifically powerful over all women. Indeed, one of the characteristics of the current form of patriarchy is the structural shift from the direct, private power of the father to the publicisation of such power, to public or social patriarchy, to collectivised fathers, principally in the professions and the state (Eisenstein, 1981; Laurin-Frenette, 1982; Brown, 1981; Holter, 1984; Burstyn, 1983; Borchorst and Siim, 1986) (cf. McIntosh, 1978) (see chapters 5 and 6).

Thus despite the various difficulties described there remains a case for retaining the concept of patriarchy that is fundamentally social structural. In particular it can be of analytical, and possibly political, use in focusing on the social structuring of gender relations, of the variety of forms of social relation and oppression between men and women. It can prompt the understanding of possible social structures underlying both institutional inequalities and everyday action. The concept above all highlights the possibility of different social bases of control and thereby oppression *by men* (and indeed of and between men in some respects) from those that arise from industrial, capitalist organisation, and the socialisation of productive labour.

To conceptualise patriarchy in this way is certainly to broaden from the specific, traditional focus upon 'the father'. It also deliberately concerns oppression *by men*, be it over women, children (or animals, plants or nature) (Gray, 1982), just as capitalism is oppression by capitalists and capital. To define patriarchy ipso facto in terms of oppression only *of women* is the equivalent of 'labourism' within socialist political economy.

Such an approach to patriarchy avoids at least some of the more obvious traps. Firstly, the concept of patriarchy 'is nothing to do with biological determinism. ... It is about socially and historically defined gender, not about biological sex' (Rowan, 1986, 49). Secondly, the concept need not suggest a fixed hierarchy between women and men that simply reproduces further dualisms. Thirdly, it is untrue to say that ' "patriarchy" does not allow either ... for repressive relations between women and men, or between different women, as well as between men and women' (Hargreaves, 1986, 115). Capitalism 'allows' 'repressive', even vicious and bloody, relations between capitalists and between workers, and 'equivalent' relations, men–men and women–women, are possible within patriarchy, albeit in the context of the overriding dominance of man. Indeed oppressive relations between men are surely part and parcel of patriarchy. After all, perhaps is it simpler just to refer to 'menarchy', or perhaps more accurately 'fratriarchy'—the 'legal' right of men in fraternities, be they marauding gangs or the institution of the state, to steal, burn, kill, and rape (Remy, 1986).

In contrast, most of the treatments of patriarchy that have been discussed so far have in their dualism, their sometime biologism, their reliance on family values or their overall lack of precision, a deeply embedded idealist aspect. Against this, specific emphasis may be placed upon dialectics and dialectical analysis in the examination of patriarchy. This necessitates attention to oppression by men, the receipt of that oppression by others, and the dialectical relation of these processes. It is not possible to simply *understand* 'women' or 'women's oppression' in an un-dialectical way, that is, without reference to and without an understanding those who, and those structures which, oppress women.

It is to this possible relation of dialectical materialism and patriarchy that attention is now turned.

PATRIARCHY AND DIALECTICAL MATERIALISM

Patriarchy and dialectical materialism are not usually considered together. From this one might infer, though I have never seen it explicitly stated, that the two projects, the exploration of the concept of patriarchy and the development of a dialectical materialist theory and practice, are somehow incompatible.

Marxism is usually seen as the expression of or attempt to realise dialectical materialism; at times the two terms are used interchangeably. By dialectical materialism I mean, following Lenin (1961, 359–60), that theory and practice founded upon

[t]he recognition of the contradictory, mutually exclusive, opposite tendencies in all phenomena and processes of nature.... This alone furnishes the key to self-movement of everything in existence. It alone furnishes the key to the leaps, to the break in continuity to the transformation into the opposite, to the destruction of the old and emergence of the new.... In the proper meaning, dialectics is the study of the contradiction within the very essence of things.
Development is the struggle of opposites.

In addition to this dominantly quantitative statement on opposites, Lenin is at pains to emphasise the qualitative nature of dialectics: 'Dialectics is the study of the opposition of the thing-in-itself, of the essence ... from the appearance' (1961, 253).

Any would-be dialectical materialist analysis of patriarchy must, therefore, encapsulate *both* the quantitative and the qualitative forms of gender relations. This is hardly attempted, let alone achieved, in most marxist or marxist-informed analyses of patriarchy. To begin with the assumption that gender divisions are of the essence subservient to or transformations of class divisions is to quantify but not to qualify those (former) divisions. This is by no means to immediately dismiss possible marxist approaches to patriarchy or approaches to patriarchy derived from marxism. There are indeed a number of clear and feasible interpretations. Three possible, and highly interrelated, contenders are initially considered, prior to the interpretation of feminist adaptations of marxism, and feminist dialectical materialisms.

The social relations of production and their reproduction

The relationship of any would-be definition of patriarchy to the social relations of production *per se* is an important and extremely elaborate issue. This latter category has in turn a number of distinct aspects, even within Marx's own writing, and a number of further forms in subsequent marxist interpretations. Many of these complexities are embedded in a short and ultimately confused chapter on 'Simple reproduction' (ch. XXIII) in *Capital. Volume 1.* Marx begins clearly enough with the statement:

> The conditions of production are also those of reproduction. No society can go on producing, in other words, no society can reproduce, unless it constantly reconverts a part of its products into means of production, or elements of fresh production. All other circumstances remaining the same, the only mode by which it can *reproduce its wealth*, and maintain it at one level, is by replacing the means of production ... by an equal quantity of the same kind of articles. ...   (1977a, 531, my emphasis)

However, in the chapter that follows at least six different interpretations of reproduction are used. These are:

(i)   biological reproduction (of the working class), as left to 'the labourer's instincts of self-preservation and propagation' (537).

(ii) maintenance of labour, through the consumption of 'necessaries' by which 'the muscles, nerves, bones and brains of existing labourers are reproduced' (537).[6]

(iii) the reproduction of labour-power, 'by converting part of ... capital' (536) and so augmenting the value of that capital.

(iv) simple reproduction of capital, so converting 'every capital into accumulated capital, or capitalised surplus value' (535).

(v)   simple reproduction as 'a mere repetition of the proceeds of production' whereby 'this mere repetition, or continuity, gives a new character to the process' (532).

(vi) reproduction of 'not only surplus-value but ... also ... the capitalist relation; on the one side the capitalist, on the other the wage-labourer' (542).[7]

It could be argued that these distinct meanings of

'reproduction' relate to each other, through reduction and relation to the 'capitalist relation'. Thus one might construct the following kind of hierarchy.

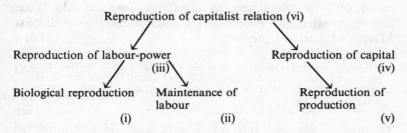

Figure 2: Meanings of reproduction in Capital

However, such an hierarchy is certainly not developed by Marx himself.[8]

These various themes are taken further in the following chapter (XXIV) with the distinctions drawn between simple reproduction, in which 'the capitalist squanders the whole surplus-value in dissipation', and reproduction on an extended scale in which 'he demonstrates his bourgeois virtue by consuming only a portion of it and converting the rest into money' (549). Marx concludes this section by stating:

In economic forms of society of the most different kinds, there occurs, not only simple reproduction, but, in varying degrees, reproduction on a progressively increasing scale. By degrees more is produced and more consumed, and consequently more products have to be converted into means of production (560).

Marx's consideration of the social relations of production and their reproduction thus brings together 'biological' questions around the reproduction of labour-power and 'economic' issues around the reproduction of capital and the capitalist relations themselves. It is perhaps by chance that the word 'reproduction' is used for both these processes. However, this recognition of the 'biological-economic' in itself does not illuminate a dialectical materialist interpretation of patriarchy. Patriarchy, as derived from the reproduction of labour-power, or of capital and the capitalist relation, or both, remains assigned to the relative superstructure of the social relations of production. As McDonough and Harrison (1978, 34) put it: 'Just as the labour process is always situated within a particular mode of production and its social relations, so too is the procreative process'. From this it is but a short step (or slide) to Marx's notorious statement:

> The maintenance and reproduction of the working-class is, and must ever be, a necessary condition to the reproduction of capital. But the capitalist may safely leave its fulfilment to the labourer's instincts of self-preservation and of propagation.   (1977a, 537)

These investigations interrelate with and are continued by Marx into the 'development' of capitalism itself.

The 'development' of capitalism

The analysis of the different forms of capital accumulation within *Capital. Volume 1* (chs. XXV–XXXIII) leads on, within *Capital. Volume 3* (Marx, 1977b), to the charting of the variety of transformations which may take place in the form of capital. This is nothing less than the analysis of the historical 'development' of capitalism. This perspective gives a further feasible interpretation of patriarchy, still within the frame of marxist dialectical materialism. The *apparentness* of patriarchy may thus become an instance, a stage, in the development of capitalism. Let us look at this possible interpretation more closely.

In 'Results of the immediate process of production', Marx (1977c) describes two phases of development of capitalism: the formal subsumption of labour under capital and its subsequent real subsumption. Such distinctions have a clear relationship, though by no means one of equivalence, with Marx's (1977b) own discussions in *Capital. Volume 3* of development from commodity-capital and money-capital to commercial capital and money-dealing capital (merchant's capital) (Part IV): from mercantile to industrial capital (338); and within industrial capitalism from capital in the process of production to interest-bearing capital (343). The last type, interest-bearing capital, is of particular concern for our present purposes for Marx argues that 'The owner of money who desires to enhance his money as interest-bearing capital, turns it over to a third person, throws it into circulation, turns it into a commodity as *capital*; not just capital for himself but also for others' (343). This point is pursued further shortly after in *Volume 3* when it is held that:

The relations of capital assume their most externalised and most fetish-like form in interest-bearing capital. We have here ... money creating more money, self-expanding value, without the process that effectuates these two extremes.... Capital appears as a mysterious and self-creating source of interest—the source of its own increase. The *thing* (money, commodity, value) is now capital even as a mere thing, and capital appears as a mere thing. The result of the entire process of reproduction appears as a property inherent in the thing itself. (1977b, 391–2)

This particular theme within Marx's work concerning the forms of capital, their transformation and their ideological appearance in effect, details the nature of social relations in relation to social forces within the capitalist mode of production. This theme is also fundamental to Lenin's discourses on capitalism and *Imperialism, the Highest Stage of Capitalism* (1964). Here Lenin charts the development from competition to monopolies, so that 'although commodity production still reigns and continues to be regarded as the basis of economic life, it has in reality been undermined and the bulk of the profits go to the "geniuses" of financial manipulation' (206–7). He continues: 'Typical of the old capitalism, when free competition held undivided sway, was the export of *goods*. Typical of the latest stage of capitalism, when monopolies rule, is the export of *capital* ...' (240), with the heightened role of the banking and finance institutions.

Lenin concludes this pamphlet with a discussion of 'The place of imperialism in history', which includes a diatribe against mystificatory descriptions of 'modern capitalism'. He asserts that:

When a big enterprise assumes gigantic proportions, and, on the basis of an exact computation of mass data, organises according to plan the supply of primary raw materials to the extent of two-thirds, or three-fourths, of all that is necessary for tens of millions of people ... it becomes evident that we have socialisation of production, and not mere 'interlocking'; that private economic and private property relations constitute ... a shell which may remain in a state of decay for a fairly long period ... but which will inevitably be removed. (1964, 302–3)

It could be argued that this socialisation of production could at least *appear* as patriarchy or a form thereof. This possible interpretation is, however, only one of *appearance*. It may be that patriarchy is *now* visible or more visible through or in relation to the socialisation of production, but the fact remains that capitalism *qua* capitalism, or capitalists *qua* capitalists, are not essentially interested in the form that the process of socialisation appears to take. It is for this reason that O'Brien writes:

> Capitalism cares not one whit for the forms of the social relations of reproduction, provided they continue to reproduce labour power, fulfil the 'ethical' function of educating children in the stability of the existing class structure, and provide a cheap labour pool of women and children which can be utilised to threaten uppish unionized male workers.   (1981, 202)

No, patriarchy may become differentially visible with the 'development' of capitalism, though it is germane to it. A more dramatic and essential analysis is (not surprisingly) the inversion, that is to see capitalism as the highest stage of patriarchy (Al-Hibri, 1981).

Within this broad perspective on dialectical materialism patriarchy is thus not specifically an instance or expression of the social relations of production themselves, as in the previous perspective, but rather a means of reproduction of social relations. In this interpretation patriarchy is but one element in the externalised process of capital accumulation within 'advanced' capitalism. Appealing though such a treatment (or dismissal) of patriarchy might be, it fails to fit the historical facts in that patriarchy pre-dates capitalism. However, it is possible that the current form of patriarchy is related to the present externalised, fetishised form of capitalism, and that investigations along these lines might lead to analysis of moves from more private to more public, patriarchal forms (Brown, 1981).

State and ideology
This perspective in many ways brings together the previous two. The (modern) state and ideology can be seen as two related forms both of social relations and of the maintenance and reproduction of those social relations.

Lenin's thinking on the stages of capitalism has been immensely important in furthering attention to the development of capital, and indeed the technical forces of production and their effects upon social relations in general and ideological forms in particular. This has led on to the search for a higher stage of capitalism still, beyond finance capitalism and imperialism, elaborated within the process of reproduction of social relations. This theme is recognisable in both marxist and non-marxist writing, such as debates on 'technocracy' and 'corporatism'.

The consideration of the role of the state in maintaining social relations is particularly significant. This includes the Miliband—Poulantzas debate on its relative autonomy, the German-based *Staatsableitung* (state derivation) debate, and the Critical Theory of Jurgen Habermas and Claus Offe on the supersession of the economic by the political as the arbiter of social decisions. The state debate has also dealt more specifically with the 'welfare state' with, for example, Ian Gough (1983) distinguishing economically 'productive' and 'unproductive' sectors; and James O'Connor (1974) social consumption and social expenses. Such emphasis on the social reproductive, some would say 'unproductive', role of the state closely parallels the work of Manuel Castells and other urban theorists on collective consumption and its spatial components. It also links with developments in the analysis of, firstly, class—the role of the middle class in the reproduction of class relations, the changing class position of state employees and so on—and secondly, ideology, in the lee of Althusserian pushes to recognise its lack of history, its autonomy and the centrality of the ideological state apparatuses (Althusser, 1971).

In all these formulations of dialectical materialism it is possible to relate the 'more advanced' stages of capitalism, whether in terms of imperialism, state formation, ideological superstructures or whatever, to patriarchy. However, such formulations tend to display a profound dualism—most clearly where the focus is upon the state or ideology, and more subtly so in the 'development' of capitalism. The shortcomings of the latter model are apparent at the international level, particularly through the resort to comparative material, such as on the interrelation of Islam and patriarchy (Al-Hibri, 1981); while the state/ideology model displays shortcomings at the more local, societal level. Particular states and particular ideologies may be patriarchal just as the family may be patriarchal. However, to see either the state or ideology as the historical explanation of gender divisions brings one back to either an Engelsian view of history or a metaphysical phenomenology respectively. The fact that both state and ideology are often patriarchal is an appearance not a material determining force: the appearance comes from the intensification of 'welfare state' and public cultural forms, not the determination of state or ideology.

To be explicit, most marxist analyses provide neither materialist nor dialectical analyses of gender relations. They are not materialist, 'since they suggest that the oppression of women is mainly (or completely) due to faulty, capitalist-imposed sets of *values*, which would disappear when capitalism disappear[s] ...'⁹ (Barker, 1977, i). They tend to consider the material production of women in relation to capital or the dominant class or dominant *mode of production* not in relation to men. Their lack of consideration of gender *relations*, as opposed to considering the oppression of women alone, is thereby un-dialectical.

Feminist adaptations of marxism, and their feminist and marxist critiques

These difficulties take on even greater poignancy when one considers the various attempts to 'update' marxism to take account of gender and women's oppression, particularly within marxist feminisms.

The very term, 'the sexual division of labour', as usually used by marxist feminists, may belie their materialism, for it is premised upon an assumed equivalence of *biological* divisions and the social divisions of *productive* work (see Burnham and Louie, 1985, 26–8). At a more theoretical level, there is the question of whether the 'division of labour' and 'labour' itself, as defined within marxism, is the most appropriate materialist focus and indeed description of material activity and interrelation when considering gender. A rather similar critique can be made against centrality being given to the 'domestic labour debate'. There, work done in the home is appreciated *as work*. Though often unpaid, domestic work creates value in addition to value created by industry and commerce. Gender divisions, however, remain subject to analysis through 'economic' concepts. Reproduction is seen as part of the productive economy. 'Labour' is not significant by virtue of its 'domesticity' or its domestic location, but by virtue of its place within and foundation of the total social formation. As noted, most marxist analyses of gender can be said to be un-dialectical, in that they are preoccupied with women's labour and its incorporation (in several senses) into 'production'. They are rarely concerned with oppression *by men*.

These issues recur in the use and construction of the concept of 'capitalist patriarchy', as within some socialist feminist analyses (e.g. Eisenstein, 1979) and some gender-conscious marxist analyses. The term, 'capitalist patriarchy', at least at present defined, is of doubtful use. It might refer to that type of patriarchy which *is* capitalist (as with *brown* bread) or that type of patriarchy which is *for* capitalism (as with *pig*-swill). In the first case patriarchy is the dominant mode implying there are other, non-capitalist forms. Capitalism is thereby subsumed within patriarchy, capitalist, non-capitalist or whatever. However, such an overarching conception of patriarchy is not to be seen within analyses of 'capitalist patriarchy'. A more usual interpretation is the latter whereby patriarchy operates *for* capitalism. Accordingly, this suggests a whole series of possible social and political institutions, capitalist social democracy, capitalist monarchy, capitalist oligarchy or whatever. Indeed, such institutions of social democracy, monarchy, oligarchy *and* patriarchy become functional to capitalism. Thus capitalism is the dominant mode which subsumes patriarchy. No major reformulation of dialectical materialism, let alone a dialectical materialist conception of patriarchy, is necessary or likely. In fact, to take the pig-swill analogy further: swill (patriarchy) does not exist as an independent object but only comes into existence *as swill* (*as patriarchy*) through its relationship to the pre-existing pigs (capitalism). Thereby theorising *merely* about pigs (capitalism) is necessary and likely. Thus in both the interpretations of 'capitalist patriarchy' presented, of which the latter is the more tenable in the eyes of the majority of the users of the term, a dialectical materialist theory of patriarchy is absent.

To put this in a slightly different way: 'Most attempts at synthesis [of marxism and feminism] attempt to integrate or explain the appeal of feminism by incorporating issues feminism identifies as central—the family, housework, sexuality, reproduction, socialisation, personal life—within an essentially unchanged marxian analysis' (MacKinnon, 1982, 10). One might add birth, children, violence, gender itself.

Socialist feminists and marxist feminists who have sought 'syntheses' of this kind have been subject to vigorous criticism not only from radical feminists but also, not surprisingly, from some marxists. Perhaps the clearest of these latter critiques is contained within Linda Burnham and Miriam Louie's (1985) *The Impossible Marriage*, published in a 'Marxist-Leninist Journal of Rectification' [*sic*]. The authors offer detailed examinations of socialist feminist (especially Hartmann's and Eisenstein's) analyses of patriarchy, use of 'the sexual division of labour', political strategy, insistent dualism, and thus philosophical idealism. Burnham and Louie's critique is founded upon esteem for the (proletarian) class vanguard party as the means to communism, and dismissal of the 'anti-leninism' of the 'autonomous cross-class women's movement'. They also recognise the importance of childbearing, particularly prior to 'the scientific mastery [*sic*] of reproductive biology and the mass availability of birth control' (81) and its interrelation with other forms of labour within the mode of production. This enables them to couple the naturalism of Marx and Engels with the materialism of 'scientific marxism' or, as they put it, the complex interpenetration of the natural and the social (77). Unfortunately, despite this the central object of their analyses remains capitalism, which itself remains theoretically unchallenged. Patriarchy is not a central theoretical object.

Feminist dialectical materialisms
A number of feminist writers have made specific attempts to produce a dialectical materialist account of patriarchy or 'patriarchy-capitalism', or indeed to dissolve the hyphen (Petchesky, 1979). In some cases these arise from the argument

that the way reproduction is organised is in its own right a source of oppression for women. For example, Juliet Mitchell's (1966) very important article, 'The longest revolution', articulates four major means through which women are oppressed: production, socialisation, sexuality, and (biological) reproduction. A less segmented explanation of patriarchy from the tradition of marxist feminism is that in Lise Vogel's (1983) ... *Toward a Unitary Theory*. She argues for the differential location of women and men 'with respect to important aspects of social reproduction' (166)—the reproduction of the *conditions* of production—as a major unifying theoretical perspective.[10]

Elements of a more detailed analysis of a dialectical materialism of gender and patriarchy are provided by Weinbaum (1978). Indeed in arguing for the central importance of age and 'kin categories'—wife, father, daughter, brother—she attempts to produce a more adequate account of *gender/economic* relations than Marx's focus on the presumed 'adult male worker'.

Christine Delphy, the French feminist materialist, goes further still in the development of much more than just a feminist adaptation of dialectical marxism.[11] She sees men as *The Main Enemy* (1977) and locates the problem in the 'family mode of production', as a form of production and consumption in itself. Her analysis is in terms of women's production of goods and services for men rather than women's (re)production of children for men. Delphy's work certainly makes great inroads into the analysis of the social relations of production and the reproduction of the patriarchal social system. On the first count, she points out the limitations of a narrowly capitalist analysis, and on the second, she establishes the importance of class relations between women and men. She is, however, less precise in her consideration of human reproduction and appears to incorporate it within the general analysis of the family mode of production.

O'Brien's work in many ways takes up this latter point. She confronts this issue directly in her article, 'The dialectics of reproduction' (1978) and extends the analysis in *The Politics of Reproduction* (1981). O'Brien's work develops from the tradition of historical dialectical materialism, and yet is more specifically concerned with reproduction than production, in the family mode or otherwise. O'Brien focuses on reproduction as an historically determined, dialectical material process. It takes place only through reproductive labour and the social relations of reproduction in turn account for different forms of reproductive consciousness of both women and men. The way in which this process occurs changes historically, for example, with men's awareness of paternity, the use of contraception, and so on. A central element in her analysis is the relating of reproduction and its domination to the social division between private and public life. Reproduction tends to be seen as primarily confined to the private world with the public world, dominated by men, paradoxically existing over and above that private realm and being responsible for the continuation of civil society. Many other insightful aspects of her analysis add to the considerable theoretical strides made in advancing a dialectical materialist approach to paternity.

However, probably the most influential account of the power of reproduction has come from Adrienne Rich, and especially her *Of Woman Born* (1977). This combines very personal, often ambivalent experiences with literary and historical references: it is a total project. It describes and analyses the way in which women's experiences, and particularly as mothers and indeed as daughters, are controlled and determined within patriarchy, often to the extent of that experience remaining hardly acknowledged. She wants to put women and women's experience first, to make 'inexorable connection[s] between every aspect of a woman's being and every other'. Although writing outside the tradition of dialectical materialism, she tellingly asserts, with clear allusion, that '[t]he repossession by women of our bodies will bring far more essential change to human society than the seizing of the means of production by workers' (284–5). I think she is right.

Some of the insights of Rich and Chodorow, as well as O'Brien's (1979) critique of Marx, are brought together in Nancy Hartsock's (1983) 'feminist historical materialism', in which she stresses the importance of women's and men's differential relation to subsistence and childrearing ('reproduction'). Although this nearly resurrects the problem of dualism, she argues that dualism itself derives from the disconnected experience of men in childrearing, both as receivers and avoiders thereof, as opposed to the relational experience of women. For her the central category is 'labour', and its 'sexual division', with reproduction, implicitly at least, the major, if not the sole, base of consciousness.

THE STRUCTURING OF REPRODUCTION: SOME IMPLICATIONS

Several implications follow from this preliminary analysis of the relationship of patriarchy, dialectical materialism and reproduction. First is the reaffirmation of the concept of patriarchy, based in these more autonomous relations of reproduction. Thus, 'patriarchy' may be used as a shorthand to refer to a complex set of social relations (of reproduction) within and by which men tend to dominate women.

A second area needing attention is the clarification and conceptualisation of reproduction. As Olivia Harris and Kate Young (1981, 142) suggest, the term reproduction 'must itself be specified much more closely if it is to be of use in theory'. Reproduction has frequently remained unconceptualised as secondary to production, in the functionalist sense of merely being reproduction rather than a form of (re)production in its own right. In contrast, Edholm, Harris and Young (1977) have distinguished *biological* (human) reproduction, the reproduction of *labour-power* and the *social* reproduction of ideas and ideologies. Useful though this analysis is, other forms of reproduction that may be identified are sexual reproduction, the social organisation and reproduction of sexual practices;[12] physical reproduction, that is including violence; and generative reproduction, incorporating the reproduction of labour-power, and based in the social processes of degeneration, nurture and regeneration.

These different forms of reproduction can be related to each other, and in turn to the social relations of production. This latter relationship varies from considerable autonomy from the relations of production, with sexual and biological reproductions, to considerable interdependence, with social reproduction. Indeed it is probably most useful to see social reproduction as a product of the general form, social relations, rather than specific to a particular form, capitalist, patriarchal or whatever. Each of these various reproductions, while partially autonomous, may be interlinked within a greater process of the reproduction of bodies and bodily contact.

Furthermore, these reproductions and their interrelations are qualitatively structured, in different ways in different historical and social contexts. This includes the differential and uneven development of reproductive classes and class struggles, reproductive technologies and their detailed social relations.

It is through these struggles and social relations that 'men' and 'women' are so defined. Strictly speaking there are many different types of 'men' and 'women'. Indeed what we generally call 'men' and 'women' are themselves shorthands for classes of persons in determinate social relations.

Individuals, individual men and individual women, are thereby themselves in a mediated relationship with such classes (see Sève, 1978).

This raises the specific problem of the practices of types of people. For example, it is possible to distinguish men's collective practice and the practices of individual men (see chapter 11). On the first count, men's collective practices may be located in social structural terms; on the second, one can try to locate particular individuals, including oneself. Different practices range from public oppressions, where men explicitly accept and profit from oppression, to private oppressions, to more liberal stances, to more thoroughgoing attempts to change to be less oppressive by public and/or private action. These last may be intensely personal matters, as with involvement in men's anti-sexist activities (see Part 4).

Finally, there is the possible implication that a central concern with what has been called reproduction, a set of social structures, necessarily implies that there is a process of reproduction, still dialectical and materialist, of social life itself. Thus reproduction is not only a *part* of social life, it is also the *form* of social life. Social life is constituted as reproduced. Whatever we may attempt to describe in social structural terms may be both experienced and changed over time in its *own* reproduction.

4 A Materialist Analysis of Reproduction[1]

This chapter outlines a materialist theory of reproduction: an attempt to theorise in a materialist way on reproduction, to begin to locate men both collectively as a gender class and individually as persons. We may thus better understand both structural limitations on action and possibilities for action.

To attempt to write on theory about reproduction, a first step is of course to make this vague term, 'reproduction', a little clearer. Reproduction can certainly mean different things to different people. For example, Maureen Mackintosh (1977) has argued for the distinctions between the social relations of human reproduction, the reproduction of the social system as a whole, and the social relations of production. Felicity Edholm, Olivia Harris and Kate Young (1977) have been even more precise in separating out biological reproduction, reproduction of the labour force (or labour-power), and social reproduction (which is an even more general notion covering the reproduction of ideas, ideology, forms of relationships and so on). I want to focus mainly on the first form, with a number of qualifications strongly added. First the term 'biological reproduction' is misleading. (If you like there is nothing strictly biological about biology!) I am concerned more specifically with the social construction or social organisation of biological reproduction; this includes such questions as who 'can' and 'cannot' have children, how birth itself is organised, with what effects and so on. Second, this means that although women give birth to children with the 'help' of men, it cannot be presumed that there is a single, natural biological form of reproduction. The most obvious factor here is the introduction of contraception, limiting and controlling birth; but there are also numerous other variations, including awareness of paternity, the use of technology at birth, artificial insemination and implantation. Thirdly, under this broad definition of reproduction I am also including early childrearing, say up to the time when children are no longer completely dependent, the age of which will of course vary considerably from society to society. So what we have is the social organisation of conception, pregnancy, birth and dependent childrearing.[2] Within all this I am not concerned with reproduction as some general occurrence, but reproduction as it is now, within the present state of affairs, that is, patriarchy. So I am trying to theorise about the nature of reproduction under patriarchy.

The debates that have taken place on this question hinge largely on two issues: on the extent to which the way reproduction is organised is seen as natural or socially determined; and the way in which reproduction is related to production, in industry, commerce and so on outside the home, as part of the 'total economy'. Most conventional treatments of the subject treat reproduction as a natural fact, about which there is little more to be said or done: women have children, thereby suffer and thereby gain, so what! Of the most critical approaches, many are strongly influenced by marxist thinking, but even there the idea of the natural way of doing things lingers on.

Many discussions of reproduction, marxist, feminist or whatever, are imbued with a strong sense of idealism, that is they are concerned primarily with the *special quality* of the ideas and experiences around, say, the family or motherhood, rather than the material basis that underlies those ideas and experiences.

A second issue is that even amongst those that adopt a materialist stance there is still often a reluctance to see reproduction as a more fundamental issue than production.

I want to argue for a materialist account of reproduction that doesn't simply subsume it within the analysis of production.

Marxism is a materialist theory and a materialist practice. But it is essentially a materialism of production, subsistence and survival; it is not materialism of reproduction, existence and essence. Whereas in production, people produce things which indirectly provide the conditions for and constraints on their future, with reproduction people both produce people and are produced by others; reproduction directly and literally provides the possibility of existence in the first place. It is this— the double dialectic of reproduction—that is usually forgotten, or thought to be unimportant.

This isn't to say biology is fixed; just that we aren't used to looking at the changes. The way we assume that the way birth as now is natural just shows we're wearing dark glasses. Sexuality, birth itself, the organisation after birth, early childwork are all different at different times and in different places. For example, in some nomadic societies women give birth under quite different conditions and with quite different personal responses to those usual in this society.

Furthermore, each birth is both life continuing and beginning again. Reproduction is both a form of relations between people, particularly between men and women, and also a form of reproduction of other new people.

Women do always (so far) actually give birth to babies. However, that is no necessary determinant of who is in control of that situation—it could be men, it could be particular women or it could be the woman herself. Similarly with sexuality. Some form of sexual encounter obviously precedes birth, except where artificial insemination is used;[3] but even forgetting AID for the moment, this tells us nothing about the nature of that heterosexuality—is it usual or unusual, is it accompanied by bisexual or homosexual relationships, is it controlled by the man or woman, is penetration[4] the norm or abnormal, is contraception used, if so, by whom, and according to whose control? The point is even clearer with regard to childwork, with some women still tending to do the majority of the work. For although there are and have been many different ways in which sexuality, fertility, birth and childwork have been organised in different societies, most of these have remained firmly in the control of men. This means that even though production may have been in the control of one class over another, reproduction has been in the control of men over women. Divisions by economic class in the organisation of production may account for the major variations in the material wealth, but divisions by sexual class in the organisation of reproduction account for the major variations in the whole material existence of different people. In other words, economic class divisions may explain why an upper-class woman is materially better off than a working-class woman, but sexual class divisions explain why both these women may know that their whole person is actually or potentially in the control of (certain) men, through the control of sexuality, fertility, birth and childwork. In this way, the understanding of reproduction provides the basis of an existential materialism—a materialism not of goods, products, commodities and so on, but a materialism dealing with who we are and with *the fact that we live at all*. It is for this reason that a materialism based on reproduction is a more basic and fundamental account that the 'traditional' form of materialism, focusing on production, as elaborated within most versions of marxism. The analysis of reproduction in particular and materialist feminism in general can thus provide the basis of a more thorough-going materialism—a materialism of existence—than marxism. In comparison marxism is superficial materialism.

At this point you may shout that I have just gone too far—for how can marxism be superficial? I admit that to say that is probably rather crude, but I have made it so to try to get a number of fundamental issues to the centre of the stage. In particular I want to avoid reproduction just being incorporated as an afterthought into another marxist analysis based on production. Having said that, it is possible to reconcile what I'm getting at with marxism. One possible argument is that marxism is centrally concerned with the creation of existence through experience, but this is understood to occur most importantly through productive labour rather than reproductive labour. A second possible argument is that this process of the creation of existence through experience may occur through both reproductive and productive labour, but within capitalism happens to be primarily structured through the distortions of commodity production. On the first argument, I would say that to see productive labour as of greater importance than reproductive labour is sexist. On the second, I would argue that capitalism may be characterised in this way, but we live in a form of patriarchy as well as a form of capitalism; and furthermore the basic building block of patriarchy is usually not commodity production.

I now want to outline three main elements that seem to me to be important in constructing a materialist theory of reproduction. These elements—class struggle and the points of reproduction; technology and the relations of reproduction; and human value and human tithes—are examples of ideas that may be useful in understanding reproduction, and particularly the contradictions that face men.

CLASS STRUGGLE AND THE POINTS OF REPRODUCTION

Economic classes are generally defined within marxism in terms of how certain people relate to production—do they own the product produced, do they own the means of producing those products, do they do the producing itself? Sexual classes or reproductive classes can also be identified in terms of how people relate to reproduction, in its various aspects. If one is going to be precise there are very many different sexual classes, and sub-classes.

Thus men and women for the time being at least are bound to have very different sorts of experiences in relation to the various aspects of reproduction, but it is also important to recognise *the different types* of experience that particular types of men, and indeed women, have. Men and women as a whole may constitute classes, but particular men and women vary in their class position and experience. Just as there are different types of capitalist production and different types of capital—competitive commodity capital, monopoly finance capital and so on—so too there are different types of reproduction.

There are thus within reproduction separate but interrelated types of material production, for example, in sexuality, fertility and birth, early childwork. For each of these there are slightly different sets of classes or sub-classes. In terms of sexuality, divisions obviously exist between men and women, but also between gays and straights and so on. Classes around fertility and birth are based not only on the biology of sex but also on the social control of fertility. So the classes controlling fertility and those controlled do not exactly match with men and women. With early childwork, there are the childworkers and the non-childworkers. *The childworkers of our society form the third proleteriat*, after women as a class and the working class. Although there are a few exceptions, for example, a relatively small number of men who are solely or primarily responsible for children, most of these classes divide crucially by sex. And furthermore the very many sexual classes overlap and impinge on each other. 'Women' and 'men' represent both the sum of all these particular class divisions, and the cumulative result of these divisions heaped one on another. Women and men are divided and 'classified' many times over—to the extent that now they are seen as obviously separate categories of people.

How and where is the struggle between these classes carried out? Where are the class struggles of reproduction? The struggles are both between the various sub-classes, for example, childworkers, non-childworkers, and the two great classes—of women and men.

These class struggles are at the various points of reproduction—sexual, including heterosexual conception; birth; early childwork—in the bed, at delivery and in the house. Just as the point of production is of special significance within marxist politics, so the points of reproduction are vital in showing up the way reproduction is organised. The house, and the domestic arrangements in it, are important in sexual politics not in a general way because of the amount of domestic labour done there, but specifically because that is where the points of reproduction for sexuality and early childwork occur.

It is also at these various points of reproduction that contradictions for me, and I suspect other men, appear. I sometimes want to engage in penetrative sex, but know this may be unwanted; I sometimes wish to be more involved in birth, but know this may be unwelcome; I sometimes seek to be more involved in childwork, but know this may be for other reasons than nurture. The essential matter is that in reproduction men often seem to stand in contradictory relations to women in a number of different ways and these contradictions, which are questions of both (sexual) class power and personal experience, often centre on the points of reproduction.

The various points of reproduction are also important in more organised ways. The closer one approaches a point of reproduction the more clearly the divisions between the relevant workers are by sex. This is most clearly seen amongst the various medical and paramedical workers concerned with reproduction. Not only is it true that midwives are the most uniformly female group, but moreover throughout the history of midwifery the many disputes that occurred have almost always been fought by sex—by men versus women. It is here that the contradictions between men and women are most public and most visible. In this sense the various intense divisions around foetal monitoring, amniocentesis, inductions and so on represent some of the sites of the class struggles of reproduction. The 'experts' on reproduction—be they a Bowlby, a Spock, a Leboyer or a Jolly—are men. For men to enter reproductive work and reproductive politics on a different, non-expert, basis also raises contradictions for the individuals concerned. It is at the points of reproduction, in sexuality, fertility, birth and early childwork, that the struggles between the classes remain the most crucial and the contradictions between and within classes remain the most intense.

TECHNOLOGY AND THE RELATIONS OF REPRODUCTION

It is possible to analyse the production of goods in terms of the technology that produces them and the relations of production, that is the way the technology is owned, controlled and organised. However, with reproduction this sort of separation is not possible. The technology of reproduction and its social organisation are one and the same. For this reason it may be that 'morphology'—the means of control of the shape of people's bodies—might be a more appropriate term than technology when discussing reproduction, but that particular issue is not considered in any detail here.

Perhaps, the first thing to establish is the difference between the capitalist organisation of production and the operation of reproduction. The way reproduction is generally organised in present society closely resembles the way production was organised in feudal society: day-to-day control of the product lies with the working group, women, and the tools, for example hands, that are used are meagre and basic; less routinely, overall control of the product lies with men, through the use of more advanced technology, such as hospitals and schools. This applies particularly to the reproduction of children, at birth or later in early childwork, though there are parallels in the sexual sphere. Many women may be allowed some degree of day-to-day control of this sexuality through heterosexual sex and masturbation but this generally occurs within the confines of the overall control of their sexuality by men, through marriage, heterosexual coupling and heterosexist ideologies. Such arrangements are truly feudal. Sexuality, fertility and birth are managed   apparently   independently   by   women   for considerable amounts of time, on the conditions that men are allowed the final 'word' and a reproductive 'tithe' when we wish. A reproductive 'tithe' may 'merely' mean sexual favours or it may mean the production of a child. More will be said on this in the next section.

The major technical development in reproduction in modern times is on the face of it the expansion of organised births in hospitals with all the paraphernalia of birth technology. Such innovations raise acute contradictions in their life-giving (or saving) potential and their life-controlling presence. They also raise further possibilities for the control of women by men, and further still determine separations between different types of men, with their own consequently different experiences.

The other major technical development of recent years would appear to be the greater use of contraception. But the fact that contraception is still not controlled totally by women and that safe abortion is not fully available means that the prevailing   feudalism   remains.   If   there   was   complete contraception/abortion controlled by women then there would certainly be a major shift in the relations of reproduction. But such control is a long way off. The control of contraception and abortion by men is one of the cornerstones of patriarchal domination.

Another possible technical change is growth in forms of sexuality that oppose penetration. These could either be from the separatist position of the radical feminists or simply a 'liberal' position. According to the latter, heterosexual penetration might continue but be the exception rather than the rule. It is here that the question of who controls artificial insemination becomes crucial. AID is not necessarily a way of changing the relations of reproduction; it only is if it is entirely controlled by women. That would mean a shift from feudal reproduction to something quite different.

If the control of fertility is one of the major questions within the broader issue of reproduction, then one can go on to ask who is in fact involved in this process—involved, that is, on both sides, as controllers and controlled. Broadly this division would correspond to men and women, but not exactly. Women who are infertile, post-fertile or in complete control of their own fertility through contraception are in different positions to other women. It may also mean that those people, *both men and women*, who are no longer involved in reproduction have a different interest to those who are. The implication of this is that *age*, or more precisely the division between those people involved in reproducing and those not involved in reproducing, is particularly important. At its simplest, older men who are not involved directly in reproduction control younger women who are.

It is partly for this reason that the experience of ageing seems to carry different meanings for men and women—differences that remain obscured in such gender-neutral words as 'youth', 'life-cycle', 'retirement' and so on. Ageing and the physical change of the body may also be used to control women in different ways. Older men may control the reproduction of younger women, but this does not mean that older women remain free of men's control over their sexuality.

HUMAN VALUE AND HUMAN TITHES

In some ways this short section has been one of the hardest to write but I think it's getting at what is a fundamental aspect of patriarchy, namely the nature of the dominant mode of reproduction. Whereas capitalism operates through the creation of commodities, patriarchy is not based primarily upon commodity production but upon what I call here the reproduction of human tithes.

Goods, services, commodities have value. They are worth something, in money terms. They can be used; they have a use value; they can be exchanged usually through money; they have an exchange value. Their value reflects in whole or in part the (productive) labour-power, that is the potential rather than the actual production of labour, invested in them.

Within patriarchy, the products of reproduction, particularly though not exclusively from the labour (power) of women, are not valued in the same way—they are not simply commodities. They have a use value: they can be enjoyed, used and consumed. But unlike commodities, this does not depend on them being bought. Babies do not usually have a money value. Most childwork remains unpaid; this is especially so for childwork done outside the state. Even sexual activity, with the exception of prostitution, is itself only paid for indirectly. The products of reproductive labour (power)—in childbirth, in childwork, in sex—usually have no direct exchange value.

To understand all this I have found it necessary and useful to put forward the idea of human value as central within reproduction. In many ways it parallels Marx's notion of value as the embodiment of abstract general labour within production. Human value is at the same time the embodiment and the product of reproductive labour. Human value is simply what is valued in humans as humans. It is socially and historically specific. Under the present form of patriarchy, it is that which is appropriated, dominantly by men from women and children, and ranges from the energy and creativity of particular people in particular situations to the whole person, their very existence.

Thus while women tend to exert more energy, are more creative and generally do more labour than men in reproduction, part of this process goes unrewarded. Some of the energy, creativity and labour brings its own direct reward, in the enjoyment of reproduction and its products, sex, birth and children, but at the same time a form of surplus human value is derived that may be appropriated by men. This process of appropriation may well be important in understanding the sources of male power; in effect individual appropriations may be accumulated.

This view of reproductive labour and reproductive labour-power (that is, the capacity to reproduce) explains why women have lower status than men in this society. The capacity to reproduce possessed by women is in effect appropriated (by men), so that women themselves are seen to have less value than men, just as workers are seen to have less value than owners or managers. It is in this way that reproductive materialism is more fundamental than productive materialism. It is the materialism of existence—of the valuing of women, of humans, of existence at all. The analysis of reproduction is badly in need of a new concept that describes the way in which human existence is turned into something like but *slightly different* from a commodity—a human 'tithe' or something of the sort. It is this 'human tithe' that we routinely and exhaustively extract from each other; and that above all men extract from women. The extraction can be little, trivial favours or whole people, babies. The essential feature of this process of appropriation of babies, children and sex is that it depends on something far less subtle than the circulation and exchange of commodities under capitalism. It depends on direct appropriation without recompense, and it is in this sense that patriarchy ultimately hinges on violence. Such possible violence lies not only in individual men, but also importantly in the state itself.

Patriarchy can thus be seen as the patriarchal or feudal mode of reproduction. The products of women's reproductive labour are appropriated directly and unusually by the state, in the case of mothers being deemed 'unfit' by the courts, or they are appropriated indirectly, *but quite routinely* by individual men in individual families, as husbands and fathers routinely receiving privileges from others without recompense for them.

It is for this reason that there can be little development of male heterosexual prostitution. This would be like workers paying capitalists to provide work for them! This raises the peculiar prospect that perhaps the most that men, aspiring to be anti-sexist, can do in a patriarchal society is to *sell* their sexual favours, and so attempt to explode the myth and the illusion. Perhaps a less drastic way of undermining heterosexism is for women and men who are sleeping together to make it clear if they are not in a sexual relationship or not having sexual intercourse (Sebestyen, 1982).

It is possible that we're coming now towards the end of the feudal mode of reproduction. Women in marriage are sexually in a very similar position to peasants within feudalism economically. Feminism is part of the transition from the feudal mode of reproduction to something else. What this is remains and continues to be fought for. The most terrifying prospect is that feminists are equivalent to the free peasant proprietors that characterised the transition from feudalism to capitalism.

Marx wrote: 'In England, serfdom has practically disappeared in the late part of the 14th century. The immense majority of the population consisted then, and to a large extent in the 15th century, of free peasant proprietors, whatever was the feudal title under which their right of property was hidden' (Marx, 1977a, 671). Will it be that by the twenty-first century sexual serfdom will have practically disappeared, to be replaced by free sexual 'proprietors'? If so what next? Will men attempt to reorganise—to form collective institutions where reproduction is commercialised? Just as in Germany and elsewhere there are 'sex palaces', will attempts be made by men to turn the production of children into a capitalist enterprise? I wouldn't put it past men. After all the hiring of women to reproduce and bring up children is something that has been done by the upper classes for a long time. It is the possible extension of this that is so terrifying—as people are transformed from unwaged serfs to waged sexual workers. In other words there may be worse or at least more blatant forms of oppression to come. To fight this will need the struggle for a sexual socialism.

SEXUALITY

In most of this chapter I have been writing about women and men in heterosexual relationships, often couples. This is not because I see this as usual or normal or whatever but simply because heterosexual relationships remain as a major way in which patriarchy is perpetuated. Thus just as Marx focused his analysis of capitalist society upon the capitalist organisation, so too can an analysis of patriarchy be developed upon the examination of heterosexual arrangements. The control of reproduction by men through the work of women provides the basis for the way we are, sexually and particularly heterosexually. As long as men control directly or indirectly, through marriage or the state or in any other way, the fertility of women then sexuality will remain defined in terms of those who are fertile and 'reproductive' and those who are not—principally women and men respectively. Control of reproduction in this way necessitates a heterosexual and heterosexist ideology—to maintain that control and to display it. Heterosexual ideology is a way of keeping control of reproduction and a way of flouting it for all to see. We can all see sexuality, we all know it, so we are fit to be subject to the control of the ideology.

5 Reproduction, Men and the Institutions of Patriarchy

Patriarchy has so far been located in the materialism of reproduction. This chapter builds on that base, in reviewing several years on some of the questions already raised. In particular three preliminary issues are addressed: some further critiques, both positive and negative, of Marx's and marxist theorising and practice; a response to some of these in the work of O'Brien; and some continuing problems in the relationship of dialectical materialism and sexuality. The remainder of the chapter draws on these discussions in outlining a structural account of the relationship of reproductive labour-powers, oppression and the division between the public realm and the private realm, and thence the major institutions that comprise patriarchy.

MARX, MARXISM AND CRITIQUE

Marx's confusion around the notion of reproduction (see pp. 46–8) is partly a matter of structural neglect and the neglect of structures; it is also a commentary on his particular brand of dialectical materialism, especially as in his middle and later work.

Early opportunities and disappointments

Marx's early work, particularly the 'Excerpts from James Mill's Elements of Political Economy' and the 'Economic and philosophical manuscripts' (1975), offers major insights as well as a lack of consistency. Their focus on alienation and people's relation with nature provides a possible entry to the question of reproduction, and yet exhibits some strange commissions and omissions. These include:

1. The remark that: 'The worker can create nothing without *nature*, without the *sensuous, external world*' (325, emphasis in original). The emphasis on the *sensuous* nature of practical activity is reaffirmed in, for example, the ninth thesis on Feuerbach. Yet Marx fails to pursue the implications of this with regard to the appeal to the senses, and especially to relations, that is *sensual relations*, between people. This is a prescription for the investigation of forms of reproduction, including sexuality (see pp. 80–3), that he fails to honour.

2. The continued reference to the *external* world neglects the nature of the sensuous, *internal* world. This is relevant to the process of reproduction, most obviously in the creation of a new internal *world* in pregnancy, and more generally in all people's flesh, blood and brains. The presence of a relationship of internal and external worlds would seem necessary within dialectical materialism.

3. The continued emphasis on production and indeed private property neglects attention to reproduction and 'familial property'. This is to be seen in numerous passages, for example, 'Man—this is the fundamental premise of private property—*produces* only in order to have. *Having* is the *aim of production*' (274); and, more pertinently, '*The demand for men necessarily regulates the production of men, as of every other commodity*' (283) (emphases in originals). Reproduction in the biological sense, is conflated with the early nurturing process, the reproduction of labour-power and supply of people to the labour market.

4. Reproduction has its own particular characteristics which are neglected. Marx's analysis is in terms of *capital*: 'Capital is ... the *power to command* labour and its products' (295) (emphasis in original). Likewise 'Man as patriarch', be he individual father or generalised agent, for example, of the state, is the power to command women and their products, children. Marx continues: 'his [the worker's] labour becomes an object, an *external* existence, ... that ... exists *outside* him [*sic*], independently of him and alien to him, and begins to confront him as an autonomous power' (324, emphasis in original).

Such *autonomous power* occurs *par excellence* with children, to become people. This is external existence as *material* not abstracted reality.

Reproduction means producing something or somebody *again*. It is a *continuation* of the producer, which can thence accomplish the same as the producer.

5. Marx neglects the possibilities of numerous sources of alienation, rather than alienation existing solely or primarily in relation (however indirectly) to production. Such sources include reproductive as well as productive ones.

6. Alienation in reproduction is both life-negating and life-affirming. It is negating both in the possibilities of particular pain, loss, violence and death; and in the characteristic loss of self, in different ways for women and men. It is life-affirming both in the possibilities of particular joys and lives; and in the characteristic of continued existence of life.

7. Sexuality, birth, nurture, childcare, care, ageing, violence and death are praxes, 'practical, human-sensuous activities' (422) *par excellence*, that together comprise reproduction. Reproduction continues through 'practical, human-sensuous activity'. Such 'activities', however, do not *constitute* reproduction as such; they exist in, around, and in relation to reproduction, in parallel to reproduction; even as a defence against reproduction. This applies *a fortiori* to men, as *relative* passengers in biological reproduction at least. Therefore the term 'parapraxis' may be more accurately used, in the sense of praxes in relation to reproduction, not Freudian 'faulty function'.

Later obscurities and blatancies
In Marx's later writings these principles and possibilities become even more obscured beneath a (critique of) political economy, the crushing 'weight' of capitalism (see chapter 3). The domination of a social structural productionism over the hope of 'practical, human-sensuous activity' could be explained away in several ways:

1. Marx developed his methodological position over time to emphasise the determinism of history.
2. The particular conditions of and concern with capitalism

necessitated a reappraisal of the possibilities of 'practical, human-sensuous activity'. Such activity like other things is liable to be commodified and fetishised: capitalism negates such activity.
3. Many or most social formations, including but not especially capitalist ones, tend to reduce possibilities of such activity.

The period of capitalist development of the mid-nineteenth century may indeed have been characterised by a domination of production over reproduction: materially, human life was drafted into the productive factory system at the earliest available opportunity; and ideologically, life was relatively unvalued as human life. The giving of lives, virtually without recompense, virtually as human tithes, to the factory (or the mines or whatever) further devalued, perhaps unvalued, life, and paradoxically in the characteristic manner of ideological inversion, made lives (falsely) seem a function of production.[1]

Not only does reproduction 'appear' invisible, but 'men' become equated with productive not reproductive classes, and defined as members of the former: aristocracy, bourgeoisie and proletariat are assumed to be men. This may be reasonable for the first two classes, with property rights through the male line predominant, but is by no means so for wage-labourers. Indeed if we look more closely we may notice that both the 'bourgeois' and 'proletarian' are implicitly male, in both linguistic and historical senses. Both are modelled on pre-capitalist male social groupings. The bourgeois is the capitalist development of the medieval burgher, the *freeman* of the free city or bourg, to become the merchant, owner of capital, or more generally member of the middle classes. The proletarian is a phoenix-like resurrection from ancient Rome over two thousand years on. He is a capitalist borrowing from the sixth century BC. Servian practice of those who, unable to serve the state with property, did so with 'their' offspring. Service by the labour of offspring has become service by the labour of the labourer. However, each remain wrongly modelled as men, as if they only had labour to offer in service.

For Marx, the proletariat is working-class men, the worker is the 'adult male' (Weinbaum, 1978): the proletariat appears as the embodiment of future Man. Not only are working-class women largely forgotten (an error corrected by marxist feminists, and then frequently re-forgotten by men marxists and socialists), but the whole conceptualisation and understanding of the proletariat is male: the model of (class) *war* waged by the *army* of labourers led by *vanguards* and *militants*, with the support of *rank and file*.[2] Many words and concepts of potential co-operation and intimacy have been appropriated by particular macho, 'socialist' rhetorics— 'solidarity', 'brotherhood', 'strength' is between vigorous, 'manly' 'brothers', not soft, gentle ones. The left in Britain at least is littered with an arch-factionalism, whereby former 'comrades' easily become 'class traitors' for each other, like squabbling and estranged 'brothers'. If political power does grow out of the barrel of a gun, or the mobile carrier of a cruise missile, then god help us.

Furthermore, Marx's own social location in both productive and reproductive terms, may have created the conditions for emphasising more deterministic explanations whatever their accuracy. Petty-bourgeois by origin, he remained often anti-worker and relatively wealthy, later, supported by the Manchester businessman, Engels. Reproductively he was a patriarch, with an oppressive relation to other members of the family. Considerable information is now available on the lives of other members of the Marx family: their subjection to domestic tyranny and their experience of 'revolutionary' activity. According to Eleanor Marx, 'even the dull routine of factory work is not more killing than are the endless duties of the *ménage*'; Laura Marx was unable to fight on the 1871 Paris Commune barricades because of her childcare responsibilities (Marx *et al.*, 1982; Kapp, 1977).

Many other unfortunate legacies of Marx's own practice and the male dominance of marxism have bedevilled left, socialist and other struggles against (patriarchal) power. This is to be felt in, for example, the conduct of meetings, the definition of 'economy', the justification of means by ends.[3]

Dialectical materialist understandings of men and masculinity are not achieved by 'reading off' the production of 'men' from productive class 'cultures', relevant though this is in the detail of men's presentation. Instead it is the production of men *qua* men, not simply as aggregations of different economic class members, that is at issue. Analysis of the latter alone facilitates a *social naturalism*. Thus important as economic class relations and productive work are for men, as for all, they do not determine the base of men; more likely they determine the ideology and ideologies of men, that is masculinity and masculinities.

O'BRIEN'S *POLITICS OF REPRODUCTION*

This theoretical and practical question of understanding men dialectically and materially is taken up, if at times indirectly, by O'Brien in her feminist theorising on reproduction. Her reproduction-focused[4] dialectical materialism is explicitly built on the notion of praxis, the unity of theory and practice, so beloved by Marx 'in theory'.

For O'Brien, reproduction is a material, historical and dialectical process, driven by praxis. In comparing production and reproduction, and their labour processes, she observes:

1. Both forms of labour are activities which mediate the separation between people and nature.
2. Both forms of labour are also mediations of contradictions *within* the fundamental processes of which labour is a necessary component.... In general, Marx's analysis of the dialectics of productive labour process is accepted as essentially correct, with some reservations in terms of the level of Hegelian abstraction to which he occasionally flies.
3. Both processes, production and reproduction, emerging as they do from necessity, contribute to the dialectical structure of human consciousness. There is a reproductive, generic aspect of consciousness, just as there is a productive, class aspect of consciousness. Again, Marx's analysis of the latter is accepted as basically correct.
4. Both forms of labour produce values and create new needs. The values and needs created are not, however, commensurable. In its abstract form, the productive process creates values and needs for the producer: in any form, reproductive labour creates another and needy human. Production in its historic development becomes socially necessary labour: reproduction is primordially *necessarily social labour*.

(O'Brien, 1981, 15, emphases in original)[5]

More specifically, she postulates that,

The actual process of reproduction is the material ground (the substructure) of: (a) reproductive consciousness; (b) the historical forms of the social relations of reproduction. The unifying process of these three aspects is dialectical because the material base is dialectically structural;

and that

Reproductive consciousness is generically differentiated in significant and identifiable ways which stand in opposition to each other.

(O'Brien, 1979, 235)

Reproduction is itself structured in a series of 'moments'—of menstruation, ovulation, copulation, alienation, conception, gestation, labour, birth, appropriation, nurture—and their characteristic forms. She notes some important differences between these moments:

[M]ost, for example, are involuntary, appropriation and nurture are the only completely voluntary moments. Copulation ... has a strong instinctual component, but a great deal of human effort has been invested historically in demonstrating that it can or at least ought to be controlled by the human will. Alienation and appropriation are male moments: copulation and nurture are generically shared moments; all of the others are women's moments.

(47–8)

O'Brien places the notion of alienation—'a technical term describing separation of the consciousness of negativity' (52)—centrally within her analysis. Alienation appears to *persist* as part of people's essential relation to nature, and likewise people appear to *resist* that alienation. For example, man (*sic*) is not negated as lover, as Hegel suggests, but according to O'Brien as parent, in alienation from his seed in copulation.[6] Men's relation to reproduction is generically alienated, women's alienation is 'simply' for the child. Women's relation to genetic continuity is not problematic; the experience of time is (relatively) continuous. Men's relation to genetic continuity is problematic; the experience of time is (relatively) discontinuous. Thus O'Brien suggests:

The fact is that men make *principles of continuity* because they are separated from genetic continuity with the alienation of the male seed. Genetic continuity constitutes one pole of the substructure of necessity which is the

material condition of human history. Unlike ... the necessity to produce ...
the reproductive pole resists male participation and control.

(33–4, my emphasis)

She continues her analysis by specifying the particular social
forms that men have developed in relation to their alienation,
above all in the wake of the 'discovery of the idea of paternity'.
Before that although men experienced separation from their
seed, they did not experience *consciousness* of negativity (52).
Thus although reproductive dialectics exist in the material
processes of biology they are social processes, as in the impact
of the idea of paternity. Whereas maternity and maternal
reproductive consciousness involve a unity of consciousness
and involuntary reproductive labour, paternity and paternal
reproductive consciousness are a process in which ideas
(principles) dominate materiality. O'Brien suggests: '[t]he
action in which men commonly annul the alienation of their
seed is that action which is described here as the
"appropriation of the child"' (37), that is, fatherhood in
marriage. She argues that 'by virtue of his need to mediate his
alienation from procreation', man (*sic*) 'has created the
institutional forms of the social relations of reproduction,
forms which mediate the contradictions in male reproductive
consciousness' (56).

The 'appropriation of the child' by fatherhood in marriage is
merely a social beginning[7] of the 'development of human
institutions and ... ideologies of male supremacy' (49). Thus
O'Brien argues that:

Man ... has created ... the institutional forms of the social relations of
reproduction, forms which mediate the contradictions in male reproductive
consciousness ... the most persistent and successful form is marriage, with all
its variations. Yet marriage in itself is not an adequate expression of the right
to appropriation.... The appropriation of the child symbolizes the rights of
the father.... The exclusive right to a particular woman is ... buttressed by
the physical separation of that woman from other men. In creating the right
to the appropriation of children, men created ... the private realm ... while
the public realm is the space where men fore-gather to make the laws and
ideologies which shape and justify patriarchy.   (56)

The creation of the public realm, the separation of the public
and private realms, and the dominance of the public over the

private realm, are thus all part of the relations of reproduction; the public–private separation is to the social relations of reproduction, as class struggle is to the social relations of production.[8] Thus, 'a huge and oppressive structure of law and custom and ideology is erected by the brotherhood of Man to affirm and protect their potency, . . . a structure which must be actively maintained, because at the heart of male potency lies the intransigent reality of estrangement and uncertainty' (60–1).

THE CONUNDRUM OF SEXUALITY

O'Brien's analysis provides a powerful critique of production-based marxism. However, one particular area of 'estrangement and uncertainty' that she fails to pursue in depth is sexuality. In keeping with much writing in the marxist tradition sexuality appears as something of a 'problem'. Against this, sexuality, along with psychoanalysis and linguistics, has become increasingly important as an avenue of critique of marxism, as in Critical Theory, Foucauldian analysis, and various post-structuralist initiatives. Within these perspectives sexuality is not exterior to the social; and its social analysis therefore contrasts with its problematic status within most marxism. This problematisation sometimes escalates to the point where sexuality, sexual relations and sexual feelings are seen as politically diversionary. The difficulties that sexuality poses for marxism include sexuality's apparent biological basis; its emotional and experiential intensity; its 'unpredictable' variability; its complex psychic structure.

Briefly these 'uncomfortable' qualities of sexuality can be responded to respectively as follows. Firstly, the argument for its biological basis has to be considered alongside both the critique of biological essentialism (for example, Rubin, 1984), and the biological basis of many other activities—walking, talking, even breathing—which are not seen as problems for marxism. Secondly, emotional power is in itself not necessarily antithetic to material relations, as instanced in the power, sometimes apparently autonomous, of stress at work. Thirdly, its variability—say, differential preferences and forms of arousals—compares well with the variability of culture and literature. Fourthly, the complex psychic structure of sexuality, which has certainly been shied away from within marxism, may just show that materialism goes very deep, as 'residues' of past material relations, and as material in the brain and body itself. In other words, there is a lot of personal work to be done here; the analysis of sexuality does not necessarily represent a critique of marxism. Indeed dialectical materialism seems a very suitable framework for understanding the dialectical material happenings called sexuality.

A more fundamental set of arguments are those that promote sexuality class analysis as a critique of marxism as economic class analysis, and possibly as dialectical materialism. Most of these are variations on critiques of heterosexuality—either heterosexual relations and people as oppressive of homosexual relations and people; or 'compulsory heterosexuality' or heterosexism over all else, or male heterosexuality over female sexuality; or heterosexual intercourse (sometimes referred to as male 'penetration') as a form of invasion over non-intercourse and/or other sexualities; or less usually non-bisexuality as oppressive of bisexuality; and so on. All the above possibilities are premised on divisions between people that cut across those of economic class, as, for example, may divisions by marital and household status (see Weinbaum, 1978), age of adult over children, and as may, but most likely will not, divisions by disability, or ethnicity.

Whether these represent a critique of marxism rests on detailed interpretations of homosexuality, heterosexuality, and bisexuality. If some people are assumed to be essentially 'homosexual' or essentially not, or if heterosexuality is assumed to be only ideology, then such analysis poses few problems for a conventional marxism: it can be 'conveniently' relegated to a biological caveat. If on the other hand a more socially grounded account is proposed, then this may lead to understanding (and indeed experiencing) sexuality as a form of material relation itself, with certain people occupying positions of power and appropriating qualities, values and desires from others. This is most clearly so in those revolutionary feminist accounts that see heterosexual intercourse as a physical assault from one class to another.

All these complications bear on an important general point, namely the dominant and deep-seated tendency to see and understand sexuality in idealised terms, indeed as an idealism. This can in fact apply as much in interpretation of homosexuality and its oppression as in mainstream/malestream understandings of sexuality. It is difficult for us (all) not to invest our sexuality with some mysterious, and ideal qualities that are all our own, so that 'I', the individual, loves 'only You', from near or from afar. Our conceptual and linguistic apparatus for thinking, understanding and describing sexuality is heavily idealised. In fact we rarely simply *describe our sexuality as what we do sexually*. However, the idealism of the language of sexuality is not a fundamental critique of marxism or dialectical materialism. Sexuality is not a discrete activity; it overlaps with other activities, even though it certainly appears powerfully autonomous. The critical arguments outlined above, although problems for marxism do not in themselves represent assaults on dialectical materialism. They speak more of the shortcomings and indeed sexism of narrowly economistic and certain other marxist traditions.

Some of these areas of difficulty may be recognised around O'Brien's treatment of sexuality, and her consequent theorising of patriarchy. Just as Marx saw his prime object of critique as capitalism, so O'Brien sees hers as heterosexual sexual-biological reproduction. The broad relationship of sexual and biological reproductions is largely non-problematic. Homosexuality, bisexuality, and self-defined autonomous sexuality[9] are not given detailed analysis in *The Politics of Reproduction*. This emphasis may derive from difficulties around what constitutes a materialist account of reproduction, defined to include sexuality. For O'Brien sexuality as *heterosexuality* is largely understood as a preliminary part of the (biological) reproductive process, that is *a priori*, by means of abstractions drawn from the material analysis of reproduction as procreation.

There remains a need to describe the detail of sexual relations materially, as material forms, to produce detailed accounts of *how sexual sexual politics is done*.[10] This is not just a matter of describing 'flesh and bones' in various permutations, it involves accounts of what these might mean, such as oppressions, to those concerned. Materialism without perceptions is anatomy, perhaps pathology. To describe sexual arrangements as perceived problematises clear separations of the perceiver and 'thing' perceived. The relevance of alienation to a materialist account of sexuality comes from the recognition of the dialectical process of separation/construction from/of material reality. In O'Brien's analysis sexuality is a matter (for men at least) of reproductive alienation. The notion of alienation that remains to be developed for a materialist analysis of sexuality is not *vis-à-vis* genetic continuity, but bodily contact/pain/pleasure *in its own right*. This is just as historically constructed as procreation.

This position is similar to that developed by MacKinnon's proposition that: '[s]exuality is to feminism what work is to marxism: that which is most one's own, yet most taken away' (1982, 1). Striking though this insight is, the exact nature of the contrast of the 'base' of sexuality with work is not straightforward. For example, sexuality is itself still a form of work, sometimes publicly paid, often indirectly paid, and more generally a form of labour (see Dorn and South, n.d. 37). More important, however, is a point made by MacKinnon herself when she says that : '[t]he substantive principle governing the authentic politics of women's personal lives is pervasive powerlessness to men, expressed and reconstituted daily *as* sexuality' (1982, 21, emphasis in original). This is crucial, for it is appearance (of powerlessness) *as* sexuality rather than sources of power/powerlessness that are described here. Sexuality, if it is to mean more than just fantasy, consists of dialectical material relations, both within and between people. Sexuality is certainly incredibly important as an apparent form of power, but it may also be the daily expression and reconstitution of something else or even of many other processes (as MacKinnon herself implies), such as violence, nurture, childcare.

One response to some of these problems is to extend O'Brien's analysis to take fuller account of areas of material reproduction, other than the biological or natal, and so include sexual and other reproductions.

REPRODUCTIVE LABOUR-POWERS, OPPRESSION
AND THE PUBLIC–PRIVATE DIVIDE

Reproduction is not a single structure or process; it needs to be
deconstructed (Ettorre, 1982: Jaggar and McBride, 1985). As
already outlined, reproduction is of several types: sexual,
biological, generative, incorporating the 'reproduction of
labour-power', and physical reproduction, including violence.
Each of these forms of reproduction is a dialectical and
material process, a material reality existing in labour and above
all labour-power, the potential to perform labour of a certain
sort. Together, these particular types of labour-power
constitute reproductive labour-power. Sexual reproduction
arises from sexual labour-power, the potential and capacity to
do labour upon others and oneself in the creation of what is felt
to be (sexual) 'desire', for bodies of others or oneself.[11] The
wrongly supposed asocial nature of 'desire' is crucial. Indeed
MacKinnon (1982, 2) sees ' "[d]esire" . . . as a term parallel to
"value" in marxist theory to refer to that substance felt to be
primordial or aboriginal but posited by the theory as social and
contingent.' Physical reproduction arises from destructive
labour-power, the capacity of bodies to do physical harm to
others or to self. Generative reproduction is based in the
labour-power of nurture, the capacity of bodies to do work on
themselves and others in the processes of degeneration and
regeneration. These processes are of particular importance in
the care of those beyond the minimum age of dependence. Thus
the term, the 'reproduction of labour-power', in marxist
parlance the (re)production of the next generation of 'workers'
for the capitalist labour process, becomes problematic. Such a
conceptualisation is probably arbitrary, for the nurturing of
young children is not separate from that of older children,
young workers, the sick, the infirm, the elderly, and so on.
Nurturing, in the marxist sense of the reproduction of labour-
power, is defined through an *ex post facto* functionalism, that is
it becomes 'reproductive' by virtue of the (proletarian) 'labour-
power' it *subsequently* produces.

   The labour-powers of sexuality, generative nurture and
violence exist for almost all; biological labour-power is in the
present 'mode of reproduction' unevenly distributed,

characteristically uneven between women and men. The bearers of reproductive labour-power in its various forms are differentially oppressed through *the exclusion of possible options* for that labour-power, by others. However, this does not mean that such bearers are dormant, rather that certain options are facilitated, and most importantly that the products of those options are appropriated. While in capitalism, the capitalist(s) appropriates the *commodities produced* from the labour-power of workers, in patriarchy men appropriate or attempt to appropriate that which is produced (as a tithe) by the various forms of women's reproductive labour-powers—be it sexual favours, nurtured 'products', or violent acts. Nurtured 'products' thus include babies, children beyond dependence, older children, the infirm and elderly.

Types of reproduction	Sexual reproduction	Biological reproduction	Generative reproduction	Physical reproduction
Incorporating	Sexuality	Pre birth, Birth, After birth labour	Nurture, Degeneration, Regeneration, and the 'Reproduction of Labour-power'	Violence
Types of Labour-power	Sexual Labour-power	Biological (Natal) Labour-power	Generative Labour-power	Violent (Destructive) Labour-power

Reproductive Labour-power(s)

Figure 3:   Types of reproductive labour-power

The creation of the public–private divide is not only a response by men to potential powerlessness in biological reproduction, but also acts as the means of separation from and male appropriation of sexual, generative and destructive labour-powers. O'Brien's exposition of the link between the patriarchal control of reproduction and the creation of the public–private divide is *based* in the process of biological reproduction, including the care of dependent children. Although there are difficulties of detail in her definition of reproduction (see pp. 112–13) the case is made that men's exclusion from biological reproduction, both from our semen and any 'subsequent' children, under the dominant mode of reproduction is all-important. It is this that creates the material possibility for the discovery of paternity, the creation of the institution of fatherhood, and the division between the private world of individual fathers and the public world of 'men', that 'underwrites' *a mutual contract between men* in 'fraternity' to sanction private inhibitions in law and public political life. This is not 'some notion of psychic need or existential yearning for fatherhood' (O'Brien, 1981, 107) (i.e. not a macro-freudianism) but a material and political struggle.

The appropriation of the products of reproductive labour-power does not stop there. Men's appropriation of the sexuality, nurture (or sexual and nurtured 'products') and violence of women may be less directly based in biology than the production of babies but it is no less material. Like birth, each of these labour-powers involves immediate, interpersonal, indeed inter-body contact;[12] and in each case, women's labour-powers may threaten and counter the power of men. Each involves work on the body, through a series of interrelating and shifting uses of touch, caress, push, press and hit, that may move from one site to another. Their 'inter-body' nature, unlike say machine work, locates them, to some extent at least, in the world of interpersonal relationships, typically the family and other domestic sites. The potential of these labour-powers of women has posed a problem of power for men, who in turn have frequently adopted a number of powerful institutional strategies. These are primarily men's appropriation of women's products; the exploitation of women's sexuality, and the conversion by men to what is wrongly seen by men as sexual 'favours', without recompense; the reinforcement of the private realm; the confinement of such labour-power to that realm, particularly the family; their strict separation into private and public realms; and the creation of public institutions, fraternities and traditions that are male-dominated and -defined, as in the professions, and the state.

These institutions produce for men spurious continuities—sexual, generative, destructive (as in 'history' seen through state wars)—comparable to the spurious 'genetic continuity', sought by men in fatherhood and public society, explored by O'Brien.

The potential sexual power of women is controlled by men in hierarchic heterosexuality, predominantly in private confinements; the generative, nurturing potential of women is controlled by men privately in the family, and publicly through the professions and the state; the destructive potential of women[13] is controlled in all these institutions, privately confined, and publicly overarched, indeed overtaken, by the state. The appropriation of women's potential violence by men to form the massive amalgamation of male private and public violence can be understood as both an autonomous control, and a *means* of control of other labour-powers, including productive labour-power. Thus men's control of destructive labour-power, and the appropriation of its 'products' and other products, is probably a fundamental dialectic of patriarchy.

The political impetus for men to control *all* these 'products' is as great as for the appropriation of the product of the semen, the child, from which men are twice removed. Sexuality, nurture and violence may pose a threat to the biological appropriations above, or each themselves may be powerful and more autonomous labour-powers. Whichever way, there are in reality innumerable reinforcing links between the organisation of procreation, sexuality, nurture and violence. In the private realm, these are principally in the complex of fatherhood, hierarchic heterosexuality and the family, again underwritten by the public world of patriarchal institutions. The control of reproductive labour-powers is the cause and the effect of the public–private divide, and the patriarchal institutions of the public and private worlds. The oppression of the bearers of reproductive labour-power sustains and is sustained by the oppression of the institutions of patriarchy, and men's oppressions within them of women, children, and each other.

Oppression in the control of labour-powers is complex, overdeterminedly by men over women and their 'products', but rarely remorseless, as indicated in the following characteristic elements:

1. *Oppression by men*
Men routinely and primarily oppress women and children, both *directly*, face to face and in direct social relations, and *indirectly*, in the creation of patriarchal institutions, public and private. Different institutional situations offer different forms of oppression of men over women, children and other men.
2. *Oppression of women*
Women are routinely oppressed by men, both directly and indirectly as 1 above.
3. *Struggles over oppression*
Men and women are routinely engaged in struggles over and around oppression, both directly in social relations and indirectly over the form of those social relations. These struggles may range from minor skirmishes to outright bloody battles. The bearers of labour-power can engage in a number of tactics of struggle in the attempt to wrest power, often from men. They may commit suicide;[14] withdraw labour; fight, attack and kill others; disrupt and sabotage the relations of reproduction; or engage in the relevant sexual politics to change the relations of reproduction.
4. *Oppression by women*
Although oppression by men overarches other oppressions, women do oppress others, including men, but *not by their sex/gender*, and thus *not as women.* They do not do this routinely, but may oppress in capacities such as adults over children, as owners and managers over workers and so on. Women may also form part of patriarchal institutions and so contribute to indirect oppression.
5. *Oppression of men*
Men may be oppressed by women, though not by them as women, as 4 above, but are routinely oppressed by other men, each other and ourselves, as oppressors. Men may be oppressed in capacities other than as men, primarily as workers, and in the past as boys. Men are also routinely oppressed by the (threat of) violence of other men, despite and because of our control of the means of violence, in armies, the state and so on.

Men may also be oppressed, in work, emotionally, in our capacity for loving others, and frequently *by each other* in the institutions created to dominate biological, sexual and generative labour-powers. More will be said on this below and in chapter 6.

To summarise so far, the labour-powers of reproduction are dominated by men, in the creation of the public–private divide and the particular public and private institutions of patriarchy. This process of domination entails the control of labour-power through a structured relation of oppression, characteristically of men over women. This structured relation is complicated by the oppression that men experience, especially from each other. A further complication is that individual men, although often individually oppressive, are not inherently oppressive, but are rather *agents* of oppression. The form and process of these public and private institutions of patriarchy and thus the form and process of oppression are now examined.

THE INSTITUTIONS OF PATRIARCHY

The institutions of patriarchy are means of men's domination of reproductive labour-powers and their products. Men dominate and oppress women and children through these institutions, yet at the same time by way of them men compete with each other; and in turn oppress each other and are oppressed. These four major institutions—hierarchic heterosexuality, fatherhood, the professions, the state—are located or based in the private or the public world. Each appears to be *based* primarily in the dominance of a form of labour-power—of sexuality (sexual 'desire'), birth (biology), generation (nurture) and violence (destruction) respectively; however, there are also multiple links and definite relations between the institutions and other labour-powers, for example, fatherhood is also a means of controlling sexuality, professions a means of controlling both sexuality, and birth and its 'products'. Although it is possible to analyse these labour-powers and institutions separately, in reality they co-exist and occur simultaneously (Hearn, 1986c). Among the sets of significant interrelations between labour-powers and institutions, the progressive incorporation of each by the next is one dominant pattern (figure 4).

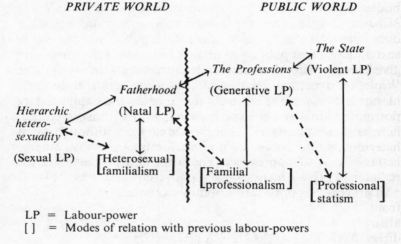

LP   =   Labour-power
[ ]   =   Modes of relation with previous labour-powers

Figure 4:   The institutions of patriarchy

Each of the labour-powers noted are organised not only through the institutions shown above, whether public or private, but also through other institutions and practices in the complementary private or public domain respectively, such as the family or organisation sexuality (Hearn and Parkin, 1987). The major institutions noted (figure 4) are, however, of special significance as they are specifically patriarchal, unlike, say, the family, itself possibly matriarchal, as a site for birth and nurture. These four institutions of patriarchy are now considered in a little more detail. The institutions of fatherhood and the professions are considered further in subsequent chapters.

Hierarchic heterosexuality
Sexual oppression by men has been analysed through a variety of fundamental concepts by feminist writers: for example, phallocentrism (Cixous, 1981); phallomorphism (Plaza, 1978);

'man's' 'desire' (Irigaray, 1978); and 'desire for the Other' (Hollway, 1983), Coward (1982) puts it clearly enough: 'In our culture male arousal is a real social problem ...'. In such formulations sexuality is not about simple relations between bodies or selves, but in patriarchal society is characteristically *hierarchic*, overarchingly of men over women, men's sexuality over women's sexuality, heterosexuality over other sexualities.[15] Rich (1980) sees these relationships of power given form in the institution of 'compulsory heterosexuality'. While it is possible for other forms of heterosexuality to exist, hierarchic heterosexuality is premised on an inequality of power between women and men. To develop egalitarian heterosexuality would necessarily mean a loss of domination of heterosexuality over other sexualities. In other words, heterosexuality that is not hierarchic undermines heterosexuality.

Hierarchic sexuality and compulsory heterosexuality derive from the domination of sexual labour-power, not in some abstract way but in the material relation of bodies, either directly in heterosexual contacts or the attempted control of male homosexual and lesbian relations by (male) heterosexuals. Men's control of such sexual labour-power produces women as adjuncts to men, in relationships and in language (Lakoff, 1975). While in the worst cases of violence women may be raped or killed, they are routinely available to men for everyday smiles, flirtations and wrongly supposed petty 'favours', for obliteration in language, or 'assignment to passivity' within a 'dominant scopic economy' (Irigaray, 1978, 163). In the face of these oppressions, 'Lesbians so violate the sexuality implicit in female gender stereotypes as not to be considered women at all' (MacKinnon, 1982, 16)—an invisibility twice over.

While the base of sexual oppression, the points of sexual reproduction, remain in the private realm, the development of sexual oppression extends clearly and visibly into the public realm. This is so in all manner of ways—from the practice of female sexual slavery and the procurement of women (Barry, 1984), to heterosexual domination of public space (Rubin, 1984), to discrimination against lesbians and gay men in employment and elsewhere, to informal practices such as men's joking and innuendo at the expense of women (Hearn and Parkin, 1987). Perhaps most important, however, is the continued interrelation of hierarchic heterosexuality and the institution of fatherhood, predominantly in the private realm and typically organised around the family.

Fatherhood
The historical discovery, the hypothesising, of biological paternity is a basic causal element in the social development of the institution of fatherhood. In turn fatherhood produces and is produced by the public world of legal and other arrangements *between men*, for paternity must always remain qualified by a social and indeed psychological uncertainty. These constructions are central parts of O'Brien's theorising on reproduction. While the specific form of fatherhood varies greatly across cultures and historical periods, the institution has usually remained in close association with hierarchic heterosexuality. Furthermore, although the power of the father, as literally expressed in the term 'patriarchy', is subject to change and questioning, it remains pervasive in this particular patriarchal culture. Despite increases in divorce and separation, the family and specifically various forms of heterosexual familialism are still the usual sites for the conjunction of hierarchic sexuality and fatherhood. Within these confines rape is possible and other violence is not uncommon (Hill, 1982), alongside references to 'love', attempts to acquire 'affection', and in contradiction with searches for intimacy. Furthermore, although the power of the father is clearly frequently located within marriage and the family, these are not necessary accompaniments: men continue to be fathers outside marriage and outside the family.[16]

The professions
The professions are based in the public realm; they have a number of responsibilities in relation to the control of reproduction, including the control of sexuality and birth, as in psycho-sexual and gynaecological branches of medicine respectively. The professions also have a broader role in relation to caring, nurturing, ageing, the reproduction of labour-power, generation, and death. All of these facets raise

problems and uncertainties, at physical, spiritual and perhaps above all, emotional levels. They are a prime institution of patriarchy in men's monitoring and control of these 'difficult' areas of 'life'. Ann Ferguson (1982, 156) specifically suggests that 'as the patriarchal family's direct, personal control over women weakened, the less personal control of a growing class of male professionals (physicians, therapists, and social workers) over the physical and mental health of women grew in strength'.[17] Although overstating the family's, that is men as fathers', loss of power, the connection between fathers and professionals is important. Professions have developed historically as public, supposedly 'neutral', 'bodies' of men, respectable 'fraternities', who can act in relation to individual fathers. Various forms of familial professionalism have been practised whereby professionals, as 'family doctors' and 'public fathers', work parallel to, by way of, and sometimes over and above the rule of fathers in families. Interestingly, like fathers, 'defrocked', 'debarred' or 'struck off' professionals do not fully cease to be professional; they are not simply sacked; their power has some life of its own.

The state
The modern state, the Absolutist (Anderson, 1974) and post-Absolutist state, is the most fully developed complex of specifically patriarchal and fratriarchal power within modern societies and nations. The state is the equivalent of monopoly capital in capitalist social relations. The state has escalated in brutality and sophistication to become the welfare–warfare state (Wilensky, 1975), and worse the nuclear state (Jungk, 1979). The state is the *concrete consolidation* of men's appropriation of violent labour-power, to make the institutions of violence, war machines, the male police forces, and all manner of 'neutral' male 'civil services'. It is the corporate potential of destruction: the organised form that however benevolent can always be redirected to produce violence and torture. Among fraternities, it is only rivalled by the multinationals. It is both a consolidation of this *potential* violence, and a means of incorporation of other reproductive labour-powers. It overarches all the reproductive labour-powers. It particularly provides the media of control of the

public realm, in government, (party) 'politics', law, and 'order'. It encompasses the organisation of sexuality, birth, generation and nurture; it underwrites hierarchic heterosexuality, fatherhood, the professions, through law and all manner of regulation. The patriarchal state proscribes homosexuality in its armed forces and in prisons;[18] facilitates and prohibits the access of fathers to children; organises public monitoring and collections through 'heads' of families; and charters professions. The state is also the context for the growth of 'bureaucratic professions' (Fielding and Portwood, 1980) and 'bureau-professionalism' (Parry and Parry, 1979, 43), a professional statism within an apparently 'humanised' bureaucratic structure.

Over and above these structures, states combine with other states to form multi-state arrangements, 'nuclear pacts', 'international defence' and the like, as patriarchal equivalents of multi-national capitalist corporations. These 'corridors of power', 'politburos' and 'pentagons' exclude women to an extreme degree.

It is truly amazing how most debates on the state, including most marxist debates on state and capital, from which a notable exception is Burstyn's (1983), fail to mention men's power in the state. Indeed if one considers the structure of state activities in relation to men's power, a number of rather obvious observations can be made, such as:

1. The state forms a major part of men's domination of the public sphere over the private.
2. The state is itself dominated by men—it is *characteristically* patriarchal.
3. There are wide variations in the generic division of labour and power between different parts of the state.
4. Those parts of the state that are more concerned with repression and violence are more fully male-dominated and male-membered than those parts which are concerned with caring, welfare and reproduction, which are usually male-dominated and female-membered. Parts of the state which are concerned with production are usually intermediate, reproducing the generic divisions of production outside the state.

These gendered divisions of the state may be analysed in terms both of sectors and of degrees of centrality. The repressive segments of the state may be more central, more base-ic, than welfare segments. Alternatively, rather than subdividing state activities as 'productive' and 'unproductive', 'consumption', 'expenses', and 'capital', they may be seen as 'reproductive', 'reproductive expenses' (repressive), and 'non-reproductive' (productive).[19] Certain state agencies perform activities both of caring and of violence, and/or exist *within* that contradiction. Gender differentials in different parts of the state may, however, be misleading if considered in isolation. For example, the labour of the military is typically premised upon the private labour of women as wives, mothers and so on, and the public labour of women as nurses, carers, caterers, even prostitutes, and formerly chatelaines. In contrast, state welfare agencies may display women's labour more explicitly and more publicly than do, say, military agencies.

State activities can also be analysed in relation to *points of reproduction*, such that the closer one approaches a particular point the sharper are the divisions of labour and power by sex/gender.

Each of these institutions of patriarchy is dynamic rather than stable, both in terms of historical change and structured contradictions, for both women and men. Hierarchic heterosexuality provides institutional access to sexual pleasure though mediated or overwhelmed by oppression; fatherhood is a means of access to children, yet a method of their appropriation; the professions give limited access to emotional, body, and people work, whilst empowering the removal of degrees of autonomy of the person; and the state provides the 'welfare state' *and* the warfare state.

OPPRESSION: STRUCTURED RELATIONS, AGENCY AND SELF-OPPRESSION

In analysing men's oppression, and the forms it takes, three major elements are considered here: structured relations, agency and 'self-oppression'.

Each of the four main types of reproduction and reproductive labour-power is a site of structured relations between women and men. The institutions of patriarchy outlined are in effect women–men structured relations. This means that whatever the activity of individual women and men, the 'terms of trade' are to a large extent structurally determined. Men may become soft fathers, liberal professionals, or kind policemen but the institution remains intact as a potential or actual means of oppression. Structured relations of oppression exist in the domination of labour-powers and appropriation of their products. The characteristic form is men's oppression of women's various reproductive labour-powers.

In addition, men do have agency. This is so in two senses. Firstly, men are *agents* of oppression. We are not inherently oppressive even though we constitute an oppressive class and a class of oppression. Secondly, men can *act differently, independently, even contrary to the demands of structured relations.* While individual men can be seen as having considerable responsibility in agency, it is difficult to 'apportion blame' for structured relations.

An interesting example of the complexities of men's agency in relation to structured relations concerns the length of men's paid working life. Men are allowed to work (for money) longer, to retire later than women, yet men tend to die younger. That extra five years of paid work enables those older men to continue to stay at the top of male hierarchies in organisations, occupations, trade unions and professions. Most are at their highest position *immediately* prior to 'retirement'. Partly through this they gain heartache, stress, money and death. Some men may seek 'redundancy', 'early retirement' or retirement in the job. Many men might prefer to have ten years of life to five of higher pay and one of retirement; collectively, however, men gain in maintaining control *as a class* over women and indeed children. A similar analysis can be made of the costs of war. Individual men fight, kill each other, die; yet through this enactment of violence men's class power is reaffirmed. Thus individual men may, sometimes in large numbers, perform individual acts that are not in their own immediate interests, perhaps *even including their own death*, but which maintain the structured relation of men's collective power over women.[20] Meanwhile other men may resist this process. In other words, men's agency may or may not be oppressive.

Another example surrounds childcare and the custody of children following separation and divorce.[21] Women's power in relation to children is constantly diminished by the power of fathers, professionals, state, law. Women's work, and particularly childwork, is not fully recognised, is taken for granted by the state. The lack of valuing of birth, children, and childwork is a major means of diminishing women. *Collectively* men avoid childcare, as through the institutions of fatherhood, yet individually some men seek it, to the point of contesting custody for children after separation and divorce. The problem is not who should be 'awarded' custody, though the award to men on the grounds of 'unfit motherhood' is a constant patriarchal threat, but the fact that *children* are *awarded* in *custody*. Patriarchal social relations involve class relations of women, men and children, whereby children exist in a 'custodial' situation, whatever individual men's actions—fleeing, assisting, lone parenting, accommodating, conflicting.

Not only do individual men enact different agencies within particular structured relations, but different individuals act differently relative to different structures at different times and in different parts of their lifespace. For example, a male nurse may also be a liberal father, and celibate. Exploring such permutations of actions is one powerful way of deconstructing men, both collectively and individually.

Men's oppression, through structured relations and/or agency has important, and indeed oppressive results for men ourselves. Although men's oppression of women is paramount, men may be 'self-oppressed' in at least the following ways:
(i) in the preparation for oppressive structured relations and agency, especially as boys;
(ii) by other men, whether they are more powerful men, or competitively by men of more similar power. The process of competition and participation in that competition can oppress as much as individual (potential) competitors;
(iii) by ourselves, whether through particular guilts or the more extensive diminution of our feelings, emotions, and

capacity for love. Such lessenings of men can occur directly, for example, in refusal of what is experienced as love; indirectly, when past pain becomes referred or transferred to another 'object' or person; or over time as oppressive relations and relationships take their toll in limiting reciprocal and mutual living and loving, in paradoxically denying the possibilities for the denial of self. Oppressive relations may also include numerous painful effects, physical and emotional, for all concerned.

This complex of 'self-oppression' may be better thought of as a reproductive and material equivalent of the almost magical Freudian process of introjection. *We men are formed and broken by our own power.* Men's structured power and agency is reproduced in men's psychodynamic development, as structure-in-psyche and agency-in-psyche.

The Buddhist text, *The Wheel of Sharp Weapons*, by Dharmarakshita appears to recognise this process in a clear light:

> All the sufferings that we have endured in the past,
> as well as our pains of the present and future,
> Are all the same as the case of the forger of arrows
> who later was killed by an arrow he had made.
> Our suffering is the wheel of sharp weapons returning
> full circle upon us from wrongs we have done.
> Hereafter let's always have care and awareness
> never to act in unwholesome ways.

LABOUR AND MATERIAL BEING

The category 'men' arises from and exists within structured relations, agencies, and indeed intra-psychic processes—fundamentally of reproduction. While 'men' persist in the base of reproduction, masculinities persist in the 'ideology' of production. This perspective casts severe doubts on definitions of labour that are patriarchal, gendered, narrowly production-based, and that posit distinctions between 'real' and merely supportive work (see Cummings, 1980). O'Brien's focus on 'reproductive labour' and MacKinnon's on 'sexuality' rather than productive work both disrupt taken-for-granted conventions of production-based (male-dominated) marxisms. Indeed if 'work' and 'labour' mediate between people and nature, *including the mediation of and between other people*, it becomes somewhat academic whether 'reproduction' is 'labour', or 'sexuality' is not 'work', or whatever. Worse still, not only are 'work' and 'workers' often implicitly 'male', but that which is separated from 'man'/people and mediated in work—'nature'—is implicitly more 'female'. To put this another way, women have often been assumed to be more a part of 'nature' than men; men are assumed to be 'conquerors of nature' (Ortner, 1974; Lewin, 1977; Gray, 1982).

In such 'nature-conquering' labours, such as sea-fishing, mining, and perhaps also warfare, men may appear obviously produced as 'men'. Yet paradoxically in such labours where men are most obviously dealing directly with nature *along with* the prospect of their own possible death, the usual, well-worn distinction between productive labour and reproductive labour (including their own reproduction in life rather than death) becomes less easy to make.

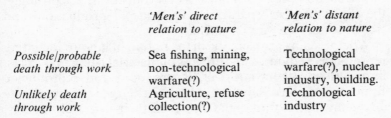

	'Men's' direct relation to nature	*'Men's' distant relation to nature*
Possible/probable death through work	Sea fishing, mining, non-technological warfare(?)	Technological warfare(?), nuclear industry, building.
Unlikely death through work	Agriculture, refuse collection(?)	Technological industry

Figure 5:   Typology of men's 'productive' work

Men's direct relation to nature, and its reproduction, is also to be found, in a metaphorical and socialised sense, in such labour as refuse collection—the repeated and continuous reorganisation of the 'dangerous' waste(s) of the social *environment*. Productive work may define different types of *masculinities*, but it does not define men *qua* men. That particular arises in relation to reproduction, to being. While marxists usually emphasise the 'natural' similarity and common interest of bourgeois women and bourgeois men, as against proletarian women and proletarian men, this perspective suggests that both types of men possess a commonality in terms of their body–being, rather than externalised, material object–related labour and relations. Class exploitation and oppression certainly concern the exploitation of labour and the oppression of the labourers. Gender, and perhaps race, exploitation and oppression extend this to the whole body–person, including incarceration, quarantine, rape. Capitalists do not need, or indeed want, the whole body; that can be left to men and fascists.

Approaching these issues from a slightly different perspective, Hartsock (1983, 259–61) concludes on the several similarities of abstract masculinity and the exchange abstraction, within the capitalist form of patriarchy. Indeed, it may be that what it now called the 'mode of production' with its consequent determining effects, including the 'production' of masculinity and masculinities, may simply be an agendered rendering and reduction of what is an inherently gendered social form. It may be that it is not only in social formations that gender appears, but rather that gendering is as much part of production, and its modes, as reproduction. Accordingly, the usual marxist separations of 'mode of production' and 'social formation' are doubtful.

What remains problematic in the notion of labour, including reproductive labour, is the process of material being that exists, impinges on others and self, is produced and reproduced. Either the notion of labour needs to be enlarged to incorporate *all* such aspects of material being, in their material impacts, without prejudgement as 'work', 'productive work', 'domestic work', 'sexual work', etc. etc., or it needs to be complemented by a firmer notion of material being that is beyond and outside narrow 'works'. In patriarchy it is these fundamentally ordinary material existences that are constantly obscured and mistakenly described, named, and lost in the fetishism of human appearance.

Even these distinctions, of production and reproduction, of labour and material being, have to be viewed with some scepticism. In actual social instances all of these occur together, so that, for example, *agencies-in-reproduction* are done by men who are simultaneously performing *agencies-in-production*.

The emphasis here on reproduction is partly as a defining character of 'men', and partly to 'redress the balance' from the ritual focus on production and the 'productive male'. Productive relations, including capitalist ones, are after all also forms and matters of sexuality, procreation, nurture, and violence.

Part 3

The Patriarchal Organisation of Reproductive Work

INTRODUCTION

Theorising patriarchy in terms of reproductive labour-powers produces not so much a determined structural edifice as an heuristic framework for understanding particular operations of patriarchy. Reproductive labour-powers and labours are organised in patriarchy in ways that are distinct and generalisable, yet particular in time and space. This section deals with some of those particularities, such as typologies of concrete actions and activities, the historical forms of individual institutions of patriarchy, and modes of construction of persons, through specific 'masculinities'. The three chapters following address these three issues in relation to men.

Chapter 6, written during autumn 1985 for this book, considers men's involvement in reproduction in terms of reproductive direct work and more distanced management. Although reproductive management is itself a form of labour, it is also a way of controlling and avoiding reproductive labours. The categorisation of men's possible and major types of management and work in reproduction is a necessary task, itself usually avoided by men. This is followed by an examination of an institutionalised form of control and avoidance, the professions and professionalisation, and their historical development through men's domination of reproduction. This line of enquiry began about 1980 initially in trying to connect the theorising of patriarchy with my experiences of men's public domination. Teaching social work students in a university, I was especially interested in how and why men become involved in social work, and yet end up dominating women, both other social workers and 'clients', and so indirectly dominating reproduction. Some ways of making sense of professionalisation within patriarchy were presented in 1981 to the Staff–Postgraduate Seminar at Bradford, and the British Sociological Association Human Reproduction Study Group in Oxford. In the light of comments there, revised versions were published in *Sociology* in 1982, and in the *Women and Social Policy* collection (Hearn, 1985b).

Meanwhile I was keen to extend this kind of analysis to the presentation of 'professional' masculinity in more everyday life. Discussions took place during 1981–2 on a possible chapter on this question for a book on 'Masculinity'. Although the book eventually changed shape to a focus on *The Sexuality of Men* (Metcalf and Humphries, 1985), the work in progress on professions formed the basis of a paper at the British Sociological Association Annual Conference in 1982. Revised extracts of this are included as chapter 8, following extensive comments from Margaret Stacey (1982), Mary Ann Elston, and others. This paper extends the structural, historical analysis of professions to the more immediate impact of professionalisation on the social construction of masculinity— a matter of clear personal and political concern.

6 The Reproductive Management and Reproductive Work of Men: Domination and Variation

The appropriation of reproductive labour-power, oppression, structured relations and agency do not just happen: each of these 'abstract concepts' has a concrete reality in the management and labour of men at, around and often at a distance from points of reproduction.

The concrete reality of men's relationship to, involvement in and avoidance of reproduction is a combination of (i) forms of domination that maintain the structured relations of oppression, and (ii) specific varieties of agency, both oppressive and otherwise. These dominations and variations entail the indirect management and control of reproduction, that is reproductive management, but they also include indirect (reproductive) labour necessary for that control to continue. In contrast agency involves a variety of forms of work, as well as avoidance of work, more direct controls, and so on. These dominations and variations exist in both specific activities and behaviours of specific men, and in the production of different types of men, for example, 'fathers', 'lone parents', 'state workers', and so on. This chapter considers the major forms of reproductive domination and agency, management and work,[1] within and in relation to the major institutions of patriarchy, and their associated forms of reproduction.

SEXUALITY AND HIERARCHIC HETEROSEXUALITY

The structured relations of sexuality (as hierarchic heterosexuality) are maintained by the following forms of men's domination:

(i) the existence of heterosexual men;
(ii) men's management and control of heterosexuality, and especially hierarchic heterosexuality, in law, organisations, ideologies and activities;
(iii) men's labour necessary for maintaining the above management and control.

To elucidate these forms of domination, it is important to make it clear that heterosexuality is not inherently or naturally hierarchic or oppressive; that is 'merely' the particular, dominant form it takes in this (and many other) societies. Thus the existence of heterosexual men assists in the maintenance of hierarchic heterosexuality, even when particular men do not act in oppressive ways. More obviously oppressive heterosexual men reinforce this process just by being, by standing in the street, by the use of cultural signs and symbols, even without harassing, speaking or moving.

Similarly, in the management and control of heterosexuality, there is no need for this to be explicitly oppressive for it to perpetuate structured relations. The professions have had an important role in managing these relations: 'between feudalism and capitalism . . . [t]he church was in charge for the most part of reproductive aspects of gender-class relations: its rules pertained to the issues of marriage, divorce and sexual practice (adultery, sodomy and the like) and . . . [it] was involved in maintaining explicit generic authority'. (Burstyn, 1983, 58). Likewise, many business and other public organisations have compulsorily heterosexual ideologies, practices and 'organisation sexualities' (Hearn and Parkin, 1987). The usually capitalist or governmental appearance of such organisations can mask their management of heterosexuality. More explicitly hierarchic heterosexual organisations, ideologies and activities may be controlled by men managers, as in 'sexploitation' and sex industries; they may also be perpetuated by men's control of sexist conversation, language and culture, as in working-class men's use of heterosexism to maintain class solidarity (Cockburn, 1983). In such situations male leaders become *managers* of sexual reproduction. These dominations also often need men's labour to maintain them, even though such labourers may themselves be oppressed.

Business ventures like the $18m. Mustang Ranch brothel (Scobie, 1985) need accounts clerks, whether men or women.

Within these structured relations men have agency and so perform more particular sexual actions and types of labour. These include:

(i)   indirect oppressive control over women, for example, the giving of sexual orders;

(ii)   direct oppressive work over women, for example, sadism, rape, infliction of pain;[2]

(iii)   implicit oppressive work over women, for example, routine hierarchic heterosexuality;

(iv)   anti-oppressive work with women, for example, men's struggles towards a non-hierarchic heterosexuality;

(v)   the avoidance of sexual work, for example, celibacy or the use of women and other 'instruments' for being touched, handled, and aroused;[3]

(vi)   sexual work with men, male gay sexuality;

(vii)   self-sexual work and masturbation;

(viii) sexual work with objects and non-people;

(ix)   action in relation to men's own sexual oppression, for example, in gay prostitution.

Several points of qualification need to be added. First, as already noted, sexuality is in part labour, upon others, self and sometimes objects. Secondly, the listing above is a severe simplification of the complexities and contradictions of sexual agency. Thirdly, while male gay sexual agency can be understood as in a generic opposition to hierarchic heterosexuality, it also is open to further forms of oppressive elaboration. These range from the capitalist domination of the 'pink economy', to oppression within gay relationships, as with 'Dilly boys' and other male prostitutes (Harris, 1972). Even so, gay sexuality threatens hierarchic heterosexuality.

BIRTH, EARLY CHILDCARE AND FATHERHOOD

The labours and dominations of (hetero)sexuality, although partially autonomous, also constitute the first part of the 'birth process', that is pre-conception. In this sense gay sexual relations, heterosexual mutual masturbation, and even coitus interruptus are forms of men's labour that are also contraceptive. Indeed, following O'Brien, it is the discovery of paternity that makes such practice conscious; that paradoxically produces contraception; and more arguably converts contraceptive practice *to labour*. From this historical juncture the contraception industries, vasectomy and more recently artificial insemination and reproductive technology industries follow, with their own patterns of indirectly reproductive management and labour.

The structured relations of birth and early childcare (as fatherhood) are maintained by the following forms of men's domination:

(i)   the existence of fathers;
(ii)   men's management and control of fatherhood in law, organisations, ideologies and activities;
(iii) men's labour necessary for maintaining the above management and control.

The existence of fathers can be oppressive simply through social association with the power of the institution of fatherhood. The management and control of the institution of fatherhood have traditionally been through the combined powers of the church, medicine and the law. Most obviously the regulation of property relations and the confirmation of 'rights' and 'duties' have usually been devolved to courts, the law, and the state with accompanying infantilisation of women (Burstyn, 1983, 58).

The epitome of these property relations is the property that are children. The threat of awarding children to men, as fathers or state workers, on grounds of 'unfit motherhood', is part of the overarching power of the patriarchal state. State law and professionals may not only overrule individual fathers, but also confirm the structured relations of fatherhood, whereby children are 'in custody', and within which individual men adopt particular agencies. Similarly, advances in reproductive technology and related techniques, such as DNA-testing in immigration control, can facilitate the reinforcement of fatherhood, both biological and social, even with men's removal from conception.

To specify the full range and variation of men's actions and labours in relation to birth and early childcare would necessitate detailed descriptions of at least conception, pregnancy, birth and early childcare (see O'Brien, 1981, 47–8). For example, conception processes may involve men in heterosexual intercourse, mechanical insemination (whether or not in the man's presence), artificial insemination by (unknown) donor, *in vitro* fertilisation, and so on. Indeed, men's necessary labour in biological reproduction is small enough in conception, and can be reduced further to convenient masturbation. During pregnancy and at birth, men's labour and even presence is not essential; men may do caring work for pregnant women, or be in attendance at birth, but the amounts of such labour are usually small. Furthermore, it is probably concentrated mostly at key points of 'crisis' and around the relieving of mothers from care of other children, rather than the care of the mother herself.[4] Even attendance at birth, now almost a norm, is mainly waiting rather than work. In the context of the institution of fatherhood in this society, increasing involvement through, say, paternity leave may be useful at the time as well as being a means to the reinforcement of paternal power (see chapter 9).

Fatherhood is an established means of men becoming involved with children and in childcare, yet usually in a closely prescribed way. It focuses a man's attention on particular, that is 'his' children, whilst at the same time giving legitimation to the avoidance of childcare, whether through paid working, in the exertion of authority, distaste for 'messy jobs', or disinterest in 'other' children. Men's limited involvement in early childcare is characterised by limitations and avoidances, together with a centring on the father role.

It is difficult to obtain a precise picture of the total and relative amounts of early childcare performed by men.[5] The majority of families in Britain, perhaps as many as 86 per cent, include two parents (NCOPF, 1982); within these, where a woman and a man are parents,[6] the distribution of childcare and day-to-day housekeeping tasks is typically very uneven (Land, 1981). There are severe limits on this labour for many men. Many women remain appreciative of even moderate 'husband's help' (Gavron, 1966). Well-off fathers may have three 'wives'—the wife-in-law, the childminder, and the cleaner

(Cockburn, 1986). Unemployed fathers do not seem to be much more involved in childcare than employed fathers (Bell, McKee and Priestley, 1983, 38), while fathers of young children may do considerably more overtime than married childless men (Cohen, 1977; Moss, 1980). Furthermore, even 'notions of "house husbands", role reversals, shared care etc. cannot simply be welcomed as progressive, but have to be treated as ... dangerous in their potential to gloss over how men maintain power ...' (Phillips, 1984, 16). Indeed 'recent research on Australian couples who actually have reversed the sexual division of labor, ... suggests the reversal is at best unstable, and often reflects no change in basic assumptions at all' (Carrigan, Connell and Lee, 1985, 573, citing Russell, 1983).

As for single or lone parents, with main responsibility for children, about eight times as many are women than men (HMSO, 1984b; Graham, 1984). In England and Wales, of households with children only 4 to 5 per cent have lone male 'heads' (most of whom are lone fathers), and about $2\frac{1}{2}$ per cent comprise lone male 'heads' with *dependent* children. However, even amongst lone parents men are on average much better off than women, with the latter about $4\frac{1}{2}$ times as likely to be in poverty (Nixon, 1979, 71). Although many 'lone fathers', and indeed some other male prime carers of young children do experience oppressions of poverty, isolation and alienating childwork (George and Wilding, 1972), it is likely that they have more access than women to assistance from women, whether from commercial or state daycare, or the help of relatives or friends. In addition, there is a relatively small group of men who seek the care of children but without women. These include divorced men who are 'missing their children', some gay men, men applying for adoption or fostering, and men willing to share care with single mothers (Renvoize, 1985, 79–84).

At this point, it may be helpful to return to O'Brien's (1981) specific theorisation of 'reproductive labour' referred to in earlier chapters. She argues on the one hand that '[o]nly women perform reproductive labour' (14), yet subsequently that 'the process of reproduction ... ends when the ... child is no longer dependent on others for the necessities of survival' (16). She is certainly correct in suggesting that '[m]en are biologically free from the *necessity* to labour reproductively' (15, my emphasis). However, to assert that '[f]athers do not labour' (36–7) seems at odds with the possibility, *though not the necessity*, that '[copulation and] nurture are genderically shared moments' (47–8), unless moments do not involve labour. Thus if nurture is a recognised aspect of reproduction then men may do reproductive labour. Despite and perhaps because of men's double (biological and social) separation from birth (see Chodorow, 1978) men do have a wide range of types of labouring and non-labouring involvements and relationships with nurture, before and after birth. Men's separateness and non-presence *as fathers* may have major social and psychodynamic consequences for the children, particularly boys, who are so fathered. Fathers' avoidance of children may produce a number of psychological confusions; for boys especially, this 'lack', this *abstraction*, may facilitate subsequent failure as a male to face and meet the self (see Dinnerstein, 1978; Arcana, 1983). This can have bizarre psychological and projective effects for the 'mature' male— including misogyny and romantic love.

These labours in families are themselves located within the broad division between the private and public realms. For pre-school children, care is overwhelmingly organised in the private realm. Of about 3¼ million children under five in Britain,[7] only about 2 per cent receive full-time care in private and state day nurseries, with a further 3 per cent with registered childminders. Up to ½ million children are probably illegally minded, with perhaps 400,000 in other informal arrangements with relatives, friends and neighbours. Nearly two-thirds of under-five children do not even have part-time daycare outside the family. The complexity of *informal* arrangements for daycare, typically between women, are accompanied by women's predominance in the public care of young children: for example, about 94 per cent of playgroup leaders (HMSO, 1984a) are women. Occasional male childminders or nursery nurses become subject to special attention and media interest. For men, whether lone parents, prime carers in marriages or other relationships, grandfather or friend, to gain access to public care, in day nurseries or whatever, means in effect transfer to the *work of women*.

Men's labours and actions in relation to birth and early childcare thus can be summarised as including:

(i)   minimum necessary work for biological reproduction (even that now may be largely obviated through reproductive technology);
(ii)   indirect oppressive control over women and children, for example, the giving of patriarchal orders;
(iii)   direct oppressive work over women and children, for example, beating and abuse by fathers;
(iv)   implicit oppressive work over women and children, for example, routine patriarchal nurture;
(v)   anti-oppressive work with women and children, for example, men's struggles for non-fatherly relationships and nurture;
(vi)   the avoidance of early childcare;
(vii)   action in relation to men's own oppression in such work.

Those relatively few men who are involved in primary early childcare outside fatherhood can also be involved in indirect, direct, implicitly oppressive, anti-oppressive work, avoidance of nurture and/or action in relation to their own oppression (i.e. as (ii) to (vii) above).

GENERATIVE NURTURE AND THE PROFESSIONS[8]

The professions are significant elements in the setting of the structured relations of hierarchic heterosexuality and fatherhood. They also have other crucial roles: in the management and labour of generative reproduction, that is nurture and regeneration beyond early childcare; in the construction of the public as against the private realm. The generic structuring of professions ranges in Britain from (virtually) all women in midwifery, to over 95 per cent for nursery nurses and early-school teaching, to 50–70 per cent for middle-school teaching, and declining numbers of women throughout upper-school and further education, to about 20 per cent of GPs, and (virtually) all men in funeral direction, though not mortuary labour. A high proportion, 85–90 per cent, of nursing, matroning, houseparenting and home help work is done by women throughout the 'life cycle' (HMSO, 1984a; DES, 1978; DHSS, 1982).

The structured relations of generative nurture (as the professions) are maintained by:

(i)   the existence of the professions;
(ii)   the management and control of the professions, including their formal professional associations;
(iii) the labour necessary for their management and control.

Not only are the professions generically structured from birth to death, they are also individually so structured so that their own management is usually almost exclusively by men. Within these structured means of appropriating the products of women's generative nurture, men 'professional' workers perform a range of actions and labours, including:

(i)   indirect oppressive work, for example, doctors' oppressive ordering of nurses;
(ii)   direct oppressive work, for example, teachers' beating of children by 'corporal punishment';
(iii) implicit oppressive work, for example, routine professional nurture;
(iv)   anti-oppressive work, for example, radical deprofessionalisation, support for feminist initiatives in the public realm;
(v)   the avoidance of work, for example, distancing from generative nurture.

VIOLENCE AND THE STATE

The state overarches hierarchic heterosexuality, fatherhood and the professions; and includes a vast array of activities:

the state ... has become for large numbers of women, especially mothers, drawn now from the petty bourgeoisie and the proletariat as well as the chronically poor, the great collective father-figure, a new representative of men-as-a-group, but now a new kind of group, totally divorced ... from these women in terms of kinship and mutual aid, a bureaucratic, impersonal pyramid of a group of men, who have taken the place of all those absent fathers. ... Policies delineating everything from employment insurance benefits to daycare subsidies to ... socialised medicine to the (lack of) abortion facilities to prosecution and persecution of lesbian mothers are all ... expressions of a generic state, in the process of developing new forms of masculinism corresponding to the really acute crisis and change in gender arrangements.   (Burstyn, 1983, 64)

The state is also the greatest concentration of patriarchal violence, even though violence is an important part of all the previously described reproductive institutions and sites of labour.

The structured relations of violence (as the state) are maintained by:

(i)   the existence of states and other states;[9]
(ii)   the management and control of the state, in the senior government administration, senior army and police officialdom;
(iii) the labour necessary for that management and control.

In analysing the (patriarchal) state it is difficult to underestimate the significance of violence. Indeed historically the state can be seen as merely the temporary status quo of the dominant distribution of the forces of organised violence. Accordingly, wars, and especially nationalistic wars, take place between 'local' patriarchies, and are a means of allocating 'patriarchal rights', such as that to hierarchic heterosexuality, at a given time. The development of warfare, and especially, since the establishment of the nation-state, the development of state warfare, is probably as significant for the 'advance' of technological change as the development of the mode of production. Warfare technology may indeed be the driving force of societal levels of technological development, the ultimate mode of reproduction/destruction.

Men's state work concerned specifically with violence and the appropriation of others' violence has a more complex form than, say, professional work. This is because the structured relations of state violence entail the mass control, oppression and even killing of other men for their continuation. Thus the variety of state labours include:

(i)   indirect oppressive work, for example, army officers' oppressive direction of soldiers or civilians;
(ii)   direct oppressive work, for example, killing;

(iii) implicit oppressive work, for example, routine 'professional' soldiering (especially in peacetime) and bureaucratic administration;

(iv) anti-oppressive work, for example, informal subversion, 'security leaks' for citizens' rights from bureaucracies, gay military organising;

(v) the avoidance of work, for example, 'skiving' by police.

The major complication is all the above can be performed upon or in relation to others, both in and outside the state, both by women and men. Thus other men state workers, particularly lower level soldiers, police and bureaucrats, are routinely liable to be subject to the above forms of oppression, as follows:

(vi) the receipt of indirect oppression;

(vii) the receipt of direct oppression;

(viii) the receipt of implicit oppression.

The potential of men's violence is immense, both in private by individual men, and by state agents, for example, in public view, for example, Orgreave Colliery 1984, or in public property, such as police stations. Certain men outside the state, especially the gay, black, young and working class, are more likely to receive the weight of this violence.

The men who inflict this violence are *not* inherently violent. They are *also* kind and caring people in most cases. They inflict damage on others and on themselves. They are agents of oppression, of violence—they carry it, as labourers of destructive labour-power. They are class agents of the class of men; above all *these men are individually dispensable*; as in war, they are of only relative value; they have no absolute value to the class of men, the patriarchal state, the patriarch. Most collective public violence—'riots', 'football hooliganism', 'wars'—remain violence between men.

Because violence is destructive of persons, it is in the interests of both the managers and perpetrators of violence to control its use, as, for example, in the elaborate codes and rules within armies (Dixon, 1976). Furthermore, male control of violence has the unforeseen consequences that particular men, such as front-line soldiers, are controlled by the (potential) violence of other men, whilst being able to inflict violence on others, both women and men, and that virtually all, perhaps all men, are brought up from a very early age in the knowledge and expectation that they may have to kill other humans like themselves. This self-imposed oppression of men is a form of oppression not experienced by women, in most societies. The shared experience for almost all men, of fear and terror, of knowing the actuality or possibility of being killed prematurely by *organised* violence, or of killing a human of the same gender, is the male birthright from citizenship of the nation-state. It is only as some men get older, past the age of immediate risk of doing violence and being violated, that they 'mellow', become 'kind old men', 'enjoy' being grandfathers, and die distanced from that fear.

THE STRUCTURING OF MEN IN PATRIARCHY

In this scheme, men's reproductive management and labour, oppressive, anti-oppressive, and oppressed, comprises one major element in the structuring of patriarchy. A much simplified pyramid of the gender class of men may be represented as in figure 6.

Heterosexual men and fathers perform the routine, largely private and individualised labour and management that support and maintain the more visible power of the public patriarchs of the class of men. A more detailed analysis of these and other types of men within patriarchy follows (figure 7). Reformulating our analytical categories in this and similar ways is a necessary part of a political economy of men and masculinity, as yet hardly developed. The investigation of the organisation of reproductive management and labour is a task for both macro societal analysis and micro studies of particular men.

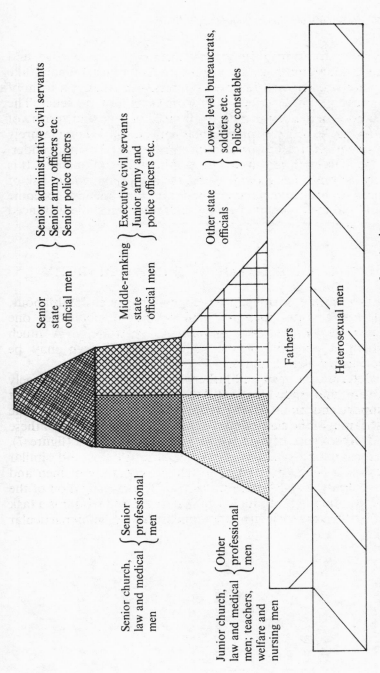

Senior state official men { Senior administrative civil servants, Senior army officers etc., Senior police officers

Middle-ranking state official men { Executive civil servants, Junior army and police officers etc.

Other state officials { Lower level bureaucrats, soldiers etc., Police constables

Senior church, law and medical men } Senior professional men

Junior church, law and medical men; teachers, welfare and nursing men } Other professional men

Fathers

Heterosexual men

Figure 6: Simplified structuring of patriarchy

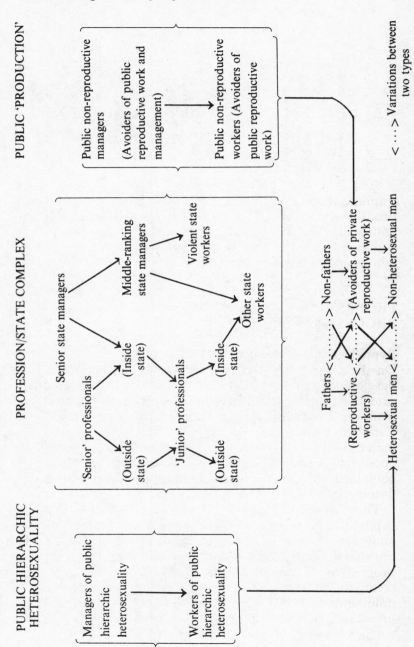

7 Patriarchy, Professionalisation and the Semi-professions[1]

Capitalism operates by conversion of wage labour to value and profit; patriarchy by the appropriation of the unwaged labour and energy of women to produce male power. Both are concerned with the control and accumulation of the creativity, labour and energy of women by men.

PROFESSIONALISATION AS A PATRIARCHAL PROCESS

Reproduction and emotionality

On the assumption that patriarchy predates capitalism, the development of capitalism can be seen to have gradually extended from the productive to the reproductive spheres, and from the simply instrumental to the more elusive emotional. Early capitalism was concerned with the satisfaction of material wants, whether food for the general society or luxury goods for the well-off. For many areas of social life, patriarchy conjoined with capitalism in a mutually reinforcing process of domination.

Those areas of social life that were not directly under capitalist domination, yet which contributed to reproduction and were where emotions were especially likely to be unleashed, became clear targets for male domination through professions. These were the very areas that the magic, creativity, indeed healing, of women had enabled them to dominate within peasant society, locally acting as the priestesses, the prophetesses, the healers, the wise women, the witches (Ehrenreich and English, 1974).[2] This domination by women certainly applied to biological reproduction, but also to other areas of reproduction, such as the management of life and death in spiritual or social terms.

The model of medicine

The case of medicine is particularly instructive. In the medieval world, the traditional medical role of women was to some extent sponsored by the Church. Indeed 'for eight . . . centuries, from the fifth to the thirteenth, the other-worldly, anti-medical stance of the Church . . . stood in the way of the development of medicine as a respectable profession' (Ehrenreich and English, 1974, 13).

According to early Christian missionary and Norman practices,

Ladies were the ordinary practitioners of domestic medicine and the skilled chatelaine could reduce fractures, probe and dress wounds or burns and prepare herbal remedies. . . . Male physicians were rare, since time and desire for study were almost confined to monks, Jews and others debarred from the supreme masculine occupation of fighting.   (Manton, 1965, 56–7)

Inroads into this pattern were made by men in late medieval times through a combination of Church, state and universities and the men who dominated those institutions (Ehrenreich and English, 1974, 3–5). This was furthered with the rise of science and capitalism. At the end of the seventeenth century:

There were still women surgeons but women healers were increasingly associated with witchcraft and the practice of the black arts. As medicine became a science, the terms of entry into training excluded women, protecting the profession for the sons of families who could afford education.
                                              (Rowbotham, 1973, 2–3)

This process was consolidated, so that

In . . . the medical occupations the seventeenth and eighteenth centuries witnessed an increasing division of labour and a concomitant exclusion of women from the higher and more lucrative branches which were gradually emerging.   (Parry and Parry, 1976, 164)

The role of education, of both a general and a more specifically professional nature, was indeed central. Clark

(1919) in her classic survey of *The Working Life of Women in the 17th Century* describes a similar process in teaching in which governesses cared for children while masters who had undergone more formal training gained professional status. 'By the end of the eighteenth century ... good-class medical practice had closed to women, apparently for ever' (Manton, 1965, 61). The barring of women from access to medical schools and the universities effectively prohibited their entry into the medical profession until the end of the nineteenth century.

The domination of the medical profession by men was paralleled and reinforced by powerful sexist ideologies surrounding the very nature of illness, 'complaints and disorders' (Ehrenreich and English, 1973). Of particular significance was the interrelation of sexist medical ideologies and class divisions, with the upper-class female 'invalid' acting as archetype of the ideal client for the male professional. Such ideologies have their legacy in the way women's health and sickness is still often seen to be a 'by-product' of their sexuality, and indeed in the dominant forms of psychiatry and psychotherapy (Chesler, 1972).

Despite the opening up of medicine in the early years of this century, the profession remains primarily and excessively in the hands of men (Elston, 1977). Thus the management of health and sickness, originally an area of female specialism has become almost a male preserve.

The mediation of conflict

The management of health and sickness became the concern of the medical profession, just as the mediation of disputes and the honouring of life and death had become the domains of the legal and clerical professions respectively. The establishment of the legal, medical and clerical professions is the clearest instance of men coming to dominate particular areas of life, by reference back to some notion of 'neutral' professionalism and service to others. In the 'settlement' of disputes, pain and mortality, a strict capitalist form of organisation was not viable and a 'professional' form a necessary, but still effective, patriarchal alternative.

Professions thereby perform certain tasks formerly

performed within the family. Typically these tasks involve the management of social conflict and tension, including illness. According to this kind of perspective the professional may be approached by a client to tackle a problem that previously may have been resolved by one or more of the family members. Typically such tasks are raised in status with their transfer from the private to the public arena; and from women to men.

The gentleman's agreement
The *domination of men in these early professions was complete* (Reader, 1966). This was not only a numerical domination but a domination of the ethos of the professions, according to which only 'gentlemen' of independent means needed to apply for membership in the first place (Elliott, 1972). A male monopoly or near-monopoly persisted in law and medicine until the last quarter of the nineteenth century. The first 'Law Society' was appropriately named The Society of Gentlemen Practisers in the Courts of Law and Equity and was founded in 1729. Male monopoly clearly persists in the Church of England and the Roman Catholic Church and male oligarchy is still maintained in most of the smaller churches.

The control of emotionality
While the mediation of disputes and the management of life and death may in structural terms be instances of reproduction, in individual terms they are a major material basis for the expression of emotions. The nature of emotionality ranges from positive feelings which may actually reinforce the enjoyment of work to negative debilitating grief. Thus in this sense the development of professions is also intimately bound up with the social organisation and control of emotionality.

Emotionality also occurs for other reasons than as an individualistic expression of reproduction. Indeed at a more abstract level, the very separation of emotionality and instrumentality or rationality can itself be explained by reference to the compartmentalising character of both capitalism and patriarchy. Strangely enough the very duality of rationality and emotionality created by capitalism and patriarchy presents inconveniences to their maintenance.

While large areas of social life are determined by the operation of 'rational' capitalist method, emotions recur in the interstices of capitalist and patriarchal relations. Emotionality created and structured by capitalism and patriarchy becomes at once a field for its further elaboration, however problematic.

MEN IN THE SEMI-PROFESSIONS

Since the development of the 'established professions' monopolised by men this process has continued apace elsewhere. It is in the so-called semi-professions that this second phase of professional development has taken place. Within nursing, health visiting, midwifery, social work and teaching are the emerging structures by which grief, joy, loss and despair are patriarchally socialised. The semi-professions are thus concerned with incipient and progressive socialisation of emotionality. Activities and experiences formerly performed privately or controlled by women became in this way brought into public control by men, and so subject to the expertise of experts.

What follows is an attempt to set out the broad types of changes by which semi-professions become more like the full professions, and so become more explicitly dominated by men.[3]

A. Feminist action
B. Initial incorporation
   (i)   Serving a man
   (ii) Serving an existing profession
C. Setting the status quo
   (i)   The patriarchal feminine
   (ii) The professional code
D. Divide and rule
   (i)   Men in the ranks
   (ii) Segmenting the market
E. Takeover
   (i)   Managerialism and men in management
   (ii) Full professionalisation

Not all semi-professions are necessarily affected by all of

these changes. In some cases one particular process may be dominant; while in another several processes may overlap and interrelate with each other.

A. Feminist action

Women have been particularly prominent in pioneering the socialisation of emotional experiences through the development of social work, care for the sick and aged, and so on. By forging the socialisation of unpredictable emotions, women have potentially posed a far greater threat to capitalism than men. Indeed in their earliest forms some of these interventions were potentially revolutionary. This is perhaps best illustrated in the early history of health visiting with its close links with radical and feminist movements (Dingwall, 1977), and the work of Sylvia Pankhurst and other suffragettes in the East London Women's Federation. A rather similar pattern is discernible in the history of social work, rooted in the activism and social reform of women in both Britain and America in the second half of the last century (Walton, 1975; Bolin, 1973). Kravetz (1976) has shown how in America this dynamism continued until the 1920s, with the ratification of the Nineteenth Amendment. A rather similar development is described by Gordon (1975) in relation to the American birth control movement. In its early days this represented a bold feminist and socialist innovation, only to be subsequently appropriated by male control in the shape of the medical profession. At the same time, it must be remembered that as soon as this process of socialising emotions began, it increased the possibility for their incorporation by the institutions of capitalism and patriarchy.

B. Initial incorporation

(i) Serving a man

If women pose a threat to both men and capitalists by taking on the socialised work on emotionality in the interstices of capitalism, then attempts are soon made to remove the threat. The simplest mechanism to achieve this is for isolated men to take on the control of the activity, as we see with C. S. Loch and his work with the Charity Organisation Society. This is the means often used in the early days of the semi-professions. In effect capitalists are employing men to manage women to work in sensitive areas of economy and society. In turn these women care for and control other men and other women as patients, clients or whatever. Women act as the agents of men. In the case of the Charity Organisation Society the control of women by men was also related to class control. Gender divisions in such early initiatives were frequently paralleled by both class division and ideological divisions. COS philosophy and development reflected the social position of its members as the professional London elite, with aspirations to form a new urban gentry. This in turn legitimated a progressive confidence in the expert and scientific nature of charity (Jones, 1971).

(ii) Serving an existing profession
Though isolated men may be an effective means of control, they are hardly reliable. A more stable and more structured form of incorporation comes from the subservience of particular semi-professions to other full professions. Thus a whole array of paramedical semi-professions have developed to service the full profession of medicine—not only nurses, as catalogued by Gamarnikow (1978), but also midwives, health visitors, radiographers, occupational and speech therapists and so on. The Ladies Sanitary Reform Association was set up as an incipient health visiting organisation initially as a parallel to the all-male Manchester and Salford Sanitary Reform Society. The latter concentrated more on the structural aspects of sanitation, while disease resulting from failures in household management and thus requiring practical instruction and home visiting was seen as a women's concern. Thus a separate ladies group was established, which was later to come under the control of the male-dominated Medical Officers of Health.

Other semi-professions can be understood in this way as serving established professions. Social workers spend much of their time serving, that is receiving referrals from and writing reports for, medics, lawyers, the courts, even the police. Even librarianship is seen at its fullest development when serving men, in universities and other 'places of learning'.

Further intensification of such subordination can often be

seen in the physical and institutional arrangements that accompany the semi-professions. Of particular significance for the medical semi-professions is the development of hospital-based medicine, with the form and layout of buildings and the gender divisions within and outside them reinforcing each other (Versluysen, 1981).

C. Setting the status quo
(i) The patriarchal feminine
Structural arrangements whereby particular semi-professions service or serve particular professions or particular men may be a major way of defining a space, a territory for the semi-professions, but they do not in themselves act as a very efficient means of controlling the ideas and aspirations of the semi-professionals. This necessitates some attention to the realm of ideology.

It has frequently been observed how the sorts of paid work women undertake tend to mirror the domestic tasks of cleaning, food preparation, clothing manufacture and so on. A similar parallel can be drawn between the social-emotional domestic tasks and the semi-professional areas of specialisation. This element of sex-role socialisation I refer to as the patriarchal feminine—feminine as it conforms to the feminine, 'caring' stereotype; patriarchal because in doing so it complements and thereby reinforces the masculine stereotype and specialisation. In this way the ideology of femininity is central to patriarchy in general and the semi-professions in particular.

This ideology is exemplified most clearly in the paramedical semi-professions, with the 'feminine' nurse 'complementing' the 'masculine' doctor (Gamarnikow, 1978; Ehrenreich and English, 1974, 38). Carpenter, writing on the historical development of the nursing ethic, suggests:

The work itself was not to be tainted with the world of Capital. It was to be carried out as a *service* and pecuniary motives were to play no part, just as home was supposed to be the place where goods and services were provided for love, not money.   (1977, 166)

The patriarchal femininity of the semi-professions has also

seen more pronounced, even authoritarian, forms. Within nursing the matron has personified a certain reinforcement of patriarchal authority by 'running a tight ship' in the areas left by the medical men. Even more interesting and complicated examples arise within the teaching profession. Indeed women teachers and headmistresses may both encourage the ideology of femininity amongst their pupils, whilst at the same time emulating their male counterparts.

In its purest form patriarchal authority is reproduced through the class structure of the semi-professions. Nursing, teaching and similar semi-professions have not only provided jobs for a mass of women, but more particularly posts with considerable authority for middle- and upper-class women. This has not only reinforced male authority, but has also brought a divisive class element into the semi-professions. In some senses this class structuring of authority *within* the semi-professions mirrors the gender structuring of authority *around* and *between* semi-professions and professions. This brings many contradictions, as Parry and Parry (1976, 181) comment:

The paradox was that the search for professionalism among nurses was more an expression of the antipathy felt by the status conscious lady-nurses towards those recruited from the working class than it was an effort to establish a self-governing profession of nursing.

This leads us directly to the question of professionalism and the professional code.

(ii) The professional code

Another effective form of ideological control (known to all teachers and prison governors) is for the practitioners, the women, to develop their own form of self-control. The principal way of achieving this is by the development of the professional code and professionalisation in general. This in effect masculinises the behaviour of practitioners, with the professional ethic expressing completely 'gentlemanly reasonableness' (Duman, 1979). The professional socialisation of the semi-professionals obliges them to conform to certain norms of behaviour (Theodore, 1971) and establishes the ideology of universalism and exclusivity.

This process has been described by Chafetz (1972) in examining the state of American social work in the post-war period. Attempts to attract more men into a female-dominated sphere have included the development of a more 'professional' base, as part of an effort to, what is misleadingly called, 'defeminise' social work. The introduction of professional codes into the semi-professions may increase the status of individual women, but in its wake brings the practical problems of career continuity, dual roles, dual career families and so on. Most importantly, however, the establishment of professional codes contributes to the possibility of more men entering the ranks.

D. Divide and rule
(i) Men in the ranks
The acceptance of masculinised versions of behaviour in dealing with emotionality not only makes such jobs more appealing in themselves to men, but also increases their status in the market. Thus indirectly they become 'more acceptable' to men as careers. The entrance of men into women's semi-professions has been seen in nursing, social work and teaching. Once in, men are available, of course, to enter the more prestigious jobs. This is perhaps most clearly illustrated by the movement of men into first and middle-school headships in recent years.

(ii) Segmenting the market
As men enter the ranks of the semi-professions, they enter in a highly discriminating way. The market is segmented in a number of directions—by status, by specialisation, by stereotype.

Within teaching there are gender divisions not only between primary and secondary education, but also by subject, with clear divisions between arts and science teaching. A rather similar development occurs within the different specialisms of social work. Women tend to specialise more in front-line casework; men more in community work, research and policy development (Brager and Michael, 1969; Scotch, 1971). The probation service is not only more populated by men than other branches of social work (Walton, 1975, 22), but it also has better conditions of service, a flatter organisational hierarchy and arguably a more reliable source of finance from the 'law and order' sector. Within psychiatric social work men have an influence out of all proportion to their relatively small numbers (Timms, 1964, 74). A more subtle and yet perhaps more significant discrimination is between practitioners and theorists, with men again tending to dominate the 'academic' section of the semi-professions, including social work (Rosenblatt *et al.*, 1970).

All of these various discriminations by specialism can be seen both in strictly economic terms as well as in status terms. Mennerick's (1975) study of organisational structuring by sex within travel agencies has the important double lesson that 'creaming' may take place not only between agencies of different status, but also within agencies. Within most of the semi-professions there is the strange contradiction of women occupying the majority of posts, as well as being diverted into the more specialist areas of work away from the centre of the profession (Mackie and Pattullo, 1977, 90–1).

E. Takeover
(i) Managerialism and men in management
The differential promotion of men and women in the semi-professions culminates in the progressive separation of the semi-professional managers and the semi-professional practitioners. Not only are the managers likely to be largely or exclusively men—for example, only 21 (out of 174) Directors of Social Services were women in 1971 (Smith, 1972)[4]—but the management ideology is heavily male-orientated.

The semi-professions can be seen as one relatively easy route by which men can reach managerial positions (Kadushin, 1976). This is particularly so in the context of British local government, where almost all departments other than Social Services are traditionally heavily male-dominated. The position for women is exacerbated by management's preference for full-time rather than part-time senior staff. There are, for example, very few part-time social workers above basic grade level. In many ways managerialism represents a further reinforcement of the male-orientated ideology of professionalism.

A detailed account of the onset of managerialism in nursing, particularly since the Salmon Report in 1966, has been provided by Carpenter (1977). He sees that Report as an implicit critique of *female* authority in nursing, and in this way sexist. He writes:

Female nurses are viewed almost as inherently unable to exercise administrative skills. They may be 'meticulous in details on which the life of a patient depends', ... 'but when, on promotion to posts in Matron's office they venture on to "administration" many seem unable to take decisions'.

The outcome of this criticism and the subsequent reorganisation was the creation of more posts in nursing management, 'made ripe for male capture'.

A comparable pattern has occurred within social work. Walton has commented:

In almonering, psychiatric social work and child care, women formed a spearhead for professional development and it is a great irony that in a profession so long fought for over many lifetimes by women that there should be the prospect of long-term subjection to men and the fact that principles carefully nursed may be in danger of disintegrating from mechanical managerial and planning systems.   (1975, 263)

Although managerialism is often linked with bureaucratisation and thus contrasted with professionalism, the dichotomy is surely a false one. In fact in the cases of both nursing and social work, a so-called 'new professionalism' has followed close on the heels of the 'new managerialism'.

(ii) Full professionalisation
Full professionalisation comes when the activity is fully dominated by men—in both management and the ranks. It is the fate that awaits the semi-professions. Full professionalisation is also signalled by the monopolisation by men of the particular area of emotional life, free from competition from other, probably more female-dominated occupations.

The process has come full circle. While semi-professionalisation indicates partial patriarchal domination; full professionalisation indicates full patriarchal domination. Once this has been accomplished, further areas of life can be opened up for sponsorship; further semi-professions can service the professions.

THE CASE OF MIDWIFERY[5]

Before continuing to some concluding remarks it may be useful to consider, albeit briefly, some of the historical changes that have affected midwifery, a semi-profession at the point of biological reproduction. Just as within marxist analysis the point of production is crucial, so patriarchy can be usefully analysed by reference to the specific points of reproduction—sexual, biological and social. Moreover, birth is one of the most emotional experiences, if not the most. Midwives, and subsequently health visitors, monitor these emotions, though not necessarily explicitly or even consciously. More importantly, they translate them from private into public terms. Birth is acknowledged as producing a certain amount of emotion, but not too little and certainly not too much. If either extreme occurs then further steps may be taken by the semi-professional to place the case within a more socialised context, that is, to bring it to the attention of other professions and senior members of semi-professions, and therefore men. In this sense the semi-professions can act as spies on behalf of men.

Interestingly enough, until the seventeenth century childbirth was effectively 'women's business', the province of the midwife. However, controls had been operative during the sixteenth century in the sense that midwives had to take an oath not to use magic when attending pregnant women (Rowbotham, 1973, 5). From the beginning of the eighteenth century the delivery of babies became for male doctors a means of entering increasingly lucrative family practice. The right to use instruments was essentially part of the monopoly of surgery enjoyed by men. This led to a division of the market, with doctors' skills reserved for those who could pay and midwives continuing to provide for the poor.

This situation persisted until the second half of the nineteenth century, with increasing interest from feminists in extending employment opportunities. In Britain the Female Medical Society was founded in 1862 and shortly afterwards it instituted a Ladies' Medical College for instructing women in midwifery and medicine. This was largely superseded by the London School of Medicine for women set up in 1874. By 1886 the Matrons' Aid Society was working under the bolder name of The Midwives' Institute. By the 1890s the relationship between the women midwives and the men doctors was becoming more fraught. In particular two issues dominated the political arena: the questions of inter-professional authority and midwife registration, which was pressed for by the Midwives' Institute in particular.

A number of Parliamentary Bills for registration were promoted during the 1890s culminating in the successful Bill of 1902. Since then there have been further intense divisions around foetal monitoring, amniocentesis, hospital inductions, the use of chemical pain relievers, home confinements, the role of fathers (as 'surrogate doctors' or otherwise) and so on.

Several conclusions can be drawn from these events. First and most important, is that in the professionalisation of midwifery, the contending parties were more clearly defined by sex than in other semi-professions. The closer one approaches the point of reproduction the more marked are sexual divisions of the related workers. Secondly, changes that took place have to be interpreted as of a dialectical nature rather than as fixed or evolutionary. Thus feminist pressure within the ranks of the midwives did not simply arise in the early days of semi-professionalisation, but continued at each point, especially to fend off the various compromises on offer. Indeed, the Act itself had complicated and apparently contradictory implications. On the one hand it represented a partial setback to the male medical monopoly, following the Medical Registration Act of 1886. On the other it meant midwives were 'unique in being subject to the licensing procedures of a local government [and] could be struck off from the ... register for a wide range of ill-defined and petty ethical misdemeanours which even included minute regulations governing their dress' (Parry and Parry, 1976, 180).

Versluysen concludes her historical survery of midwifery:

female midwives found their subordinate status confirmed by the ... Act which put a majority of medical men on the council responsible for the

training and registration of midwives, thereby making clear that neither
skilled women nor mothers could regard birth as their own concern anymore.
(1981, 43)

The case of midwifery acts as an important reminder that
changes towards greater professionalisation should not be seen
as part of some remorseless evolutionary process. Rather
professionalisation is a shorthand term for a variety of
processes by which men move into and increase their influence
on the semi-professions.

CONCLUDING REMARKS

The professions, both established and emerging, both fully and
partially dominated by men, and indeed the whole process of
professionalisation are bastions of patriarchy. This is
particularly so in the sphere of reproduction and the control of
emotionality, areas of life that present difficulties for capitalist
organisation and patriarchal domination.

The major purpose of this paper has thus been to
demonstrate the impact of the professions in the maintenance
and development of patriarchy. It is in the context of this
relationship that the semi-professions, staffed mainly by
women, managed mainly by men, in turn assume a greater
significance than is usually attributed to them. The traditional
professions have grown to dominate important areas of
reproduction. Indeed medicine, the church and the law
effectively control the management of life and death, in
biological, spiritual and social terms respectively. They operate
close to and with jurisdiction over the various points of
reproduction. They are concerned with the socialisation of
what were formerly private, emotional experiences around the
points of reproduction.

In contrast to the overarching role of the professions, the
semi-professions have a much more limited area of interest and
work. They either act as the 'handmaidens' of the professions
in performing specific duties, for example, radiography, or they
focus on particular points of reproduction, for example,
midwifery, or they assist in extending professional concerns

into new areas, for example, psychotherapy. The male-dominated professions define the limits of action and ideology and so control both reproduction and the semi-professions indirectly, almost without having to be there. The (numerically) female-dominated semi-professions do particular types of, often arduous, work and control particular aspects of reproduction directly. Indeed the closer one approaches particular points of reproduction, whether sexual, natal or whatever, the greater may be the ideological need to demonstrate apparent control by women, through the semi-professions, although the greater may be the material need to exert actual control by men, through the professions. The semi-profession of midwifery is clearly crucial, particularly in terms of the gender division of occupations in relation to the points of reproduction, in this case that of birth itself.

A final more speculative point is that professionalisation, already analysed as patriarchal, is one of the major ways in which two apparently disparate realms, institutional science and personal sexuality are linked. The church, medicine and the law still effectively define sexual limits. Sexuality may yet become more fully 'scientised' through the action of professionals.

8 The Professions, the Control of Emotions and the Construction of Masculinity[1]

Reproductive labour is characteristically sensual—it appeals to the senses; it involves work on oneself or towards other people rather than towards the production of objects. It entails the enjoyment and oppression of the body, the expression and repression of the emotions. Such emotional work and bodywork has necessary consequences for those working at and around reproduction; here the focus is upon the implications of working with emotions for professional men, and so the impacts of professionalisation for the social construction of masculinity within patriarchy. As before, the professions, and particularly the people-related professions, are understood as one of the means of control of women by men through the control of reproduction.

By masculinity I refer to those sets of signs indicating that a person is a 'man', or 'not a woman', or 'not a child'. These signs may include differential expressions and even experiences of 'emotion'. Thus I specifically reject the rationalist use of the notion of 'masculinity' (and 'femininity'), as within psychological testing. For example, it is not possible to link emotions and their expression to objective measures of 'masculinity' and 'femininity' (Constantinople, 1973), at least not in any direct way. It is also clear that women are not simply 'more emotional' than men (Allen and Haccoun, 1976). Rather masculinity is diverse, socially constructed and certainly not reducible to a referent continuum.

Emotions are themselves notoriously difficult to theorise. On one hand, they are objectively definable 'mental states accompanied by intense feeling and involving bodily changes of a widespread character' (Koestler, 1967, 226). On the other, a strict separation of emotionality and, say, rationality into mutually exclusive qualities is mistaken, as actions can be both emotional and non-emotional (rational) at the same time (Eichler, 1980, 121). Furthermore, emotions can be felt, consciously or less consciously expressed, and be more or less visible to various others. They are clearly not a unified phenomenon, but rather several different, if related, types of phenomena. They also and importantly have frequent social associations, both positive (joy?) and negative (anxiety?), and with masculinity (anger?) and femininity (sorrow?), alongside the broader, social conflations of emotionality and femininity, that ideologically obscure the contradictions of gender relations.

The place of emotions in relation to reproduction and reproductive labour is necessarily complex. While 'emotions are involved in every aspect of living, emotions of varying tone of intensity' (Stacey, 1982, 24), particular intensities of emotion recur around reproduction. Thus experiences at the specific points of reproduction, for example, childbirth, may be among the most emotional (while simultaneously the most instrumental). Subsequent phases of reproduction, for example, early childcare, may be sites for emotional development in a more extended way. Emotions may *seem* at their most intense when experience and valued expectation or fear are either completely convergent (the 'successful' birth) or completely divergent (the 'unsuccessful' birth). Yet even this is not enough, for often contradictory emotions may accompany experiences of life, illness, death, and so on; and more importantly still, while reproductive labour and experiences may be emotional for all concerned, there are clear differentiations in what emotions may be expressed, in what manner, in what circumstances, and by whom. It is in this arena that men as professionals, reproductive managers, reproductive workers, 'people workers' of various sorts, act: both in dealing with the emotions of others ('clients'), and perhaps defining their experience; and in the, at least potentially emotional, encounter of professional and 'client'. Two main types of professional involvement are initially considered, in terms of their constructions of masculinity: as managers of people work; as the labourers of people work.

While this division largely parallels the 'professional'/'semi-professional', there are men in the latter occupations who are managers of people work and vice versa.

THE CONSTRUCTION OF PROFESSIONAL MASCULINITIES

Professionals as managers of people work

Men in the male-dominated 'established professions' of medicine, the law and the church, are characteristically engaged in the selective control of the emotions of themselves and others, both workers and 'clients'. In this sense they act as specific emotional managers. Some of the major types of emotional control of these professions are represented in figure 8 below.

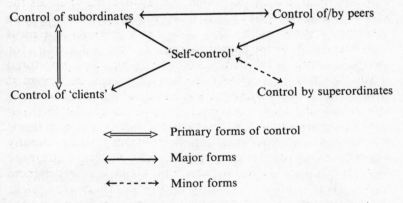

Figure 8:   Professional emotional control (1): 'people managers'

Professional work is often accomplished with and through the work of 'semi-professionals', such as midwives, who are mainly women. Such professions also have distinct hierarchical control over other workers. They may define the limits of action and emotion for other workers, often without having to be there.

A second form of control of others' emotions is towards

'clients', who may be women, men or children, though in certain areas of work they are significantly and predominantly women. On those occasions when 'clients', and particularly women, are brought into contact with the professions, they may express their emotions, and even be encouraged to do so, as long as this is within certain limits. If not, they may move from being voluntary to involuntary 'clients', or face other sanctions.

On the other hand, these professions assist in the 'self-control' of men and their emotions, so contributing to definitions of masculinity. For men 'being professional' may mean not showing certain emotions, especially in the control of others' emotions; it may also in the longer run limit certain emotional experiences; or more likely their transfer from one form to another (say, from anger to depression). Such men may apppear to 'not be emotional' or subscribe to a professional code that values 'not being emotional'. They may display 'affective neutrality', even talk *about* emotions, become 'expert' on emotions, yet not be *seen* as emotional. A degree of controlled friendliness may conjoin with this denial of emotion. In effect, the problem of emotional control of such professionals is primarily located *through others*—subordinate staff and 'clients'—in the form of an institutionalised defence *structured in interpersonal relations and other persons*. These professions and their masculinities are havens of occupational extraversion and projection.

This leaves such professional men 'free', despite their 'self-control', to be just as emotional in private or even in certain aspects of their public practice, for example, shouting at nurses. It is the public presentation of the ideal or value or supposed practice of this non-emotionality that is important ideologically. In fact, while 'excessive' emotional displays in public may be considered by many as inappropriate, unmanly, or simply ineffective, there are circumstances where men commonly express anger in public and might be judged (by other men) to be 'reasonable' to do so. It is tears that are 'not very professional'. Furthermore, this selective 'denial' may be mutually reinforced by other professionals, again in rather contradictory ways. One professional may control or sanction another for expressing emotion, but do so with a mixture of 'self-control', and indignation, even (emotional) upset (Stacey, 1982, 23–4). What is called 'masculinity' for professional men is not a fixed formula, but rather that combination of actions, part powerful, part arbitrary, performed in reaction and relation to these complex emotional and other demands, and recognised by others as signifying this is a 'man'.

This approach sheds light on other literature on professions as implicit constructions of masculinity. Professional behaviour thus often becomes a euphemism for a patriarchal model of masculinity. The trait approach to professions becomes an itemisation of the traits of one model of masculinity. The professional service ethic can be reinterpreted in terms of objectifying others and particularly others' emotions. The double-edged nature of this ethic, providing service and reinforcing superior knowledge, is sharpened. Professional models of masculinity can also be subjected to critique on the basis of their underlying search for and assumption of control, of others and themselves, as in instrumental rationalities. The legal profession and even the police, in presenting a supposedly non-emotional stance towards violence is thus the embodiment of patriarchal authority, with the task of the supposedly non-emotional resolution of situations involving the expression of, often intense, emotions. Such a 'resolution' is in practice likely to be highly emotional for the men concerned.

Similarly, the supposedly asexual nature of masculinity within the professions deserves some comment. Bland *et al.* (1978a, 66) note that 'in [some] jobs female sexuality as sexuality on display is part of the *use value of the commodity labour power itself.* For some secretaries, receptionists, boutique assistants, it is essential to be attractively feminine as well as to serve.' Perhaps the professions are the opposite case with their (usually male) asexuality as asexuality on display as part of the service sold. Whereas women workers are often 'sexualised' or 'eroticised', some men workers are specifically 'asexualised', in keeping with their supposed neutrality and the supposed neutral competence of masculinity presented.

Professionals as labourers of people work
In contrast to the 'established professions' professional

managers just described, the people work of teaching, nursing, midwifery, health visiting, social work, youth work, community work, even therapy is mainly done by women or seen as 'women's work'. These professional workers have a much more limited area of interest and work. They are also engaged both in the control of the emotions of others, particularly of 'clients', and in the control of their own. Their own emotions are controlled both by professional managers and by themselves.

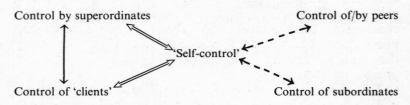

Figure 9:   Professional emotional control (2): 'people labourers'

Professional labourers typically work more directly with clients' emotions though often with less control; they are closer to the points of reproduction, often completing the routine emotional work, and referring to more powerful professionals in disputes or when a crisis cannot be resolved. The control of the professional labourers' own emotions comes partly from the control by other staff, particularly other professionals, and partly from 'self-control'. This may involve the use of deferential indirect responses rather than more direct and potentially more emotional responses by, say, nurses to doctors (Bullough, 1975). Unlike the structured 'occupational projection' of the 'established professions', these labourers of people work experience more direct emotional control, in relation to both professional superordinates and 'clients' themselves. Their emotional economy is not located in other persons but *in relation to themselves.*[2] This practical mixture of control and emotional, and sometimes very stressful, work leads to a somewhat different form of institutional defence, in rules, procedures, standards of dress, work routines and so on (Menzies, 1960). The emotional threat of direct emotional labour is not displaced in the structure of authority relations; the means to this have almost to be dug out of the available organisational resources.

Such 'self-control' is complicated by the fact that the *numerical* domination of women in those professions may be accompanied by a 'personalistic' ideology. This can mean that an even more thorough socialisation process takes place than in the 'established professions'. For the prospective professional labourer the whole person is available for assessment and resocialisation: personal values, character, attitudes, moods. All of these are material which professionalisation may work on and change, in a more conclusive, less cynical way than in the 'established professions'. This may reflect a sense of occupational insecurity that comes from their status ambiguity as professional yet proletarian jobs.

This is clearly illustrated in 'counselling out' within social work education, in which educators and indeed practitioners see it as their business to dissuade students who do not appear to be appropriate future members of the profession from continuing with their chosen career. However, the important factor in 'counselling out' is its performance by informal or 'personalistic' methods rather than by formal procedure or assessments. There is even provision on some social work courses for 'options' by which such successfully counselled students may graduate without the 'professional' part of the qualification. This is rather like a doctor becoming qualified, but without the qualification to practice—an expert on medicine but not a medic.

The relative minority of men who enter such occupations may do so with contradictory motives. They are generally entering what is seen as a form of women's work. Their immediate 'people-orientation', the work's supposed expressiveness, perhaps working with women, may appeal. On the other hand, such a career choice may result from or even engender a highly instrumental motivation. Men may achieve career advancement, often over women, and so away from emotional work towards administration, a significant process both structurally in men's control of professions and personally for those concerned. Additionally, working with or in relation to others' emotions may affect their own emotionality, reflecting partly the self-selection of men and partly job-induced change, that is from the 'clients'. Distress with and of 'clients' can be distressing for the worker.

Such professional men may provide more 'liberal' models of masculinity. Such contradictions may cause such men to liberalise their self-presentation, to be more accommodating to their, often women, co-workers, to survive organisationally. So we find professional men learning to work as peers alongside women, doing the photocopying to avoid burdening the secretary, and subsequently progressing above their women co-workers and away from their secretaries in pay, status and so on.

These 'liberal' models of masculinity may appear different from, say, more traditional models but are in fact rather similar. Life-styles may change but objective gender relations may be much more resistant to changes, and men's control of reproduction may even be intensified with their professional promotion. Nevertheless, working with others' emotions and one's own emotions can for some men challenge and question traditional models of masculinity and their own masculinity in a more thoroughgoing way. This may lead some to become involved in men's consciousness-raising and other groups, and develop a general interest in sexual politics. It is in effect the work-based equivalent to domestic pressures from women on men. More usual is the continuing development of the contradictions described, so that men develop various ways of coping and forms of compromise. These may range across the integration of work/non-work friendships, the compartmentalising of very expressive work, job sharing, development of unofficial support groups, interest in serial careers, extended unpaid or study leave where possible, and other liberal fragmentations in the face of the emotional.

THE PROFESSIONAL CONSTRUCTION OF MASCULINITIES

In addition to this structured self-construction of masculinity, the professions are crucially involved in the construction of the masculinity of others, especially boys, young men, and men, individually or collectively in their charge. Teaching provides particularly explicit models of masculinity, in terms of authority, fairness, punishment, and so on. More generally, the professions accomplish, and may even create, a particularly important type of generative work that is across the public–private boundary, between the realms of private families and public professional activity over separated 'clients'. In a multitude of 'homes', schools, as well as custodial, medical, psychiatric, military, and paramilitary institutions, in public privacy, boys are made masculine and 'men'. These institutions are partly sites of male culture and 'character formation' (Fromm, 1974), and so of their temporal and generational transmission; they are also sites of individual experience, of oppression in the present, of control by older boys and men, of separation from others of the same or different gender.

These productions of masculinism in the public–private[3] take their most serious and sophisticated form in the combination of militarism, 'man management', manners, and killing taught in the military 'academies' of Westpoint, Sandhurst, and the like. More widespread are the varieties of 'social skills training' in schools and educational establishments, often constructed *through* economic class, historically specific (Radley, 1985; Armstrong, 1985) and productive of distinctive masculinities. Within professional schooling, discipline, physical punishment, arrangement of bodies (in classes, lines, and so on), and sport have recurrently been paramount.

These constructions take place in the public realm, yet around the public–private boundary. Whereas Ardener (1978) suggests that men's presence in large numbers in a space designates it as 'public', a more accurate description of many of these sites is as places of public privacy. Schools and other similar institutions are thus professionalised equivalents of such other public privacies as pubs, men's clubs, freemasonry lodges, even sport itself. The mild and heavy brutalisation of boys and men in these public–private institutions is a means not just of male socialisation, but of the contested struggle of gender itself (Hargreaves, 1986). The social statement, near stamping, of boys and men persists through an implacable, naive differentiation and arrangement of persons, in deliberate 'mixing' or 'segregation': the continual, acausal reproduction of material beings as gender(ed).

Part 4

Politics and Practice

INTRODUCTION

Finally and primarily, we come to politics and practice—the rationale of theory. Practice is after all virtually all we have. This section includes some short statements on four areas of practice in which I have had direct involvement: fatherhood, childcare politics, men's anti-sexist politics, and social science. In *Birth and Afterbirth* I concluded from a good deal of personal struggle: 'the notion of fatherhood must be smashed or more precisely dropped bit by bit into the ocean' (1983, 51). This conclusion, however, clearly also had to be a starting point: it was necessary to spell out its implications for practice. During the winter of 1983–4 I wrote out some of these for the journal, *Radical Community Medicine*; an edited and slightly revised version of that article appears as chapter 9. In this perspective what is called 'fatherhood' is largely an illusion (Hearn, 1984a), a patriarchal camouflage of alienation in reproduction. Moving from this involves facing alienation and changing our (men's) relationship to childcare and other aspects of reproduction. The political nature of this question has been brought home both from my own domestic experience and through more public action, especially childcare campaigning. The latter issues are discussed in chapter 10, originally written in the period 1980–81 for *Birth and Afterbirth*, with the particular focus on the need for a more explicit politics of childcare.

The more general question of possibilities for men's practice had been the subject of papers in 1982 at the Critical Social Policy conference in Sheffield (1982b) and the Conference of

Socialist Economists in Bradford (1982d). At those sessions I
was concerned mainly with the problem—when men realise we
live in a patriarchy, what do we do about it? Chapter 11 is a
development of those ideas, particularly following work in the
Low Plains Drifter newsletter collective, conversations with
Mark Long, correspondence with Keith Mothersson, and the
opportunity to review and present some of this information at
the University of Hamburg in April 1986.

Finally, and not primarily, I consider some of the
implications of all this for changing men's practice in the social
sciences. Chapter 12 is adapted from the 'Changing men's
studies . . .' papers given in 1986 at the University of Bradford
and the British Sociological Association Conference at the
University of Loughborough (Hearn 1986a). Social science is
still primarily practice, be it patriarchal or anti-patriarchal.

9 The Problem of Fatherhood[1]

There appear to be two major ways in which men come to be involved at childbirth: through providing medical care and what is generally called 'fatherhood'. While medicine, hospitals and technology are the major means of men's access to and control of birth in the public sphere, the major means of access and control arising out of the private sphere is fatherhood. Just as a wide range of opinion supports the medicalisation of birth, so the increasing involvement of fathers in birth has been acclaimed by a wide range of opinion as a good idea. The natural childbirth movement has been campaigning for father participation in birth for fifty years (Reid, 1934). In 1972 Sheila Kitzinger (1972) made clear recommendations for the father's role in childbirth and his continuous presence during labour. Over the last twenty years there has been a revolution in attitudes towards fathers' presence at birth, so that now the great majority of births are attended by fathers—over 70 per cent in a recent Equal Opportunities Commission survey of 282 births, with another 14 per cent attending labour only (Bell, McKee and Priestley, 1983). Other surveys have reported fathers' attendance at birth in up to 80 or 90 per cent of cases (Woollett, White and Lyon, 1982).

A similar enthusiasm for the importance of fathers has developed amongst many health educationists; in fatherhood classes; in involving fathers in ante-natal relaxation; in a variety of literature and publicity. Interestingly it is also found throughout much of the media—both the 'popular' and 'quality' press—with stories of fathers who have had vasectomies reversed, had heart operations, who actually look after children, who are also pop singers or TV personalities. Fatherhood goes down very well these days. There is now talk of 'pregnant fathers', 'fathers in labour', 'expectant fathers', even 'pregnant couples' and 'pregnant families' (Parke, 1981; Richman, 1982). While the family may be having a hard time in many other respects, not least the level of separation and divorce, this is one area where it seems to be having a definite boost.

So what are the implications of this trend and why are they problematic? As with medical and technological change the implications are several, not altogether consistent, perhaps even contradictory. For example, on the face of it fathers' acceptance into labour and birth is part of the attempt to resist the medicalisation of birth. Yet as Charlie Lewis (1982) points out: 'fathers have appeared at the same time that birth has become increasingly "unnatural" '. For the fact is that although many men may experience hospitals and medical personnel as relatively unaccommodating to them at birth, fathers' presence at birth now has major support from within medicine. The medical profession now accepts that fathers have a 'right' to see 'their' child being born, and indeed according to Lewis has itself perhaps been the greatest agent of change in allowing fathers' access. Many medical men also recognise that other men can be useful at births, if only in that they can make 'a highly medicalised experience into a humane and family one' (Woollett, White and Lyon, 1982). Thus medicine is now not only responsible for the medicalisation of birth, but also for underwriting the involvement of fathers.

An interesting recent case that bears on the relationship of medicine to fathers is that of Brian Radley, fined £100 under a little-used section of the 1951 Midwives Act stating that 'being a male person, you attended otherwise than under the direction and supervision of a duly qualified medical practitioner', after he had delivered 'his son' at home without calling a midwife. What is particularly significant is that the case was generally interpreted in terms of fathers' rather than mothers' rights of control. The mother, Michelle Williams, apparently wanted 'to give birth in the "natal crouch" position ... did not want a catheter routinely used to clear mucus from the baby's throat, and emphatically did not want the use of any drugs'. The midwife was reportedly 'aghast' at these plans, and refused to arrange a planned home delivery (Adams, 1982). Medicine seems to have the upper hand in law, but fathers may be gaining ground and have much appeal to popular consciousness. Meanwhile mothers' control over what happens at the births of their children appears to remain as a secondary issue.

Another set of contradictions surrounds the connection between men's experiences at a birth and broader definitions of fatherhood, and indeed of masculinity. By being at a birth men may be opened up to a new, and perhaps very emotional, experience. Thus at a birth many fathers can be seen to break the 'first commandment' of masculinity, 'Thou shalt not cry or expose feelings of emotion, fear, weakness, sympathy, empathy or involvement before thy neighbours' (Richman, 1982). This all sounds very well and very promising in challenging conventional models of masculinity. Men who are privileged to be present at a birth may have a powerful and potentially changing experience. However in some cases men, fathers, have been reported as 'collapsing after labour, complaining of not receiving enough "emotional support" ... and becoming ... furious that they could not feed *their* babies' (my emphasis) (Robert Feiss, quoted in Gathorne-Hardy, 1981). Such vigorous emotional responses may follow a high level of identification with the foetus, and attempts to take control of the pregnancy, and lead on to engrossment with the child and a belief that this baby is distinct from all others. A father reported in Sheila Kitzinger's (1973) study of parents' emotions in childbirth spoke at length of how he established 'harmony of breathing with contractions ... insisted that she breathe properly and relax', felt 'her breath was my breath', and proceeded with bearing down, 'the most painfully beautiful experience', and finally the exclamation: 'I had given birth along with my wife, I was exhausted. It was a glorious ... ecstasy.' Meanwhile the mother concludes: 'It was very much a joint effort. Without John I'm afraid I never would have made it. He played the most important part.' Yes, truly amazing.

Thus, what on one hand can be a challenge to conventional masculinity can on the other be a reinforcement of fathers and fatherhood. This is so much so that one group of commentators have gone as far as suggesting that *fathers'* presence at birth 'has improved enormously the *quality* of the childbirth experience for mothers' (my emphasis) (Woollett, White and Lyon, 1982). Fathers now appear to some as almost indispensable; masculinity isn't so threatened after all.

These contradictions are not so surprising when seen in the broader context of social change. For example, in recent decades the nature of the role of fathers has become subject to increasing doubts and questioning. There are now several different types of fathers and father roles to 'choose' from. Not only are there distant, silent, tyrannical, demanding fathers but there are also liberal, affectionate, eccentric, bizarre fathers. Perhaps above all there are confused fathers. As Maureen Green (1976) has written: 'The number of men who would now enjoy playing the role of stern Victorian paterfamilias is probably very few.... They much prefer being a modern father, if only they could be a little more certain what that is.'

These changes and uncertainties would seem to result both from the realignment of sex roles and the upsurge in divorce and separations. Thus we have the reinforcement of fathers and fatherhood, described above, occurring alongside other social changes which would tend to confuse or undermine them. It is particularly significant that all this has occurred whilst the other main 'family' role of men, the economic 'breadwinner' role, has taken a considerable battering, with men's 'flight from commitment', that is economic commitment, during the post-war period. More recently this has been exacerbated with rising levels of unemployment. The 1984 Matrimonial and Family Proceedings laws reduce men's economic responsibilities still further. It seems in fact that within the family, while men's economic role is going in one direction, men's authority role is going in the other—even if the latter is liberalised or softened in some senses. Perhaps women's loss of economic support both in and after marriage is at the expense of men's assertion of authority in reproduction, what Lewis (1982) calls a 'conjugal symmetry'.

The most important long-term outcome of all these changes is that it is now increasingly recognised that fathers and fatherhood is a political issue. In other words, many women and some men are becoming more aware of the politics of fatherhood, and that fatherhood brings not only joys but also dangers. Indeed the whole idea of fatherhood may itself be subject to question, scrutiny and opposition. There is in short a case *against* fatherhood. In practical terms, involvement before and during birth is not the same as involvement after birth. There is no guarantee that the relatively short and easy involvement around birth will continue after birth, in terms of taking responsibility for children. Men's involvement is not with birth in general but birth in the particular, the birth of 'their' child. It is an involvement not as a man, nor even as husband or lover, but as a *father*. Being at a birth in effect means being *affirmed* as a father. It is a privilege accorded to fathers of the child to be born, rather than to friends, lovers, brothers or even fathers of the mother.

Involvement around birth may not be as much a guarantee of subsequent involvement (and above all, work) in caring for children, as a means of changing men's perceived *relationship* to children and to women as mothers and wives. Being at a birth can certainly be an emotional experience for men as fathers. It probably increases the feelings of subsequent involvement with that and perhaps others of 'one's' children— but these are *feelings not deeds*. To put this another way, men's fatherly relationship with children is one often based on an illusion. Men's relationship with children is not made closer or deeper by being present at birth, nor indeed by being present at conception, but *by doing work with and for them*. That is why women have a closer relationship to children. I suspect that it is significant, and a sign of our oppression of women, that there is no single word, such as 'childwork', for all the work done in caring for children.

Thus one of the dangers of recent developments is a reinforcement of fatherhood at a time of increasing divorce and separation. While many men are questioning their economic responsibilities, many are more reticent in questioning the fatherhood role. Men's involvement around birth may in the long run be not so much a means of sharing childcare and losing power to women as of actually increasing power, especially in the face of women's independence. We may be seeing the development of a new family form—the dispersed nuclear family, the nuclear family exploded. Here relationships are not so much based on direct contact between men and women, as on indirect contact via children.

This analysis has implications throughout the whole process of (biological) reproduction. As things now stand, it is generally assumed that a 'father' is necessary at each stage of reproduction, at pre-conception, conception, pregnancy, birth, subsequent authority over children. Medical personnel of all types have a particular responsibility and opportunity to question dominant assumptions about the necessity for fathers. Their involvement and indeed their power at each stage enables them to play an important role in either reinforcing or challenging current assumptions about fatherhood. Medical personnel also clearly have a complementary ability to influence, even interfere with, women's own control of their bodies, and of reproduction. In most routine involvements medical personnel assume a father; instead they might develop their practice of *not* assuming there is a father and *not* opposing attempts by women to produce and care for children without men's involvement *as fathers*.

In the light of this critique, suggestions for 'support systems to facilitate (fathers') involvement', such as

1. The development of educational programmes in school,
2. fatherhood preparation classes,
3. open visiting,
4. instruction in infant care for father during the postpartum hospital stay,
5. paternity leave,
6. more flexible working hours, and
7. postpartum support groups   (Beail, 1982)

become much more problematic. For example, 'fatherhood preparation classes' could well be extremely reactionary unless conducted in a critical way. They could simply reinforce individual men's interest in and power over individual children and, indirectly, individual women. Much more satisfactory would be classes focusing critically on 'men and childcare', such as that at Leeds WEA (Harris, 1982–3), which do not assume that men's only interest is with sons or daughters. This sort of course is an opportunity for a broader understanding of men's relationship to children.

Similarly, the idea of paternity leave, currently so popular with many 'enlightened' shades of opinion, including many trade unions, begs the question of why such leave should hinge on *paternity*. There is no reason why demands for paternity leave could not be reformulated to be demands for statutory leave for a person, relative, friend, lover, woman or man, named by the mother. There could be a simple clause that no one person could be named more than so many times a year, to avoid abuse.

However, the implications are more far-reaching than arrangements for 'fatherhood preparation' or paternity leave. At its most fundamental, the very need for fathers at conception itself is obviated by AID (artificial insemination by donor). Fathers do not have to be created in the creation of children. In this respect it is interesting that AID has been given publicity largely as a remedy to the 'childless couple', on the question of paternity rather than issues around maternity, and on the 'childless' heterosexual couple rather than other possibilities. The radical importance of AID lies in the possible demolition of fatherhood.

In the longer term, we, as men, have to face the fact that births and children are not *ours* in any sense, however closely we are involved with them. We may live with children, take responsibility for some, but they are not ours. We do not have rights over children, nor do we gain rights through separation from them. Being a father in two families is no more satisfactory than in one. This issue is at its most crucial in that most blatant area of male control, the attempt to disqualify women as mothers because of their sexual orientation (Harne, 1984; Rights of Women, 1984). Put plainly, families do not need fathers.

To say this is not to devalue particular fathers, less still to devalue them *as men*. Nor am I suggesting that men should not take responsibility for children, rather the opposite that men should take as much responsibility as necessary, whether the father or not. Men, as 'fathers' or not, need to demonstrate a commitment to children, beyond the relatively temporary demands of 'their' children through fatherhood. As things stand, a long-term commitment to children is for men constantly and collectively in doubt. In contrast, women know their greater collective involvement or potential involvement, as grandmothers, paid workers, childminders, 'babysitters', and so on. It is these 'facts of life' that provide the differential social contexts of actions towards children.

Individual fathers are not inherently oppressive; the structured relation is. It may not be impossible to transform fathers, especially within different relations of reproduction— fatherhood, however, remains beset by problems of history, being long established as a home of violence. The risk of fatherhood is that even 'nice' fathers can change back to 'nasty' ones.

A POSITIVE APPROACH TO CHILDREN

I have tried to argue that fatherhood is a problem, and certainly so for men. Saying this may be disturbing, even bewildering, to some men, and perhaps some women. However, I say it simply because it makes sense in my own experience. This is not out of any sense of guilt (for which I have no time and no inclination) from being a 'father'. Rather it comes from a material involvement, doing work for children and a slow realisation that the potential of relationships with children is enhanced by getting away from fatherhood. Instead of relying on the authority of the father, we can better work towards forms of responsible friendship with children. This applies to friendship both with the children we live with and those who generally live elsewhere. In fact breaking down that distinction itself seems worth striving for. This may be difficult and we may have to begin in small ways, such as encouraging children we don't live with to stay over or come to the park with children we do live with.

Most importantly, by seeing ourselves and acting not as fathers concerned just for 'our own' but simply as men with different involvements with different children, a more positive approach to children is possible. This is a way of locating ourselves and changing ourselves; of building from our own experience; and of reaching out to other men with their own negative and positive experiences of children. Many men seem either uninterested in children or only interested in 'their own', so that their relationships with children are minimal and/or fatherly. This is a major block and a major loss to us, especially as and perhaps because many of our relationships with our own fathers have been so unsatisfactory. As Anna Coote (1981) has written: 'While men continue to segregate themselves from children, they are cut off from a range of experience which would no doubt broaden their understanding and no doubt alter their political priorities (and which they might even enjoy).' Paradoxically, fatherhood assists that segregation from children. We will find our own, more enjoyable, relationships with children without fatherhood and without the power of the father.

10 The Politics of Childcare[1]

Above all else children produce work of a certain sort. And just as with productive work, wage labourers sell their labour-power and are likely to be alienated, to feel powerless, so something comparable is involved in doing childwork. In this society at least, the childworker, usually a parent, usually the mother, is necessarily alienated from the product of the work, the child. This may occur for many reasons, including the control of men over women, husbands over wives, the state over 'citizens', professionals over the 'general public'. I think most men need to be alienated through childwork and housework in order to get through this massive assumption and possession of power we have. This may help us to find the 'powerless' part of ourselves. This means accepting the power of others and particularly women, appreciating the interconnectedness of things and everything, knowing oneself as part of deep calms and flows, and changing one's posture and relationship to one's body, back, feet and the ground itself. Finding the powerless part of ourselves may also enable us to re-enter politics on a more humble basis, and with a different interest in mind.

The experience of alienation is to me a vital one in shifting work to become politics. Work is no longer just something that you don't want to do, that alienates the self from the object of the work, in this case children; instead work becomes the process from which one looks beyond to the reformulation of subjects—self, children and other social arrangements.

It is only with the experience of the full weight of that power and the recognition of some of its sources, that one can realise what one can and can't do as a subject. We have got to live through the full weight of what oppresses us and what is in us oppresses others, in this case women and children. This reformulation of subjects who do and make social arrangements is a reformulation on the basis of powerlessness, not of power. So on to politics.

Politics, in which children are central not peripheral, are very different from what we usually mean by 'politics', especially party politics. The recognition of the link between children and politics makes politics more alive and immediate. For example, in childcare campaigning, politics ceases to be an activity separate from other activities—political organising, meetings, events involving children, making arrangements for looking after children, having fun—can all blend confusingly into each other in a way that is rare in, say, trade union politics.

The practical political point of all this for me and I believe for other men striving to be less sexist is that the political struggles around reproduction should become the centre of attention. Putting it pretty crudely, men do not become less sexist or 'anti-sexist' simply by expressing their sexuality more or exploring their most intimate fears and feelings. They do so by working against men's domination over women through children. Of course sexuality is one aspect of the whole business of reproduction but it is only one part and for many sexual change is to say the least inhibited by rather obvious material conditions—like looking after several children without relief and the physical, nervous and sexual wearing down that comes from that.

Most men, including many who see themselves as anti-sexist, seem to have hardly begun to face the prospect of powerlessness that comes from dealing with children, let alone act on that prospect. Out of that powerlessness comes the politics of birth and childwork. The politics of production have been recognised, the politics of reproduction are of great, perhaps greater, importance. The latter are not new, but what is new is their recognition on a par with or above productive politics.

Not surprisingly these uncertainties are to some extent paralleled by uncertainties around the place of men in the politics of reproduction. The clearest danger is that men should try to take over any political arena in the face of women. If men are to enter these politics then we should do so with the utmost humility that comes from some considerable amount of work with children, paid or unpaid. Without that our involvement is likely to be posturing.

In one sense the politics of birth and childwork, the politics of reproduction, is the way in which feminism has meant most to me; but feminism is also much more than that. It is a root and branch reconstruction of every area of life, in a way that sometimes attempts specifically to separate women from reproduction, for example in the exploration of their sexuality. This inevitable diversity of feminism is thus its strength. However, for men the individual political campaigns around reproduction—on abortion, home confinement, illegitimacy, etc.—can provide political reference points and guidelines for practice. It may be useful for men to recognise the links between the various individual campaigning areas in terms of the political control of reproduction. This is a way for me of making sense of a whole array of particular campaigns and issues. It is also for me a way of approaching sexism that is blatantly materialist.

So what precisely are these politics of birth and childwork all about? First it has to be said that very little serious attention is currently given to birth and childwork by virtually all the dominant political perspectives—from the mainstream political parties to most varieties of marxism. Secondly, even where children are seen as a major public issue, the debate tends to be seen in terms of 'care' or 'family life' not political power—of adults over children, and of men over women through the latter's work for children. Thirdly, there is the question of resources. The organisation of childwork is one of the main ways in which resources are created and in turn distributed. The domestic labour debate has shown this above all else. The state intervenes in primary education from five years upwards and in the organisation of birth, however inefficiently or patriarchically; but for the intervening years childwork goes on often unaided for the majority of parents, usually mothers. This isn't so much left to the market, as to the family. Fourthly, there are the structures which constrain birth and childwork. By these I mean the material and power relations between men and women, of different types, married, unmarried and so on, that provide the social framework within which arrangements for birth and childwork are made and discussed.

Within this framework I see the politics of reproduction as about violence, sexuality, contraception, abortion, ante-natal services, birth, post-natal provision, day care, nurseries, childwork, family structures, 'substitute care' and early education. In each of these fields men oppress women either directly or indirectly, often with the help of other women. Material relations are fixed, with men benefitting from the structuring of each and women not benefitting. For example, pressure for more day care provision may mean that some of the labour of caring for children is shifted from mothers in the home to other women, who still remain relatively poorly paid. Men may still benefit from those material relations. Each aspect of reproduction is bound to the others within the whole realm of reproductive politics. The campaign for a woman's right to choose is the same campaign as that for universally available, free, twenty-four-hour childcare.[2] Both would if fully successful constitute a restructuring of each other and thus of the whole realm of reproduction.

Reproduction and the way it is socially organised can thus provide an umbrella framework for thinking and acting in sexual politics—a way of locating what is happening and what if anything one and others are doing. At its most basic and most general this means contributing to the struggle by which reproduction is controlled by women totally and completely. In the short term the provision of twenty-four-hour childcare is obviously crucial. In the longer term the actual form of control of such provision, by women, for women, is perhaps a more important qualitative prospect. In this context the current cuts in nursery education, day care, support for childminders and so on only indicate how far off is a structural change in the organisation of reproduction. Such cuts mean less socialised provision for childcare (and that necessarily means certain women will be worse off), but they are also reducing provision that was far from ideal in the first place. This raises all sorts of dilemmas, such as whether one wants more of something one doesn't really approve of in the first place. Or, more precisely, does one mind having less of something one didn't approve of?

It is not enough to campaign for nurseries, if those nurseries are to be run as part of the patriarchal state—inflexible hours, insufficient equipment, means-tests for parents, and sexist organisation and practice.

The role of the state in all this is indeed bewildering, especially if one sees the state as dominated by men and serving the interests of men. On the one hand the state is one of the major providers of institutional childcare in the form of day nurseries, nursery schools and so on. On the other hand this provision is usually sadly lacking in quantity and quality. In the face of this, demand for more nurseries can easily slip to providing playgroups from people's, that is women's, own resources. Reproductive politics can thus change to self-help. This is why the National Childcare Campaign formed in 1980 from local campaign groups is so important. This is also why all the various attempts to change the quality and form of nurseries and day care must be carried forward and expanded—in nursery centres, combining education and care; in comprehensive day care projects, for pre-school children and older children after school and in school holidays; in feminist playgroups, lone-parent playschools and childsharing schemes; in communal and co-operative living arrangements.

However, on top of these basic struggles, it must be added that a number of fundamental issues persist. First, it is difficult for those with children to organise, partly because of simple practicalities and sheer exhaustions, and partly because of the way in which we tend, quite wrongly in my opinion, to see children as slightly separate from and therefore distracting from 'real (political) life'.

Secondly, there is the difficulty of the ideology of 'femininity' in thinking about, discussing, caring for children. Many of those who might appear to be allies within reproductive politics are in fact deeply imbued with a sense of rightness that women's main place is in the home. It seems very hard to combine a thorough concern for children and the adults who look after them with a revolutionary critique. The problems with the ideology of femininity as it relates to birth, children and indeed motherhood itself is how these issues can become central within sexual politics, without falling unwittingly into the traditional language, concepts and practices that pervade them. Men have got to rethink our whole relationship with birth and children, including the words we use about them, while respecting some women's decision to remove themselves from that area of life.

This brings me on to the questions of qualitative and structural change. In many ways the ideology of femininity and the role of men in reproductive politics are both issues that are bound to throw up severe contradictions. Neither is resolved by just more effort or provision or more care or more nurseries or more anything. They are only resolvable with a qualitative change in the organisation and control of reproduction—a radical restructuring of the social order imagined and derived from greater consciousness, no doubt feminist-inspired, around reproduction.

11   Patriarchy and Men's Practice

Patriarchy is not 'out there': it exists in our practice as men. Living *in patriarchy* has numerous implications for men's practice, and most importantly its change. This chapter considers some of these implications for men's practice, in relation to earlier statements on the private and the public, the personal and the political.

TYPES OF MEN'S PRACTICE

Men's practice resides in both the public world and the private world. Men's various dominations of reproduction, of the public world over the private world, arise from and produce particular practices. The dominant male notion of *practice* involves a transposition from the ways of the private world to the public, from the 'private moralities' of hierarchic heterosexuality and fatherhood to 'politics'. The structured relations of reproduction and men's agency within them provide the conditions and possibilities of what men do, can do and cannot do. The implications of this relation are both deeply structural and intensely personal.

Thus in simple terms we can recognise:
(i) Men's collective practice
Here one can ask how does one locate men's collective practice structurally? What sort of social and political phenomenon is it? Is it possible to distinguish superficial and deeper changes in practice?
(ii) The personal practice of individual men
How does one locate oneself? What sort of politics, if any,

should one do? With what political method or style?

'Men' exist as a category within social relations, and men exist individually, in particular personal situations. These two levels are clearly connected, though by no means directly. There is no necessary one-to-one relationship, nor is it possible to argue for a crude determinism of individual practice by social structure. Men's collective practice is structurally determined, overarchingly patriarchal, while the variety of individual practice is related to determined structures in individual ways, experienced individually (see note 3, p. 199)

While men cannot be feminists and cannot not be oppressors, we can do different things. Possible types of men's practice, both collective and individual, include:

(i) *explicit oppression*, whereby men explicitly accept and profit from that oppression, publicly and/or privately;

(ii) *liberal oppression*, whereby men make themselves (superficially at least) more acceptable to women, yet still maintain that oppression;

(iii) *conspicuous liberalism*, whereby men involve themselves in what is seen as women's arenas, work, campaigns, yet maintain a modified oppression by taking leadership;

(iv) *inconspicuous liberalism*, whereby men involve themselves as above, yet attempt to reduce that modified oppression by not taking leadership;

(v) *change against patriarchy*, whereby men try to change themselves, inconspicuously by private activities, and/or conspicuously by public activities.

Just as different strategies and positions within socialist politics—radical, revolutionary, reformist, and so on, can be developed, so men may adopt different positions *vis-à-vis* reproductive politics. The difference is that most men, being members of the oppressor class, will be on the metaphorical Right. Even attempts to move from complacency face contradictions and re-incorporations at every stage. Such processes occur for men ranging from the Director of Social Services, relatively more concerned with reproduction than productive counterparts, to the individual man doing more housework, taking it over and then asserting *his* rights over home, children, women. That said, possibilities for men's practice against patriarchy exist in the private world; the public world; and across the public–private divide, as more self-conscious anti-sexist practice.

PRIVATE PRACTICE

The 'private' and the domestic, the form of arrangements and relationships for living with and relating to others, is in many ways the most difficult area of practice for men to face and change. One important block is that the home and the personal are seen as 'private' in the first place—the private sphere is itself private, beyond influence. The private may include facets of sexuality, procreation, nurture and violence. Each of these is open to change in men's practice—the diminution of hierarchic (hetero)sexuality, the abolition of fatherhood, the reformulation of caring, the abandonment of violence. Opening up these 'private' issues, making them more 'public', is, however, complicated by the implications that may follow for other people, who may or may not seek involvement in 'personal politics'. A politics of personal relationships, with all their complexities, dependencies, loves and hates, seems hardly to exist.[1] Political change applies just as much to the critique of personal relationships as of macro social phenomena. Perhaps above all the private also contains multifarious experiences, talk, conversations, use of language, touch, chores, childcare, housework and so on, that are usually considered 'trivial'. Changing these so they are no longer seen as such is an important possibility for men's practice, and in itself political. Making a mess of them, as when men trivialise women and relationships, so that can be begun, rearranged, and disposed of 'at will', is as serious as public political abuse.

PUBLIC PRACTICE

Men's practice in the public world is both facilitated and constrained by the fact that this is the arena of conventional 'politics'. Despite its historical domination by men, the public realm presents possibilities for political change against patriarchy. Possible arenas of the public realm include paid work; the street; men's 'private' clubs and associations; and reproductive politics (see chapter 10).

Within trade union, political party and similar political organisations, there are characteristically multiple issues of sexism, ranging from men's domination of executive positions to the persistence of alienating structures and methods of working. This applies in both 'normal' committee procedure, so popular in the Labour Party, and in the masculinism of Leninist party organisation: both have much to answer for. Thus not only is men's involvement important in specific campaigns, such as against sexual harassment,[2] but so too are changes in everyday political practice. Direct attempts to change practice include placing men's anti-sexism more centrally within political debate, and the creation of men's groups within political organisations, like Big Flame; and the effective banning of men's candidature for councillors by the local district Labour Party (Johnson, 1986). A basic problem is that routine 'political' activity of meetings, committees and so on, is usually seen by men as of higher value than 'mere' anti-sexist activity. One almost has to 'come down' from the political level to the personal, from the theoretical to the practical. Indeed, the theoretical is itself often considered as the political, so that paradoxically much time and effort can be spent in such political/theoretical discussions/activities without individuals having to make political positions clear to anyone, perhaps including themselves.

There are also pronounced differences between the politics of production and reproduction. In the case of productive politics, both of the revolutionary class and labourist, trade union varieties, relations and activities, including political ones, are usually conceived as means–ends relationships, reproducing the dominant mode of production under capitalism, in which means (exchange values) both facilitate and obscure access to ends (use values). In reproduction, and thence reproductive politics, these relationships no longer apply. The comparable relation in reproduction is between the *experience* of life and the *possibility* of life. This would-be means (the experience) can no longer be seen as a mere instrument for the achievement of would-be ends (the possibility of life). In reproduction, the experience of life is both part of the process of reproduction, and an end in itself. Reproduction is a process in which 'means' are an *end* of the process: practice is paramount.

ANTI-SEXIST PRACTICE

A third major way in which men may attempt to act against patriarchy is through the more conscious creation of anti-sexist activities, groups and networks. As already discussed, such initiatives have arisen largely in relation or response to feminism and feminists, in some cases, in support of or alliance with specific campaigns by women. Men's action of this sort although more apparent in recent years is not new—for example before the First World War, the Men's Federation of Women's Suffrage was established in London, '[t]o secure for Women the Parliamentary Vote as it is, or may be, secured for Men' (Strauss, 1983).[3]

Increasingly and especially since the late sixties the basic unit of men's anti-sexist practice has been the consciousness-raising group. Men join these groups for what often appear contradictory reasons. They may have experienced personal difficulties in their own lives, sometimes with *particular* women or men, during or following separation, divorce or sexual relationships. Such groups may become a way of finding support, getting closer to other men, simply making sense of themselves and their own history. The same men may also possess a considerable *general* commitment to support women's and/or gay liberation. A general theoretical solidarity may clash with personal practice, in men's own lives. This contradiction can be a powerful motivating force for the re-evaluation of men's lives and commitments (Bradley *et al.*, 1971; Hearn, 1980).

Groups are places for the sharing of experience, for reflecting on it and its common and dissimilar elements, and for changing it. 'Topics' that are usually dealt with include being brought up as a boy, teenage experience, relations with mother, with father, gayness, women, men, friendship, fantasy, violence, and so on (Hornacek, 1977; Eardley, Humphries and Morrison, 1983; Côté, Dare and Muzychka, 1984). In Britain by 1975 there were between twenty and thirty groups, and five national conferences had taken place (Harrison, 1975). By the mid-eighties, most medium-sized towns and some small towns, and rural areas have at least one group; towns like Bradford (300,000 population) have usually had two or three at any one time; larger centres like Leeds have generally had four or five. In addition to ongoing CR groups, there are also other groups doing similar work, such as men's co-counselling or gestalt groups, and focused campaigns, and weekend workshops.

These groups have in turn created a new genre of men's magazines, and other writing against sexism.

A series of publications under the general title 'Brothers Against Sexism' came out between 1972 and 1974, spurred on by the energy of a number of national conferences of mens groups which met over that period. Between the summers of 1975 and 1977 an internal newsheet called 'Mens News' has been circulated among London groups and in Manchester at least a similar local newsletter has been produced.   (Achilles Heel Collective, 1978, 3).

1978 saw a regional Men's Conference in London and the setting up of the Men's Centre there. It also saw the beginning of a national *Men Against Sexism* newsletter, subsequently retitled *Anti-Sexist Men's Newsletter* and then *Men's Antisexist Newsletter*, or *M.A.N.*

Another important development in 1978 was the production of the *Achilles Heel* magazine, by a group of London-based men. The first issue begins:

This journal has been produced by a working collective of socialist men who have been involved in men's groups and mens politics for some time. For all of us it is a process of making public a very private and very important experience—that of consciously redefining and changing the nature of our relationships with women and with each other as men. In making this experience public and in beginning to develop an analysis around it, we are in a sense 'coming out' politically as men and realigning ourselves with the women's and gay movements in the struggle against sexual oppression.
... this is a new venture based pretty squarely in our own particular experience of men's politics and quite consciously committed to the development of what we see as an essential connection between socialism and sexual politics.   (Achilles Heel Collective, 1978, 3)

The first three issues of the national newsletter centred around the lead-up to a national conference in Manchester; several subsequent issues contained reflections on it, particularly the production of a series of anti-sexist commitments, such as support for the Women's Liberation Movement, the Gay Liberation Movement, taking responsibility for and involvement in childcare, and breaking down traditional father/mother/child roles. The third published draft of the 'Commitments' appeared in issue no. 9 of the newsletter (1980), and they were subject to further discussion at the national conference at Bristol in 1980. In the event that gathering produced several different versions of 'Commitments', raised critiques of the 'manifesto' approach as both too far-reaching and too limited, and agreed that local groups should go away and discuss them for next year's conference, which in fact did not take place. The Bristol conference did, however, approve *by acclaim* a statement, 'Our common ground . . .' prepared initially by Paul Morrison, and revised by a variety of suggestions (Appendix). Reaching this 'common ground' was probably an end to a particular phase of men's political activity, and probably still represents the most accurate statement of what unites men who are against sexism. There have been no full-scale national men against sexism conferences since, representing a loss of momentum in some ways, but also a decline in the need to prove that men's antisexist activity existed. There have been several regional gatherings in Manchester, London and elsewhere; and generally a diversification of practice, a going on and looking outwards, on the basis of commitment, rather than institutionalisation or manifesto.[4] In some cases networks have developed around the production of more local newsletters, such as *against sexism against patriarchy*, *Against Patriarchy* and *Low Plains Drifter*.

Meanwhile seven issues of the *Achilles Heel* journal were produced during the five-year period to 1983; since then the original collective has gone in different directions, including writing and film-making,[5] and a new collective has been formed. The national *Men's Antisexist Newsletter* (*M.A.N.*) continues, with each of the twenty-four issues produced to January 1987 by different local collectives and so having different formats and viewpoints.

Likewise individual men's groups have developed their own particular concerns, and sometimes public action around specific issues, such as sexuality or bisexuality. Some have seen childcare as the priority, leading to playgroup work (*Out of the Pumpkin Shell*, 1975) or crèche work for feminist or other events (*Please Can I Stop Being a Tree Soon?* 1977). In 1984 a national network of (mainly men's) crèche groups throughout Britain was established.

Another more focused area of struggle has been against men's violence. In some cases this has taken the form of campaigns, such as Men Against Pornography in Leeds, and Sheffield Men Against Sexual Harassment (Anon, 1986). Other groups, such as the Bristol MOVE (Men Overcoming Violence) project (Mason, 1986) and groups against violence in Birmingham and elsewhere, have begun to do direct work counselling men, violent or potentially so, following American ventures like EMERGE and RAVEN (Gondolf,1985; Jones, 1982). The Hamburg-based *Männer Gegen Männer-Gewalt* (Men Against Men's Violence) acts as both a counselling service and a self-help group for violent or potentially violent men ('Schneller Schlag', 1986). In the United States there are a number of men against rape, or men stopping rape groups.[6]

The emphasis on personal change is an important element in many men's groups and related activities, so much so that some groups redefine themselves as primarily therapy groups for men. This often leads to a more concerted use of particular psychotherapies, such as gestalt or Reichian, or to co-counselling. Other types of groups, all of which I have experienced, are based on workplaces, occupational interests (e.g. education), other common interests (e.g. poetry, dance, performance) or consist of men who are themselves involved in or leading other groups.

As already noted (pp. 29–30), there are dangers with men's groups. In particular, they can be used as a resting place from which to continue oppression, 'a reference point for a new style of male supremacy' ('Personal politics', 1982, 13), a way of avoiding confronting power over women by hiding with men. In the United States this tendency has seen explicit expression in the Coalition of Free Men group, seeking 'men's rights', asserting 'male liberation', and reasserting male bonding, with a consequent split from pro-feminist, anti-sexist groups and organisations, such as the National Organisation for Changing Men. In Britain, differences of emphasis have certainly existed between 'more political', more socialist men, as in Achilles Heel, Big Flame, and so on, and men who are more concerned with therapy and personal change. Such tensions are also often present within individual consciousness-raising or other men's groups, and even within individual men. Over the last ten or fifteen years some of these differences have diminished, as 'more political' men realise the importance of personal change, and *vice versa*. Even the term, 'men's liberation', is beginning to be reclaimed by certain men as indicating opposition to both women's and men's oppression, rather than the 'Free Men' stance.

It should not be all that surprising to find tensions between the individual and the collective, in the context of the long established practice of men's 'solidarity' with each other at paid work, at school, in sport and so on. This 'solidarity' is often at the expense of other similar 'teams' of men, *with whom there is competition*, and who in the ultimate military case may be killed. Such oppressions both by and of men remain, and are difficult to dispel from practice. Accordingly, simply labelling practice 'anti-sexist' is not necessarily significant; what is important is the growth of non-oppressive, loving practice by men *between the public and the private worlds*. This is just as possible between neighbours, friends, lovers, relatives, shoppers, workmates, pickets, and men on the street, as it is in more formally organised men's groups. It is just that such groups are more consciously founded. It is more difficult for police and soldiers. I mourn for the loss of my brothers into these public oppressions.

BEYOND THE PRIVATE AND THE PUBLIC

Taken together, men's anti-sexist practice constitutes a variety of attempts to act differently, with women, children and each other. These moves from competitive and privatised patterns towards more open support for women's liberation, gay liberation, and anti-oppression, are typically faltering, as is associated personal change. Privately, the crucial questions include, 'Do men really change? Are men able to stop oppressing women?'; publicly, we are obliged to address such questions as, 'Are men publicly against sexism, changing each other, doing anything to change patriarchy?' In addition, anti-sexist activity can contribute to change in the relationship of the private and public worlds, often by bringing private experiences into a more public forum, in campaigns, group discussion, writing and so on. Shifting the public–private divide itself assists changing definitions of 'politics'. As Metcalf (1978, 8) writes: 'The question is no longer whether the personal is political, but how we can enrich the struggle for socialism with the often *privatised knowledge and experience* of years of struggle against traditional "personal" relations and sacrosanct life patterns' (my emphasis). The public–private divide can also be reconstituted by politicising the private; bringing the public into the private; by bringing the private into the public; personalising the public. The problem is that for men *forever holding on to the private and the public, the personal and the political* is difficult, sometimes arduous. Moreover some men get so enthralled by one side of the divide ('discovering their emotions' or 'discovering politics') they become immersed in that alone, and 'move on' from anti-sexism.

The reasons men leave men's groups and men against sexism activities are as many and varied as the reasons for joining in the first place. They include straightforward return to former lifestyles and priorities; disillusionment with 'other' men; movement to privateness, domesticity, and perhaps childcare; and various moves 'beyond' to personal or group therapy. Involvements in therapy can, in the short term at least, lead some men to convince themselves that they can just *be*, and deserve to be accepted as such. This does not necessitate their being against sexism or much else, nor for much apart from themselves. Some men decide that the best way of men opposing sexism is to keep out of the public area of sexual politics. Occasionally and *paradoxically* this position is argued publicly by men with experience of men against sexism activities.

Another way for men is into other public arenas, such as gay, trade union, party or community politics. These may be entered or re-entered as a way of carrying the opposition to sexism *into effect* in practical situations that potentially affect a large number of other people, for example, in assisting anti-discrimination employment policies. They may alternatively represent a movement from 'personal politics' into 'real politics', to the supposed priority of class, race, party. For some, such moves may carry both proactive and reactive motives, in a profoundly contradictory way. For others, the priority of 'non-sexual' politics may be unfortunate but necessary in the short term, for example, to fend off fascist initiatives. A final possible way out is into a form of politics seen as more *universal* than men's anti-sexist politics, for example, peace politics, anti-nuclear politics, anti-militarism, world development, anti-hunger and third world campaigns. The dire and urgent problems faced by these politics are some of the most horrific and visible products of the world patriarchal 'order'.

These possibilities indicate the need to extend men's anti-sexist practice and politics—to distrust privatism, to be aware of the limitations of a simple libertarianism, to be critical of the often patriarchal traditions of labourist socialism, and to link with public and private oppositions to oppression. To do this involves hard and loving work on ourselves, critical vigilance in our practice, leadership without hierarchy and with love, and a commitment against oppression. We haven't got to just 'enrich the struggle for socialism with ... privatised knowledge and experience', but prefigure a socialism that starts from being against patriarchy.

12 Changing Men's Sexist Practice in the Social Sciences

'MEN'S STUDIES UNMODIFIED'

Writing this book has been a form of practice, at odds with, yet part of, that broad body of activity called the 'social sciences'. Indeed one obvious area of men's practice that invites attention and change is that within the social sciences. This collection of disciplines has historically developed in close association with the professions of the church, medicine, law and indeed science itself. They have traditionally comprised another bastion of the 'progressive' male establishment, producing malestream depictions of 'society', governing reproduction, dominating education, and 'standing above' and avoiding various reproductive labours. In other words academia and academic discourse have long been part of malestream patriarchal public discourse (see O'Brien, 1981). Indeed, according to Mary Daly (1978, 112).

patriarchal scholarship is an extension and continuation of sado-ritual ... manifested—often unwittingly and witlessly—by its language. This language betrays, or rather, loyally and faithfully displays, the fact that the 'authorities' are apologists for atrocities.

In the social sciences, 'men' have generally remained untheorised. The ignoring and ignorance of men has perhaps been most profound in the *abstract universals* of philosophy, the *documentary public worlds* of political science, and the *market forces* of economics.[1] This careless neglect has been less pronounced in psychology, social psychology and anthropology. Psychological studies have traditionally

177

attended to the individual, the interpersonal, the intrapersonal, even if this often means 'private behaviour in public'. This focus has given massive legitimacy to the study of 'masculinity' and 'femininity', even if these are often cast within another set of universals.

Anthropology has despite and perhaps because of its Victorian imperialist heritage been more explicitly concerned with the social construction of men and masculinity,[2] usually in other societies, often of black people. The relativist and comparative strength of anthropology is sometimes applied to white dominated Western societies, and their women and men. For example, the willingness to seriously engage the cultural meanings has clear application to interpreting the 'myth of masculinity', amplified in superman, cowboy and other 'heroes', yet visible in mundane form daily. In comparison sociological inquiry has typically been constrained by a particular direction of emphasis upon 'industrial society', with 'economic class', 'division of labour', 'status' and so on the 'normal' building blocks of analysis. Assumptions about the nature of men and masculinity have usually remained implicit (Morgan, 1981; Pearson, 1984). History and literature provide endless stories about men and masculinity, and huge creative opportunities in teaching and learning if only these subject matters become more focused (August, 1982; Bowen, 1985). However, above all there is a huge wariness in using the concept 'patriarchy' within the social sciences.

These 'men's studies' have been shown to be man-made, badly in need of 'modification' (Spender, 1981). Faced with the multiple implications of feminism for men in the social sciences, a small group of men met at the 1982 British Sociological Association Annual Conference on 'Gender and Society'. This led to a joint letter to *Network*, summarising some of these issues as seen then:

(1) *The political impact of feminism on men*: the implications of linking the personal and the political; the nature of that relationship; the question of whether the political is totally personal; the importance of 'political' stance against sexism.
(2) *Problems in doing sociology*: the advantages and limitations of experiential approaches; the link between self-knowledge and sociological knowledge; the problems of obtaining knowledge, other than that that relates

to one's own experience; further difficulties raised by the notions of false consciousness and ideology.

(3) *Teaching and assessing sociology*: the adequacy of traditional, experiential and other methods of teaching; the validity of traditional or other criteria in assessment; the relationship between teachers and taught.

(4) *The structure of academic sociology*: the, often hierarchical, conventions of academic conferences and modes of writing and speaking, and the structure of the organisations of sociology.

(5) *Work relationships*: relationships between sociologists at work; trust, isolation and support.

(6) *Substantive issues*: for example, masculinity and the male sex-role.

(Hearn *et al.*, 1983)

MEN'S (ANTI-SEXIST) STUDIES—SOME PROBLEMS

Several possible avenues present themselves for men social scientists in the light of these issues, from pretending to be 'male feminists', becoming 'expert' on women's studies, promoting 'gender studies' as some 'overarching' discipline for both women and men to 'fit into', to developing the study of men and masculinity. There are many other rationales that can prompt an interest in the study of gender by men, from fascist experimentalism to liberal voyeurism. There are, for example, many good liberal reasons for men to take a(n) (un)healthy interest in the affairs of women, just as there are similar motivations for white people to 'know' the minds of black people.

Of particular interest are the increasing signs of the development of the specific study of men and masculinity in further and higher education. In the United States there are about a hundred men's studies courses in universities and similar institutions (Bliss, 1986; also see Weisberg, 1984). There are special issues on men in academic journals, and bibliographic sourcebooks on men and masculinity. In Britain there is a gradual development of occasional day courses, study groups, and taught units within formal educational programmes.[3] Thus the situation is not the hypothetical one of should men's studies exist, for they do; but how they should exist.

Having said that, it is necessary to view such developments with caution. For example, the specific study of men may well attract (men) researchers with no particular commitment to critique, or worse with some form of anti-feminism. On the other hand, the growth of this area of study is to be welcomed as the specific critique of men is seen as a priority for men in opposing sexism in the social sciences. My own concern is that men opposed to sexism and interested in studying 'gender' should focus primarily on the critique of men and masculinity, not the study of women; and similarly men studying men and masculinity should do so with an anti-sexist commitment, that is both critical and loving.

The reasons for this are several, and hinge on the acceptance of other men as our brothers, from whom we are separated, in the public domain, in the private domain and by the public–private divide. The most drastic action that men can take politically, personally, or academically is not to try and solve the problems of women for women, but to recognise our love and responsibility for each other, to change our relationship with each other. Thus by changing social science, itself a part of the public domain, in such ways, men can contribute to changing the form and nature of the public–private divide. Thus I would criticise the work of, for example, Bouchier (1983) and Charvet (1982), as concentrating almost wholly on women, women's material and the critique of feminism in the first case, and in reducing feminism to an ideology paralleling liberalism or conservatism in the second— in effect externalising and entrenching the problem. In contrast, Griffin (1982, 280), writes 'when a theory is transformed into an ideology, it begins to destroy self and self-knowledge. Originally born of feeling ... it organises experience, according to itself, without touching experience.'

In making these suggestions I am certainly not advocating any form of male academic separatism. Indeed I see collaboration with women as an important possibility in certain sorts of social research, for example, where women interview women who have suffered violence from men, and men interview the violent men concerned. Similarly in recent years I have co-researched with a woman researcher on the same topic—the dynamics of sexuality within organisations (Hearn and Parkin, 1987). This collaborative approach has enabled us to interpret the same phenomena from two gender perspectives, within the context of a firm awareness of patriarchy. For me it has particularly meant focusing on the understanding of men in those organisational settings. Thus at times strict divisions between women's studies, 'gender studies', and men's studies may be difficult to draw—studying, say, men's control of women will benefit from studying both women and men. What I wish to make clear, however, is the need for men social scientists to clarify what we are doing in relation to feminism, women's studies and the study of gender, and why. Indeed the emerging emphasis of men's studies is historically and politically specific; it only arises as a priority with the establishment of women's studies as an identifiable area. In my experience, the rationale for (my/men's) involvement in studying gender comes most convincingly and unequivocally from a focus on the understanding and changing of men and masculinity. The more a commitment is made against sexism the clearer this focus becomes.

PRINCIPLES AND APPLICATIONS—SOME POSSIBILITIES

The recognition of the case for men's focus on men and masculinity is, however, only a beginning. Because of the contradictions and ambivalences outlined, care and attention is needed on the form and quality of this development. As a result of working on these issues, especially with friends and colleagues in the Men and Masculinity Study Group at Bradford, the following broad ground rules are suggested in the study of men and masculinity.

1. Men must not seek to appropriate feminism or feminist theory. We must respect the autonomy of feminism/women's studies, while not seeking to establish as a matter of principle a converse autonomy of what might be conveniently called 'men's studies'.
2. Men's studies must be open to all, women and men. While men are likely to constitute the majority of participants in men's studies, women are to be welcomed too. The forms, procedures, findings and theories of men's studies must be open to women's scrutiny, criticism and guidance. Men

need to listen to, learn from, but not sit back and depend upon women.

3. The major task of men's studies is the development of a critique of men's practice partly in the light of feminism, not the development of a critique of feminism. This means that while men's studies are inconceivable without feminism and while they are bound to utilise, and must recognise feminist work, the basic concern is not to engage feminism on its own terms but to see what implications feminism has both for men's position in the world and the practice of the existing malestream disciplines. The critical target is men, and men's discourse, not women or feminism. For these reasons, the very term 'men's studies' may itself be open to objection as expressing an unwarranted symmetry between men's and women's studies. It may be preferable to use an alternative term, such as 'the critique of men', that makes this distinction explicit.[4]

4. Men's studies, or whatever preferred term is used, must span traditional disciplinary divides; it cannot avoid being interdisciplinary. Psychology, economics, political science and the rest are all relevant to an understanding of men and masculinity. Similarly it is unlikely that a single methodology will be able to encapsulate all that has to be said.

5. Men doing research, learning, teaching, study, theorising and academic discourse about men and masculinity need to subject our own practice to scrutiny. The relationship of researcher to researched, learner to learned, teacher to taught are problematic and need repractising (not just rethinking) in ways that do not reproduce the patriarchy of disinterested positivism. They need to be subject to consciousness-raising, *even become forms of consciousness-raising*. This is not meant as a root to the unfolding of Spirit, but in recognition that gendered subjectivity is part of material relations. Collective self-reflective theorising of how gendered subjectivities exist within those material relations, of the male-dominated public domains, called academia, appears a necessary part of reproducing an anti-patriarchal 'social science'.

These broad principles seems to apply whether one is involved in formal social science courses, short courses on men and masculinity, theorising of and on men, related research projects, or simply informal academic discussions. We need to improve the quality of our activity.

FACING OPPRESSION: EXPERIENCING, LOVING AND CHANGING—SOME PROMISES

To face oppression, primarily *by* us as men but also *of* us, we need drastic action. Men must address our power and the sources of oppression by men, alongside our own oppression and alienation. This requires committed attention to the structures of power, the enormities that are so obvious and so taken for granted in the social sciences. How can there be so many books, articles, treatises written on government, parliament, industry, the money markets, the state, the police, the professions, and so on, that *do not even mention* the power of men?

Against this we have various resources: our materiality, our practice, our experience, our critique. In developing critical men's theory, we can ask how this makes sense in terms of our own and others' experiences; how it helps to relate theory and practice; how our construction of theory becomes part of our own practice, and thus subject to consciousness raising. These are useful tests of 'academic practice'. In this sense experience should not be so embarrassing to the social scientist, that is, if it is available as a resource for critical reflection and enquiry. It is unfortunate that experience has become devalued in the social sciences to mean uncritical story-telling, the recitation of prejudice, and so on.

It is surely time to legitimate practice and experience as serious matters for theory. In feminism, theory, practice and experience are your own resource, what you have and can critically explore, an interrelating praxis. Men's experience is rarely honestly shared; *it is usually a missing element*; it is time for men to elaborate critical story-telling, help each other overcome the recitation of prejudice, develop *more accurate* men's theory. Such critique of experience may begin to indicate how things are for men, how complex, contradictory, and multi-layered. For example, men's relations with each other may be part competition, part fear, part solidarity, part longing. Attention to men's experience, as it is, is likely to take time, effort, commitment, pain, repetition, and a tolerance of detail—a continual re-turn to gendered subjectivity existing in relation to the enormities of material powers. Conducting men's studies on this basis in the public domain necessitates activity across the public–private divide, as with other anti-sexist practice (see chapter 11).

Perhaps most surprisingly, and yet most importantly, my experience tells me that a commitment to the critique of men and masculinity will probably develop in association with love—not a romantic or privatised love, but an openness for all humans and all life. To speak of love in academic discourse is near heresy. Indeed unconditional positive regard to the perpetrators of violence, whether institutionalised or individualised, is very difficult and liable to create major contradictions in research and personal terms. However, just as within psychoanalysis, practice without love is technique, so too social science without love is methodology. Love is the unspoken necessity for men changing our practice in the social sciences; researching our brothers and ourselves, and co-researching and co-learning as brothers are opportunities for changing and meeting others and ourselves. This necessitates changing relationships in working, that are more than working relationships—moving towards egalitarian rather than hierarchical research, teaching and social science.

Finally, and optimistically, we can, in doing social science as elsewhere, be allies to women in opposing sexism and oppression. Despite and probably because of our biological fix, we men can socially change sides; however disconcerting this may sound and be to both men and women, it is possible for us to do this.

Afterword

So why, after all, should men change and oppose patriarchy? There may or may not be something called altruism; there certainly are principles of justice and equality invoked by men of many political persuasions; there is also the sheer anger at men's brutality and violence, to women, children, each other. In addition, from both my own experience and from discussion and analysis with others, there are also *material* reasons for men to change against patriarchy:

1. the increased possibilities of love, emotional support and care for and from others, particularly other men;
2. the privilege and emotional development that may come from increased contact and work with children;
3. the possibility of improved health, the reduction of certain illnesses, and the extension of life;
4. the creation of the conditions for the transformation of the capitalist mode of production (that being inherently gendered) to more liberating productive relations;
5. the avoidance of other men's violence and of the fear of men, of killing, of being killed; and most importantly,
6. the reduction of the likelihood of nuclear annihilation, the grimmest legacy of patriarchy.

This process of understanding and changing men needs to be well informed by both marxism and feminism. However, for different reasons—the patriarchalism of marxism, and the speaking-of-and-to-women of feminism—neither usually addresses directly what men are or should do. For this task, men need to learn from both, yet be more willing still to confront our own power, as our own problem. We need to

185

construct our own action upon ourselves. Similarly with men's anti-sexist politics, in Britain at least, the two main political influences, other than feminist and gay politics, have been socialism and libertarianism. Again we need more than just one of these. Both the structural rigour of marxism, socialism, radical feminism and radical gay politics, and the personal tolerance of liberal feminism and libertarianism, are necessary in being against and actively dismantling patriarchy.

Moving from simply being *against* something, sexism, patriarchy, the sordid lot, to being for something else is not so easy. As is sometimes sung, 'What are we fighting for?' There are few clear signs for men of where this leads, though several contenders have been offered. To be sure, it is not possible to reduce men's contribution to the changing of patriarchy to a utopian strategy. It is tempting to just hold up hands and await a continual, everyday struggle of contradictions. Significantly, there is no single word for this seriously structural, intensely personal project for men—'masculinism' is an obvious parallel to feminism, but has been appropriated by the Right; 'effeminism' is appealing yet stereotyped, perhaps undialectical; some fall back on 'socialism' or 'communism' and their idealist mystiques.

I prefer several words—the positive, rigorous, and loving critique of ourselves. This involves identifying who and what we value—women, children, other men, ourselves, even valuing anti-sexism as a positive activity not just an excuse for negativity. It also involves locating all those positive valuations in their strict material contexts, and struggling critically and lovingly both with our experiences of them and with the material relations themselves.

Finally, that which we value, including ourselves, is not just set in material locations but, as has been stressed throughout, is material, that is material relations themselves. And this is a further reason for men's difficulty in facing our materiality. Our existence as material relations confounds us. Following this daunting line of praxis, Keith Motherson (1984, 9) expresses the hope that:

more and more . . . 'men' will come to see through the separatist spells cast in the Men's Huts[1] and cease to hallucinate ourselves as Men . . . for Real Men aren't. As we re-identify as SONS, the flesh-of-earthling-flesh loyal mummy's boys that we once were, then we will no longer imagine that we 'need' to hold onto our privileges—as—Men. Nor will we hold out against the Mothersphere for fear of losing our 'male identities' or our individual autonomy 'as men'.

As we remember the maternal roots of our identity, may we also be re-member-ed as accountable and co-responsible members of the long-suppressed matri-tribe which is now resurfacing.

Our collective self-reflection as sons within a possible matriarchy overwhelms the illusion of fatherhood. The self-recognition of sonhood is but one element in the dismantling of patriarchy: others, especially important in modern society at least, persist counter and beyond the patriarchal institutions of hierarchic heterosexuality, the professions, and the state. To see ourselves as 'mere' sons is threatening indeed to 'adult' men. To imagine and re-create the material relations of equivalent 'threat' in the realms of sexuality, nurture, and violence may be more difficult for men, yet no less urgent.

To respond to all this demands positive and creative action from men; being 'nice' is no longer enough. Indeed in writing a critique of a naive 'gentleness' as a prescribed style for men ('anti-sexist' or not), Sally Roesch Wagner (1985, 46) argues that

Instead of renouncing male behavior, . . . [the] 'gender warrior' turns around, faces the enemy within you, and transforms it: claiming the strength, the assertiveness, the personal power of maleness (all good virtues, I believe, and ones men shouldn't give up, we women are working like crazy to get them) and using it to destroy the system that makes it corrupt. Going to war against gender, like going to war against war. Holly Near's line, 'The greatest warriors are the ones that fight for peace'. Take the passion of the crusades, the fierceness with which men have done injustice, and turn that power against injustice. My god, we don't need an army of wimps to fight against this war against women: if you want to fight on our side, and join us, then we need you to come with all the spark, all the passion, all the fire you can muster. And I'm not talking violence. Non-violence is not wimpy, it is as strong as tempered steel, it is gentle soldiers. . . .

This is surely a time for men to change against patriarchy.

Notes

FOREWORD

1. As Tony Eardley (1985, 87–8) explains the use of 'we' or 'they' when writing of men and masculinity is an important issue. He writes:

   > To talk as 'we' can suggest a false confessional, a communality of feeling with other men that I don't often share, since I have learnt in quite a self-conscious way to distance myself from and question male assumptions. To retreat into 'they' supposes a spurious separation, a making of exceptions, which men are inclined to use when dealing with uncomfortable political ideas. It also denies the shared experience and understanding which should and does link me with other men.

   For these reasons I shall generally refer to 'we' and 'ourselves', except where the text is reproduced from published sources and where I am referring to particular types of men which do not include me, for example, the military.

2. This point is developed in chapter 10.
3. Parts of this story are included in *Birth and Afterbirth: A Materialist Account* (Hearn, 1983).
4. These issues are discussed further in chapter 3.
5. To avoid any misunderstanding, it has to be clearly said that this is in no way a criticism; it is a statement of fact; indeed feminism has quite rightly in the struggle for liberation put women and women's experiences first. The criticisms noted are more against the limiting nature of certain marxist frameworks within marxist feminism.
6. This term is used by O'Brien (1981) to describe the patriarchal domination of ideas, usually neutered as 'mainstream'.
7. Oakley's (1972) *Sex, Gender and Society* remains an excellent introductory text on this question.
8. Brittan and Maynard (1984, 1–4) offer a succinct discussion of the term, drawing on Frye's (1983) emphasis on the element 'press' within oppression.
9. I am indebted to Alan Carling for discussions on this line of enquiry,

particularly around his paper 'Exploitation, extortion and oppression' (1987).

10. The ordering of this book like all others is a political matter. It does not really reach a 'great, single climax', as in the characteristic male narrative (Dyer, 1985). An extended critique of the male narrative is developed in the text, *'Sex' at 'Work'* (Hearn and Parkin, 1987).

CHAPTER 1. THE PERSONAL IS POLITICAL IS THEORETICAL

1. This extension of 'the personal is political' may appear cumbersome, yet a more complete statement would read: 'the personal is material is political is theoretical'. Each of these realms is part of the others and yet each may encapsulate the others.

2. The wearing of jewellery, make-up, etc., are of course no necessary sign of a relinquishing of male power. This is apparent from even the most cursory exercise in cross-cultural or historical analysis of male images. Similarly, writing on the association of masculinity and sport, Jennifer Hargreaves (1986, 114–15) notes '[s]traight men as well as homosexual men, some of whom are sportsmen and some of whom are not, wear flamboyant clothes, braces woven with flowers, ... fragrances and elaborate hair-styles—cropped, punk, long, tousled, sleek, dyed and gelled.'

3. As Frank Mort (1985, 43–4) writes:

   The whole area of style, fashion and youth subcultures has fractured dominant representations of masculinity.... street styles and fashion have opened up a space for men to look at other men as objects of desire and to experience pleasure (around the body, clothes and self-presentation) hitherto seen as exclusively feminine.

4. In the United States there are magazines such as *Gentlemen's Quarterly*; in Britain both the women's magazines, *Cosmopolitan* and *Options*, have developed supplements for the 'new man'. The emphasis is very much on consuming new products, adornments, and preparations rather than political change.

5. It is probably more accurate to refer to dominant *masculinities*, even if there sometimes appears to be an ideological hierarchy between them.

6. It would be more accurate to describe these social movements as often raising contradictions with gender relations and male power.

7. The juxtaposition of radical questioning and managerialism in the context of social services is explored in Hearn (1982c), and Hearn and Jones (1981).

8. Stanley and Wise (1979; 1983) have produced ample evidence of the impact of academic study on personal life; some comments on my similar experiences and those of my co-writer, Wendy Parkin, are described in Hearn and Parkin (1984; 1987).

9. An invaluable feminist critique of this literature has been produced by Eichler (1980).
10. This issue is explored more fully in chapter 4, by way of the argument that materialism must surely address the fact that we live at all not just how we survive.
11. This is one of the central themes of Mary O'Brien's (1981) *The Politics of Reproduction*, such that what constitutes practice and politics is historically (and reproductively) specific (e.g. pp. 189–91).
12. This is despite the fact that '[i]n Old English the word *man* meant person or "human being", and when used of an individual was equally applicable to either sex. It was parallel to the Latin *homo*, "a member of the human species", not *vir*, "an adult male of the species" ' (Miller and Swift, 1981, 9).
13. The central place of work, and of production, in Marx's theorising is discussed by Isaac Balbus (1982, ch. 1).
14. This perspective is clearly much informed by O'Brien's theorising of malestream discourse. This raises the more than interesting question of how men's auto-critique might contradictorily relate to the malestream: how it can be public without being patriarchal. One way might be for it to always have one foot contradictorily in the private. (See chapters 11 and 12).

CHAPTER 2.   CAUSES, EXPLANATIONS AND CRITIQUES

1. The connections between war, public violence and masculinity are complicated in North America and many other places of 'colonial' expansion by the continuing importance of the 'Frontiersman' (Gerzon, 1982).
2. The United Kingdom, a doubly inappropriate national title, has abolished conscription, yet is the last European country to abolish corporal punishment in schools, in state schools at least from August 1987.
3. A short and absorbing analysis of the relationship of masculinity and war, genocide, rape, and specifically the arms race is Penny Strange's (1983) *It'll Make A Man Of You*.
4. As economic crises are probably endemic to capitalism, many men are presumably likely to experience such threats to 'sex-role' over a lifetime.
5. There is increasing evidence that men's unemployment has disproportionately negative effects on wives, girlfriends and other women (Hunt, 1980; McKee and Bell, 1985, 1986; Morris, 1985; Beuret and Makings, 1986), and may indeed solidify rather than challenge gender roles.
6. Some men appear to experience degrees of confusion in the association of technology, masculinity and sexuality. For example, Cynthia Cockburn (1983, 139) reports how men operating automated printing

machinery may feel 'reduced' to women operating keyboards, yet write off men clerical workers as 'a bunch of poufters'; Game and Pringle (1983, 86) note how men computer programmers look down on men computer operators as 'sex-starved animals'.

7. I am grateful to Jan Pahl for raising this point (see note 5 above).

8. Jennifer Mason's (1986) research into 50- to 70-year-old married couples suggests that renegotiation of roles takes place within well-defined, male-dominated limits, typically reproducing pre-retirement patterns in slightly altered form.

9. Some of the 'male hazards' literature has to be treated with some caution. Men's own oppression, for example, in terms of paid work, unhealth and so on, has to be understood in relation to men's oppression of women, not as an excuse for further male privilege.

10. Various feminist texts (for example, Elshtain, 1981) give accounts of different strands of feminism. Most typologies include most of the following: radical feminism, marxist feminism, socialist feminism, liberal feminism, psychoanalytic feminism. Often such accounts note that these are classifications for analysis, and that specific practices transcend such categories.

11. Effeminism is concerned with opposing the oppression of women and effeminate men 'by any means except those inherently male supremacist or those in conflict with the goals of feminists intent on seizing power'. (Dansky, Knoebel and Pitchford, 1973).

12. An extensive critique of this genre, and especially the work of Joseph Pleck, is provided in Carrigan, Connell and Lee (1985, 570–2).

13. Other texts in this tradition include Hocquenghem (1978), and Deleuze and Guattari (1977).

14. This collection comprises nine chapters by different authors, most of whom were associated with *Achilles Heel*, the socialist anti-sexist men's magazine, published in London from 1978.

15. Arguably some of these criticisms have been taken up in some recent action and writing by men (see Reynaud, Connell, Metcalf and Humphries).

CHAPTER 3. THE DIFFICULT CONCEPT OF PATRIARCHY

1. It is interesting to speculate on Marx and Engels' differential use of 'naturally' and *natural* predisposition. As an example of the latter they give 'physical strength', so that one is reminded of Plato's (1955) treatment of 'The status of women' in *The Republic*. 'Natural predispositions' therefore presumably refer to fundamental biological sex differences, whereas the 'natural' character of developments are derived therefrom. Thus social 'naturalness' in development is presumably the means through which the more fundamental 'natural' differences became visible (see Lange, 1979).

2. Marx and Engels appear to posit the historical and logical primary of sex (or gender?) class over economic class (see O'Brien, 1981, 168–9).
3. Engels' work has been subject to major critiques particularly on the grounds of its teleology, in addition to straightforward disputes over the accuracy of his and Morgan's empirical material (for example, Aaby, 1977; Delmar, 1976; Sacks, 1975; Leonard, 1984). Diana Leonard Barker (1977, iii) goes as far as arguing that 'recourse to explanations in terms of ... events in the prehistorical past ... are endemic to explanations of sexual divisions in society in this country'. Despite this there has been both a revival of interest in Engels' work especially through the work of Claude Meillassoux (1981) and other anthropologists, and a resort to comparable hypothesising of a prehistorical matriarchy in O'Brien's (1981) feminist theorising. Whether set within the tradition of marxist anthropology or feminist theory, the presumption of a prehistorical matriarchy suffers from the same difficulties as any 'Golden Age'-ism (Brown and Adams, 1979). Engels himself was 'honest' enough to argue tautologically that: 'With the patriarchal family, we enter the field of written history ...' (1972, 122). Marx (1975) was appropriately critical of the ideological nature of the search for first causes. In the 'Economic and philosophical manuscripts' he writes:

> We must avoid repeating the mistake of the political economist, who bases his explanations on some imaginary primordial condition.
> Such a primordial condition explains nothing. It simply pushes the question into the grey and nebulous distance. It assumes as facts and events what it is supposed to deduce.   (323)

and then a little later, more precisely:

> Who begot the first man, and nature in general? I can only answer: Your question is itself a product of abstraction ...
> My answer is, Give up your abstraction and you will give up your question. (357)

Here, Marx is following Hegel, when the latter writes:

> A so-called fundamental proposition or first principle of philosophy, even if it is true, is yet nonetheless false just because and insofar as it is a fundamental proposition, merely a first principle.
> (Hegel, 1931, 85)

A modern feminist restatement of this view from Christine Delphy (1984, 17), writing against the historicist conception of patriarchy:

> Many people think when they have found the birth of an institution in the past, they hold the key to its present existence. But they have in fact explained neither its present existence, nor even its birth (its past appearance), for they must explain its existence at each and every moment in the context prevailing at that time, and its persistence today (if it really is persistence) must be explained by the present context.

4. The tension of 'particularism' and 'generalism' in the analysis of patriarchy has been commented on by Middleton, who writes: 'The concept is useful because it reflects the almost universal tendency for some men to exercise social power over women, and to enjoy the privileges which accrue therefrom' (1981, 130). He continues following a brief consideration of the range of usage of the concept of patriarchy to argue, however, that all *particular* usages are premature as they are insufficiently based on comparative historical research, and as such tend to close off discussion.
   It should be added that the generalised, biological issue, the problematic equivalence of men as a sex and as a gender, is in some respects less of a problem than is often supposed. There is the hypothetical and actual possibility of men living effectively as women; there are also the complications of transsexualism, and of indeterminate sexing. However, in most cases the question is simply which people are socially defined as men, which as women, and the respective powers that follow. On the other hand, a materialist analysis of real differences between bodies could be a fruitful perspective on patriarchy, that remains to be developed.

5. Refining the concept of patriarchy is inevitably a different kind of project when undertaken by men and by women. For men to *refute* patriarchy is dishonest. It is not possible to separate statements about patriarchy from everything else, including who says them, their social context, others' actions, and so on. Statements about patriarchy, like other social statements, are not epistemologically or ontologically privileged (Keat and Urry, 1982, 19–20). If a particular man is, for example, a rapist, or a women beater, certain statements he might make might be received with doubt. Rather than trying to dismiss patriarchy men can usefully bring issues of men's power to the attention of other men.

6. This usage parallels the following passage in Marx's discussion of 'The buying and selling of labour-power': 'Labour-power ... becomes a reality only by its exercise; it sets itself ... only by working. But thereby a definite quantity of human muscle, nerve, brain, etc., is wasted, and these require to be restored' (1977a, 167). The reference to 'a definite quantity' and more arguably its 'waste' is indicative of the quantitive approach to reproduction within Marx's thought, with the associated neglect of quality.

7. Arguably other distinctions could be made in rereading this chapter, most obviously the actual process of incessantly converting 'material wealth into capital, into means of creating more wealth and means of enjoyment for the capitalist' (Marx, 1977a, 535).

8. The interrelation of these various types of reproduction may indeed by one of the central issues in developing a dialectical materialist analysis thereof. While Marx is supreme in noting the interrelation of different aspects of production, exchange and distribution, he is less explicit in dealing with reproduction. Above all he is unclear about the interplay of quality and quantity in reproduction, while it is absolutely central in his

productive scheme and especially the analysis of commodities. One of his most promising statements on reproduction in this respect is found within his discussion of 'the buying and selling of labour-power' and from which can be imputed a number of these relationships, most likely interpretations (i), (iii) and (vi) above. He writes:

> The owner of labour-power is mortal. If then his appearance in the market is to be continuous and the continuous conversion of money into capital assumes this, the seller of labour-power must perpetuate himself 'in the way that every living individual perpetuates himself [*sic*] by procreation'. The labour-power withdrawn from the market by wear and tear and death, must be continually replaced by, at the very least, an equal amount of fresh labour-power. Hence the sum of the means of subsistence necessary for the production of labour-power must include the means necessary for the labourer's substitutes, i.e. his [*sic*] children, in order that the race of peculiar commodity-owners may perpetuate its appearance in the market. (Marx, 1977a, 168)

The lack of an adequate account of quality and an adequate account of the interplay of quality and quantity remain major shortcomings of marxist analyses of reproduction and patriarchy (see note 6 above).

9. The statement neatly sums up the ambiguity of the idea of 'values', ignored completely within bourgeois and patriarchal theorising, and largely ignored within marxist theorising. Value(s) as a normative precept and an economic concept, derives from the same structural sources. The point is made, albeit negatively, in O'Brien's discussion of de Beauvoir's analysis of reproduction:

> The implication of de Beauvoir's model of human development is not only that parturition is non-creative labour, but that the product, the human child, *has no value*, that the value of children must want to be awarded by the makers of value, men.... The low value of reproductive labour is not necessarily immanent in that form of human labour, but may well be assigned to it by those who are excluded from it. Men assign low social value to 'mere' biological reproduction, yet value children. (1981, 75, emphasis in original)

The relation of normative values and economic value is somewhat neglected in Marx's own writing, except of course indirectly in analysing ideology. A more explicit, yet by no means complete, treatment is to be found in *Capital*. *Volume 1*, and particularly around the construction of 'value' in commodities. The issue hinges on *that which is equivalent* between commodities—this 'something' is both an apparent value and a consequence of values, such that 'we must ... have recourse to their guardians, who are the possessors of commodities' (Marx, 1977a, 88). This equivalence problem has been discussed by Elson (1979, 151ff.).

A further parallel to the value(s) 'ambiguity' is between the recognition of private, personal needs and the operation of private enterprise (see O'Brien, 1981, 178).

10. Useful comparison can be made here with the work of the French anthropologist, Meillassoux (1981). He has argued that the control of reproduction can be more important than the control of production. In certain societies at least human reproduction can be a *pre-condition* of production rather than merely a necessary adjunct. He works to some extent from reproduction to production. Against this, he assigns a passive role to women and fails to work within any notion of patriarchy (Mackintosh, 1977).

11. Delphy's pamphlet *The Main Enemy* was first published under the authorship of Christine Dupont, the same adopted surname as all the other contributors, and entitled *Libération des femmes: année zéro*. This was an attempt to avoid the star system and thereby presumably to acknowledge the sisterhood of feminist scholarship and ideas.

12. Despite their interrelation, the conflation of biological and sexual reproduction is heterosexist. It should be emphasised that the term sexual reproduction is used here to refer to the reproduction of sexual practices, and thus in quite a different sense to biological reproduction by sexual means.

CHAPTER 4. A MATERIALIST ANALYSIS OF REPRODUCTION

1. This chapter is an edited extract from the chapter 'Theorizing on reproduction' in *Birth and Afterbirth* (Hearn, 1983, 39–50). The footnotes have been added.

2. The reader is reminded of the narrower definition of reproduction used here as compared with the preceding and succeeding chapters.

3. I am less sure now of the usefulness of this statement. Rape might be simply violence rather than sexual encounter; artificial insemination may be (part of) a sexual encounter, even when it is self insemination performed alone.

4. The word 'penetration' does seem in retrospect offensive; 'enclosure' might be just as appropriate; on the other hand, 'penetration' might be a more accurate definition of male heterosexual practice and ideology.

CHAPTER 5. REPRODUCTION, MEN AND THE INSTITUTIONS OF PATRIARCHY

1. This would seem a fertile perspective for further detailed historical research, not only on the valuation or lack of valuation of human lives under capitalist transformations, but also on such horrors as the First World War.

2. These and many other linguistic traps and legacies of patriarchal marxism are listed by Keith Motherson (1979, n.d.(a)).

3. Motherson (1979, n.d.(b)) has highlighted the shortcomings of most of the industry dealing in the study of Marx, as: an uncritical acceptance of Marx's own word; a blindness to socialist alternatives; a lack of historical pattern, particularly in the relation of different political movements; the split between ideas and practice; the lack of views from other sectors and constituencies, especially non-'straight, white male' perspectives; and academicism.

4. This is something of a simplification: production and reproduction are dialectically related; the separation of their inseparability (Jaggar and McBride, 1985) may be a characteristic of patriarchy (Sørensen, 1984, 94).

5. Unless otherwise stated, pagination in this section refers to O'Brien (1981).

6. Whereas the marxist concept of alienation appears to be derived from labour and production in particular, O'Brien's feminist concept of alienation is distinct, with *labour becoming the mediation of alienation*. Alienation in effect precedes labour, alienation is in existences, in bodies, in parapraxes. We are made in reproductive parapraxis rather than labour.

    An area of ambiguity in her work is the relation of alienation and maleness. For women, alienation from the child is mediated through *reproductive labour*; for men, alienation from the seed is not mediated. In her detailing of 'moments' in the reproductive process, alienation is a male moment.

7. This is not meant literally, although O'Brien argues for the historical connection. It is meant in that the fatherhood in marriage is the simplest social and legal form that arises in the private realm and is recognised in the public: 'fatherhood [is] ... the paradigm case of the possibility of getting something for nothing' (60).

8. O'Brien warns at several points against too close an analogy between production and reproduction in her analysis.

9. At a more detailed level of analysis it would be useful to distinguish narcissism, masturbation, celibacy, and lovemaking with the self (Bevson, 1977).

10. This is the subject of the special issue of *Women's Studies International Forum*, as explained in Wise and Stanley's (1984) introduction.

11. See Hearn and Parkin (1987, 58–62) for further statements on 'sexual labour-power'.

12. Exceptions might include narcissism, masturbation and self-love; self-nurture; and masochism and self-mutilation.

13. This is not to suggest that women are 'naturally' violent, or indeed non-violent; merely it is men's restriction of women's potential violence, an exercise in men's short-term interests, that is at issue.

14. This may seem a surprising inclusion, yet in certain dire situations, suicide may appear the only means available to thwart the powerful. In Durkheimian terms, this may be either personally 'fatalistic' or 'altruistic' for sake of similar others.

15. Zita (1982, 162) and MacKinnon (1982, 16) comment on the

relationship of hierarchy and heterosexuality. Also see Reynaud (1981) on hierarchy and men's fear of homosexuality.

16. Indeed current British Parliamentary legislation on Family Law Reform promises 'rights' to unmarried fathers comparable to those of married fathers.

17. Ferguson (1982, 157–8) links this development both with Foucault's (1981) thesis that the control of sexuality was part of changing forms of bourgeois class control, and with the reorganisation of patriarchy.

18. Homosexual relations are illegal in the armed forces in Britain, sometimes with dire results for those concerned (Tatchell, 1985). Homosexual activity is generally considered contrary to the rules of prison discipline, although a court ruling in 1982 held that in the absence of contrary indication disciplinary offences under the Prison Rules should be construed no more harshly than equivalent criminal offences (Hearn and Parkin, 1987, 76–7). Homosexuality is legalised in the Swedish and some other national prison systems.

19. A possible interpretation of these divisions in patriarchy is that some activities, like caring, convey use values, which are converted to exchange values, like violence.

20. This perspective raises many complex questions, in terms of different relations of men's immediate interest, that may apparently be sacrificed, and men's collective power. A more complete analysis would necessarily consider sacrifice *in* life and *of* life; shorter and longer term interests of individual men; and the presence and absence of pain, physical and mental. Apparent sacrifice may also bring other rewards, material or otherwise, from other men or women.

21. I am indebted to John Barker for discussions on this question.

CHAPTER 6. THE REPRODUCTIVE MANAGEMENT AND REPRODUCTIVE WORK OF MEN: DOMINATION AND VARIATION

1. There are clear parallels, though analytical distinctions, between 'structured relations' and 'agency' as abstract concepts: 'domination' and 'variation' as respective characteristics of those 'structured relations' and 'agencies'; and 'management' and 'labour' as particular concrete activities done.

2. These are the more obvious examples of a diffuse 'phallocentrism', the symbolic and practical use of the phallus as a weapon of power.

3. Irigaray (1978, 162) writes: 'the man ... needs an instrument to touch himself: his hand, the women's sex, language.... Woman ... is in touch with herself, by herself and in herself.... Woman 'touches herself' all the time, moreover without anyone being able to forbid her to do so, for her sex is made up of two lips which embrace each other continuously.'

4. Longer-term crises, such as unemployment coupled with the care of handicapped children, may also bring extra efforts from fathers (Pahl

and Quine, 1985, 45–50). Thus fathers may temporarily or permanently become male parents 'as heroes'.

5. This is partly because social statistics, official and otherwise, are usually collected by family/household structure not labour, responsibility, caring or time.

6. Further complications in the interpretation of statistics of 'family structure' are the inclusion or exclusion of two (or more) parents of the same sex, or communal care.

7. Information in this paragraph is from, *inter alia*, Hughes *et al.* (1980).

8. This section is minimal, as the professions are examined further in chapters 7 and 8.

9. Individual states exist in relation to other states, each patriarchal. This 'network' of relations between men is a largely unrecognised and unanalysed aspect of 'international relations', the world patriarchal system.

CHAPTER 7.   PATRIARCHY, PROFESSIONALISATION AND THE SEMI-PROFESSIONS

1. This chapter is a shortened and slightly revised version of the paper, 'Notes on patriarchy, professionalization and the semi-professions' (Hearn, 1982a). Although I am dissatisfied with the patronising and patriarchal term, 'semi-professions' (Etzioni, 1969), it is retained here for the sake of textual consistency. I have, however, made some modifications in the references to capitalism, and the deletion of the term, 'capitalist patriarchy', as like Stacey (1982, 20), I now see patriarchy as independent of capitalism. Some changes have also been made in the footnoting.

2. Stacey (1982, 20–1) has quite rightly pointed out the shortcomings of this and some of the subsequent section. She draws attention to the constructive criticism of Ehrenreich and English's work in Versluysen's (1980) analysis of women healers in English history. Stacey explains:

> In particular the relationship between witchmania and women healers is questioned and two medieval images of women as both pure and *evil* is drawn out. Not only did upper class women healers avoid the stake, they ministered to the rich as well as the poor and were revered as saints of the sick, unlike the peasant wise women who were seen as a dangerous and powerful witch ... [I]n the medieval period ... [w]omen assisted each other in child birth and older women certainly had an important and influential role.... Despite their subordination Price and I (1981) have argued that such women had more power than women in today's allegedly egalitarian society. (emphasis in original)

3. An important methodological caveat must be added at this point, that the analysis of the relations of reproduction does not take place through the analysis of particular individual people, in this case men and women. The point is made most clearly by Marx in *Capital*:

> The principal agents of this mode of production, the capitalist and the wage labourer, are as such merely embodiments, personifications of capital and wage labour; definite social characteristics stamped upon individuals by the process of social production; the product of these definite social production relations. (1977b, 880)
>
> I paint the capitalist and the landlord in no sense *couleur de rose*. But here individuals are dealt with only insofar as they are personifications of economic categories, embodiments of particular class-relations and class-interests. My standpoint ... can less than any other make the individual responsible for relations whose creature he socially remains, however much he may subjectively raise himself above them. (1977a, 20–1)

There are clearly connections albeit indirect and mediated, between the structure of social relations and the experience of individuals within it (Sève, 1978). In this section, the descriptions of processes of change in the semi-professions are meant as examples of the more obvious forms of organisation of the semi-professions, and specific historical references should be interpreted accordingly. It is not suggested that all men are the embodiment of patriarchy nor all women the personification of patriarchal oppression. Neither is this to suggest that individual women, including professional women, do not experience contradiction and pain as a consequence of patriarchal social relations. (Howell, 1979)

4. In 1977, 83 per cent of all social work assistants and 64 per cent of all social workers employed by local authorities in England were women; while 71 per cent of area directors and 91 per cent of Directors of Social Services were men (Popplestone, 1980) (quoted in Ungerson, 1985, 195).

5. This section draws heavily on historical information contained within Donnison (1977) and Parry and Parry (1976).

CHAPTER 8. THE PROFESSIONS, THE CONTROL OF EMOTIONS AND THE CONSTRUCTION OF MASCULINITY

1. This chapter is a revised version of the paper 'The professions and the semi-professions: the control of emotions and the construction of masculinity' (1982e).

2. There are several possible parallels between this primarily social account and psychoanalytic interpretations. These include understanding relations with and projections onto people managers, people labourers, and 'clients' in terms of super-ego, ego, and id; the categories of parent, adult, and child of transactional analysis; and family roles. However

perhaps the most striking parallel is between people managers and Jung's concept of extraversion: '(h)e (who) lives in and through others'; and between people labourers and introversion, of 'being directed to the subject not to the object' (Jung, 1983, 140). The act of direct labour on and for other people, whilst bringing human social contact, is also a point of reproduction, *and of separation*, both social structurally and *intra*personally.

3. The concept of the public-private used here is similar to that of the 'intermediate zone' between, or spanning the boundary between, the public and private domains (Stacey and Davies, 1983; Stacey, 1986, 21–2).

CHAPTER 9.   THE PROBLEM OF FATHERHOOD

1. This chapter is an edited and slightly modified version of the paper, 'Childbirth, men and the problem of fatherhood' (Hearn, 1984b).

CHAPTER 10.   THE POLITICS OF CHILDCARE

1. This chapter is an edited extract from the chapters on 'work' and 'politics' in *Birth and Afterbirth* (Hearn, 1983, 28–36). I now see them as somewhat reductionist in their emphasis on the 'politics of birth and childwork' as the true (heroic?) site of struggle. Accordingly, the term reproduction is used in this chapter and in chapter 4, in a narrower sense than elsewhere in this text.

2. This is one of the four original demands of the Women's National Co-ordinating Committee in 1971. This demand—for 'free 24-hour nurseries'—and some of its misunderstandings, are discussed by Anna Coote and Beatrix Campbell (1982, 24).
Comparison can be made with the *TUC Charter on Facilities for the Under-Fives* (1978, 6), which argued for 'A comprehensive and universal service of care and education for children from 0 to 5 . . . made available by public authorities'. The Charter is, however, less clear on the precise meaning of such 'universal service', the question of community control and the role of 'non-parents'. In particular the case for childcare for children living with women not in paid work is left open. It is also unclear why fathers should have paternity leave, rather than any other named adult.

CHAPTER 11.   PATRIARCHY AND MEN'S PRACTICE

1. Examples of recent writing by men on this area include the *Achilles Heel*

(1982–3) special issues on sexuality, Chris Knight's (1980) pamphlet on impotence, and Ben Stout's (1984) on bisexuality, gayness and celibacy.

2. Information on forms of harassment and action against harassment is included in 'Men's sexuality at work' (Hearn, 1985a).

3. Invaluable historical information is contained in the anti-sexist men's history column, 'Before Us', co-ordinated by Sally Roesch Wagner in the journal *M./Changing Men*. More general surveys of the 'crisis' of masculinity in late seventeenth and early eighteenth century England, and in late nineteenth and early twentieth century United States have been compiled by Michael Kimmel (1987).

4. A more recent statement of this type is 'newmanifesto' (1985) produced from Brussels.

5. For example, Paul Morrison's 'About Men' Channel 4 television series and booklet (Eardley, Humphries and Morrison, 1983), *The Sexuality of Men* collection (Metcalf and Humphries, 1985), and films, such as 'True Romance Etc' from The Newsreel Collective. Back copies of *Achilles Heel* are available from 79, Pembroke Road, London E17 9BB.

6. Public action by men against pornography and violence is not necessarily from an anti-sexist stance (e.g. Taylor, 1976). Campaigns against media rather than, say, military violence are frequently conducted from reactionary positions.

CHAPTER 12.   CHANGING MEN'S SEXIST PRACTICE IN THE SOCIAL SCIENCES

1. Tribe (1978, ch. 5) provides an absorbing discussion of the relationship of household economy and the development of economic discourse. Recent revivals of the analogy of the household in monetarist economic management are closer to this tradition than much post-war Keynsianism.

2. For Slocum (1975) this is itself part of the discipline's male bias.

3. Special issues of journals include:
   Impact of Science on Society (21, 1, 1971); *Black Scholar* (2, 10, 1971); *Journal of Social Issues* (34, 1, 1978); *The Counseling Psychologist* (7, 1, 1978); *The Family Co-ordinator* (28, 4, 1979); *New Dance* (14, spring 1980); *Women's Studies International Forum* (7, 1, 1984); *Therapy Now* (summer 1985); *Ten-8* (17, 1985); *American Behavioral Scientist* (29, 5, 1986); *Journal of the National Association of Women Deans, Administrators, and Counselors* (spring 1986); and *University of Dayton Review* (1986–7).

   Bibliographies on men and masculinity include those by Grady, Brannon and Pleck (1979); Massachusetts Institute of Technology (1979); August (1985); and Ford and Hearn (1987). Networks of and newsletters for men's studies scholars exist in the Netherlands (*Nieuwsbrief Mannenstudies*), the United States (*Men's Studies Newsletter/Review*) and Britain (*Linkman*); and collated syllabuses from the United States are available from San Femiano, 22 East Street, Northampton, MA 01060 USA ($10).

Courses and more academic study groups on men that have taken place in Britain over the last five years include those on 'Men and Childcare' (Leeds WEA) (Harris, 1982–3); 'Men's Studies' (Coventry WEA) (Gurden and Hardman, 1982–3); 'Men and Sexual Politics' (Huddersfield); 'Men and Masculinity Study Groups' (Goldsmith's College, London and University of Bradford). 'Images of Masculinity' (Dayschool Leeds University Extra Mural Department); (Masculinity in Crisis' (Manchester Cornerhouse) 'Men and Masculinity' (Option, MA Social and Community Work Studies and MA Women's Studies (Applied), University of Bradford); 'Men's Studies' (Youth and Community Work Courses, Manchester Polytechnic); 'Men's Studies' and related adult education courses (Islington Adult Education Institute) (Adkins, 1985); 'Myths of Manliness' (Nottingham WEA); 'Male Awareness Workshop' (Division of Education, University of Sheffield); 'Men about Men Seminar' (Keele University); 'Masculinity' (Dayschool Centre for Contemporary Cultural Studies, University of Birmingham); 'Thinking About Men' (Manchester WEA) (Cooke, n.d.).

4. These first three points are slightly adapted from my memorandum with Alan Carling 'Studying Men', November 1983, University of Bradford.

AFTERWORD

1. According to Motherson (1979, 26),

> workplaces, along with the Council buildings of the City Fathers, the Courts, Universities, Hospitals, Churches, Stock-Markets etc. are *extensions of the men's huts.* Anthropologists who have studied non-industrialised patriarchal tribes describe men's huts as the place where men go to flee and repudiate women, to initiate boys into manhood by beating them as the 'wives' of the older men . . . , to guard phallic objects containing the 'soul' of the village . . . , and from which to launch rival ceremonies of the 'couvade' (mock-birth rituals) to upstage women's creativity and communal work. . . . (emphasis in original)

Appendix

A minimum self-definition of the anti-sexist men's movement

(Paul Morrison, 'Our common ground ...', *Anti-Sexist Men's Newsletter*, 1980)

This conference of men places itself unequivocally in support of the women's and gay movements in the struggle against sexism. We realise that men's power in our society means that we are not an equivalent or 'parallel' movement. We are certainly not a competitive one.

Yet we have discovered that the power we have over women also cripples and distorts our own lives. Learning how to give up this control and grow out of our masculine straightjackets [sic] is a frightening but very positive process.

We are traditionally expected to be unemotional, tough, aggressive, individualistic, and not to admit weakness, yet we all contain the opposite qualities—gentleness, co-operativeness, lovingness, receptiveness, which we can reclaim and allow.

The main vehicle for our personal changes has been men's groups, in which we can look at our negative patterns of relating to women and gay men, and learn to draw support from other men. Becoming close to other men reduces the exclusive emotional burden that men have traditionally placed upon women. Recently some men have found therapy and co-counselling valuable in helping to resolve deep patterns and oppressive blocks in themselves.

We want to change our relationships with children, to take our full and equal share of responsibility for children. We have been discovering the positive benefits of being close to and learning from children.

This means looking to change patterns of work and pay that are dominant in our society; and confronting eventually the huge gulf between the workplace and domestic labour and life.

The main public expression so far of our support for the women's liberation movement has been in helping to organise crèches for women's events, and in attending mixed demonstrations. We would like to find other ways of supporting Women's movement campaigns and demands, when invited, and in developing the particular contribution we can make as men—for example, in confronting rape and male violence, and in support of a women's right to choose, equal pay, adequate nursery provision, and so forth.

The many of us who are heterosexual are committed to exploring our prejudices against gay men and lesbians, and our fear of our own gay feelings. We would like to find ways of linking up with and supporting the Gay Liberation Movement, and specific gay movement campaigns.

We have been developing ways of reaching out to other men; and confronting the sexism that we meet in other men in our own lives and workplaces. We want to create a positive anti-sexist culture that men can draw support from in their changes. We want to develop campaigns in our own interest as anti-sexist men—against media stereotypes of men, around unemployment, men's health, for well-paid part-time work, for jobsharing, paternity leave, etc.

Patriarchal culture has become synonymous with the 'conquering' of the natural environment. We want to live in harmony with the natural world, including our own bodies, and to redirect our skills and technologies in such directions as to make this harmony possible, eliminating poverty and enabling each individual to live to her or his fullest potential.

We realise that in our society sexism is inextricably linked with class and racial oppression, and with imperialism. We are working towards a society free of all these.

The anti-sexist men's movement is small in number, and it is young. We are only now beginning to feel confident to move out of relative isolation. We need to recognise our limitations, *as well as our very real strengths*.

In coming to take collective political initiatives, we don't want to create new hierarchies of leaders and led.

That's it.
Love and struggle,
Paul Morrison

Bibliography

Aaby, P., 'Engels and women', *Critique of Anthropology*, 3 (1977).

Achilles Heel, Special Issue on Sexuality, 6 and 7 (1982–3).

Achilles Heel Collective, 'By way of an introduction ...', *Achilles Heel*, 1 (1978).

Adams, C., 'Perils of delivering one's son', *The Observer* (8 August 1982).

Adkins, G., 'Educating Peter', *Men's Antisexist Newsletter*, 21 (1985).

Al-Hibri, A., 'Capitalism is an advanced stage of patriarchy: but Marxism is not Feminism', in *Women and Revolution. The Unhappy Marriage of Marxism and Feminism*, ed. L. Sargent (Pluto, London; Maple, New York, 1981).

Allen, J. G., and Haccoun, D. M., 'Sex differences in emotionality: a multidimensional approach', *Human Relations*, 29 (1976).

Althusser, L., *Lenin and Philosophy and Other Essays* (New Left Books, London, 1971).

Anderson, P., *Lineages of the Absolutist State* (NLB, London, 1974).

Anon, 'Sheffield Men Against Sexual Harassment', *Men's Antisexist Newsletter*, 23 (1986).

Arcana, J., *Every Mother's Son. The Role of Mothers in the Making of Men* (The Women's Press, London; Anchor, Doubleday, New York, 1983).

Ardener, S., *Defining Females: The Nature of Women in Society* (Croom Helm, London, 1978).

Armstrong, A. J., 'Social skills training', *Bulletin of the British Psychological Society*, 38 (1985).

Atkinson, P., 'The problem with patriarchy', *Achilles Heel*, 2 (1979).

August, E. R., '"Modern men", or, men's studies in the 80s', *College English*, 44 (1982).

——, *Men's Studies. A Selected and Annotated Bibliography* (Libraries Unlimited, Littleton, Col./London, 1985).

Balbus, I., *Marxism and Domination* (Princeton University Press, Princeton, 1982).

Barker, D. L., Introduction to *The Main Enemy*, C. Delphy (Women's Research and Resource Centre, London, 1977).

Barker, J., and Downing, H., 'Word processing and the transformation of the patriarchal relations of control in the office', *Capital and Class*, 10 (1980).

Barrett, M., *Women's Oppression Today* (Verso, London, 1980).

Barry, K., *Female Sexual Slavery* (New York University, New York, 1984).

Beail, N., 'The role of the father during pregnancy' in *Fathers, Psychological Perspectives*, ed. N. Beail and J. McGuire (Junction, London, 1982).

Beechey, V., 'On patriarchy', *Feminist Review*, 2 (1979).

Bell, C., McKee, L., and Priestley, K., *Fathers, Childbirth and Work* (Equal Opportunities Commission, Manchester, 1983).

Beuret, K., and Makings, L., 'Love in a cold climate: women, class and courtship in a recession', Paper at British Sociological Association Annual Conference, Loughborough University. Mimeo, North Staffs Polytechnic (March 1986).

Bevson, J., 'Lovemaking with myself', in *A Book of Readings for Men Against Sexism*, ed. J. Snodgrass (Times Change, Albion, Ca., 1977).

Bland, L., Brunsdon, C., Hobson, D., and Winship, J., 'Women "inside and outside" the relations of production' in *Women Take Issue*, Women's Studies Group, Centre for Contemporary Cultural Studies, University of Birmingham (Hutchinson, London, 1978a).

Bland, L., Harrison, R., Mort, F., and Weedon, C., 'Relations of reproduction: approaches through anthropology' in *Women Take Issue*, Women's Studies Group, Centre for Contemporary Cultural Studies, University of Birmingham (Hutchinson, London, 1978b).

Bliss, S., 'Fathers & sons', *The Men's Journal* (spring 1985).

Bliss, S., 'Changing men's publications', *Mens Studies Newsletter*, 3 (1986).

Bolin, W. D. W., *Feminism, Reform & Social Service: A History of Women in Social Work* (Minnesota Resource Centre for Social Work Education, Minneapolis, 1973).

Borchorst, A., and Siim, B., 'Women and the advanced welfare state—a new kind of patriarchal power', in *From a Woman's Point of View*, ed. A. S. Sassoon (Hutchinson, London, 1986).

Bouchier, D., *The Feminist Challenge: The Movement for Women's Liberation in Britain and the U.S.A.* (Macmillan, London, 1983).

Bowen, J., 'Speaking of men', *New Statesman* (24 May 1985).

Brackx, A., 'Out into the open', *Spare Rib*, 84 (1979).

Bradley, M., Danchik, L., Fager, M., Wodetzki, T., *Unbecoming Men* (Times Change, New York, 1971).

Bradshaw, J., 'Now what are they up to? Men in the "men's movement"' in *On the Problem of Men*, ed. S. Friedman and E. Sarah (Women's Press, London, 1983).

Brager, G. and Michael. J. A., 'The sex distribution in social work: causes and consequences', *Social Casework*, 50 (1969).

Brittan, A. and Maynard, M., *Sexism, Racism and Oppression* (Basil Blackwell, Oxford, 1984).

Brown, B., and Adams, P., 'The feminine body and feminist politics', *m/f*, 3 (1979).

Brown, C., 'Mothers, fathers, and children: from private to public patriarchy' in *Women and Revolution. The Unhappy Marriage of Marxism and Feminism*, ed. L. Sargent (Pluto, London; Maple, New York, 1981).

Bullough, B., 'Barriers to the nurse-practitioner movement: problems of women in a women's field', *International Journal of Health Services*, 5 (1975).

Burnham, L., and Louie, M., *The Impossible Marriage: A Marxist Critique of Socialist Feminism*, Line of March, 17 (The Institute for Social and Economic Studies, Oakland, Ca., 1985).

Burstyn, V., 'Masculine dominance and the state', in *The Socialist Register 1983*, ed. R. Miliband and J. Saville (Merlin, London, 1983).

Campbell, B., 'Brotherly love', *City Limits* (16–22 September 1983).

Carling, A., 'Exploitation, extortion and oppression', *Political Studies*, 35 (1987).

Carpenter, M., 'The new managerialism and professionalism in nursing' in *Health and the Division of Labour*, ed. M. Stacey, M. Reid, C. Heath and R. Dingwall (Croom Helm, London, 1977).

Carrigan, T. J., and Connell, R. W., 'Freud and masculinity', Mimeo, Macquarie University (March 1984).

Carrigan, T., Connell, B., and Lee, J., 'Toward a new sociology of masculinity', *Theory and Society*, 14 (1985).

Chafetz, J. S., 'Women in social work', *Social Work*, 17 (1972).

Charvet, J., *Feminism* (Dent, London, 1982).

Chesler, P., *Women and Madness* (Doubleday, New York, 1972).

Chodorow, N., *The Reproduction of Mothering. Psychoanalysis and the Sociology of Gender* (University of California, Berkeley/London, 1978).

Cixous, H., 'Sorties', in *New French Feminisms*, ed. E. Marks and I. de Courtivron (Harvester, Brighton, 1981; University of Massachusetts, Amherst, Mass., 1980; first pub. 1975).

Clark, A., *The Working Life of Women in the 17th Century*

(Routledge & Sons, London, 1919).

Clements, J., 'A feminist's view of anti-sexist men', *Anti-Sexist Men's Newsletter*, 9 (1980).

Cockburn, C., *Brothers. Male Dominance and Technological Change* (Pluto, London, 1983).

Cockburn, P., 'How the pecking order is changing', *The Guardian* (2 September 1986).

Cohen, G., 'Absentee husbands in spiralist families. The myth of the symmetrical family', *Journal of Marriage and the Family*, 39 (1977).

Commitments Collective, 'Anti-sexist commitments for men ...', *Anti-Sexist Men's Newsletter*, 9 (1980).

Connell, R. W., 'Men and socialism', in *Labor Essays 1982*, ed. G. Evans, and J. Reeves (Drummond, Blackburn, Victoria, 1982).

——, *Which Way Is Up?* (Allen & Unwin, London/Boston, 1983).

Constantinople, A., 'Masculinity–femininity: an exception to a famous dictum?', *Psychological Bulletin*, 80 (1973).

Cooke, D., *Thinking About Men*, (WEA North Western District, Manchester, n.d.).

Coote, A., 'The AES: a new starting point', *New Socialist* (November/December 1981).

——, and Campbell, B., *Sweet Freedom. The Struggle for Women's Liberation* (Picador, London, 1982).

Côté, P., Dare, B., and Muzychka, M., *Men Changing. A Resource Manual for Men's Consciousness Raising* (Alternative Futures Institute, Ottawa, 1984).

Coward, R., 'Pornography: two opposing feminist viewpoints', *Spare Rib*, 119 (1982).

——, Lipshitz, S., and Cowie, E., 'Psychoanalysis and patriarchal structures', in *Papers on Patriarchy*, Patriarchy Conference (Women's Publishing Collective, London, 1976).

Cummings, J. E., 'Sexism in social work: some thoughts on strategy for structural change', *Catalyst: A Socialist Journal of the Social Services*, 8 (1980).

Daly, M., *Gyn/ecology; The Metaethics of Radical Feminism* (The Women's Press, London; Beacon, Boston, 1978).

Dansky, S., Knoebel, J., and Pitchford, K., 'The Effeminist Manifesto' in *Double F: A Magazine of Effeminism* (1973), reprinted in *A Book of Readings for Men Against Sexism* ed. J. Snodgrass (Times Change, Albion, Ca., 1977).

Deleuze, G., and Guattari, F., *Anti-Oedipus: Capitalism and Schizophrenia* (Viking, New York, 1977).

Delmar, R., 'Looking again at Engels's *Origin of the Family, Private Property and the State*' in *The Rights and Wrongs of Women*, ed. J. Mitchell and A. Oakley (Penguin, Harmondsworth, 1976).

Delphy, C., *The Main Enemy. A Materialist Analysis of Women's Oppression* (WRRC, London, 1977). First pub. in French, 1970.
——, *Close to Home. A Materialist Analysis of Women's Oppression* (Hutchinson, London, 1984). First pub. in French, 1970 onwards.
DES, *Primary Education in England. A Survey by H.M. Inspectors* (DES, London, 1978).
DHSS, *Health and Personal Social Services Statistics for England 1982* (HMSO, London, 1982).
Dingwall, R. W. J., 'Collectivism, regionalism and feminism: Health visiting and British social policy 1950–1975', *Journal of Social Policy*, 6 (1977).
Dinnerstein, D., *The Rocking of the Cradle: And the Ruling of the World* (Harper & Row, New York, 1976; Souvenir, London, 1978).
Dixon, N., *On The Psychology of Military Incompetence* (Jonathan Cape, London, 1976).
Donnison, J., *Midwives and Medical Men* (Heinemann, London, 1977).
Dorn, N., and South, N., *Of Males and Markets: A Critical Review of 'Youth Culture' Theory* (Centre for Occupational and Community Research, Middlesex Polytechnic, Middlesex, n.d.).
Doyle, J. A., *The Male Experience* (Wm. C. Brown, Dubuque, Iowa, 1983).
Duman, D., 'The creation and diffusion of a professional ideology in nineteenth century England', *Sociological Review*, 27 (1979).
Dyer, R., 'Male sexuality in the media' in *The Sexuality of Men*, ed. A. Metcalf and M. Humphries (Pluto, London, 1985).
Eardley, T., 'Violence and sexuality', in *The Sexuality of Men*, ed. A. Metcalf and M. Humphries (Pluto, London, 1985).
——, Humphries, M., and Morrison, P., *About Men* (Broadcasting Support Services, London, 1983).
Easlea, B., *Fathering the Unthinkable* (Pluto, London, 1983).
Eberhardt, E., Hamilton, K., McKechnie, S., 'Amen', *Red Rag* (August 1980).
Edholm, F., Harris, O., and Young, K., 'Conceptualising women', *Critique of Anthropology*, 3 (1977).
Ehrenreich, B., *The Hearts of Men. American Dreams and the Flight from Commitment* (Pluto, London, 1983).
——, and English, D., *Complaints and Disorders. The Sexual Politics of Sickness* (Feminist Press, New York, 1973).
——, and ——, *Witches, Midwives & Nurses. History of Women Healers* (Feminist Press, New York, 1974).
Eichenbaum, L., and Orbach, S., *Outside In, Inside Out* (Pengiun, Harmondsworth, 1982).
Eichler, M., *The Double Standard. A Feminist Critique of Feminist*

Social Science (Croom Helm, London, 1980).

Eisenstein, Z., ed., *Capitalist Patriarchy and the Case for Socialist Feminism* (Monthly Review Press, New York, 1979).

Eisenstein, Z., *The Radical Future of Liberal Feminism* (Longman, New York, 1981).

Elliott, P., *The Sociology of the Professions* (Macmillan, London, 1972).

Elshtain, J. B., *Public Man, Private Woman* (Martin Robertson, Oxford, 1981).

Elson, D., ed., *Value. The Representation of Labour in Capitalism* (CSE, London; Humanities, Atlantic Highlands, N.J., 1979).

Elston, M. A., 'Women in the medical profession: whose problem?' in *Health and the Division of Labour*, ed. M. Stacey, M. Reid, C. Heath and R. Dingwall (Croom Helm, London, 1977).

Engels, F., *The Origin of the Family, Private Property and the State*, ed. and with an introduction by E. B. Leacock (Lawrence & Wishart, London, 1972).

Ettorre, B., 'The "perks" of male power: heterosexuality and the oppression of women', in *On the Problem of Men*, ed. S. Friedman and E. Sarah (The Women's Press, London, 1982).

Etzioni, A., ed., *The Semi-Professions and their Organization* (Free Press, New York, 1969).

Farrell, W., *The Liberated Man* (Random House, New York, 1974).

Ferguson, A., 'Patriarchy, sexual identity, and the sexual revolution', in *Feminist Theory. A Critique of Ideology*, ed. N. O. Keohane, M. Z. Rosaldo, and B. C. Gelpi (Harvester, Brighton; University of Chicago, Chicago, 1982).

Fielding, A. G., and Portwood, D., 'Professions and the state—towards a typology of bureaucratic professions', *Sociological Reveiw*, 28 (1980).

Firestone, S., *The Dialectic of Sex* (Jonathan Cape, London, 1971; Morrow, New York, 1970).

Ford, D., and Hearn, J., *Studying Men and Masculinity. A Sourcebook of Literature and Materials* (University of Bradford, Bradford, 1987).

Foucault, M., *The History of Sexuality. Volume One: An Introduction* (Penguin, Harmondsworth, 1981). First pub. in French, 1976.

Franklin II, C. W., *The Changing Definition of Masculinity* (Plenum, New York/London, 1984).

Fromm, E., *The Anatomy of Human Destructiveness* (Penguin, Harmondsworth, 1974; Holt, Rinehart & Winston, New York, 1973).

Frye, M., *The Politics of Reality: Essays in Feminist Theory* (Crossings, New York, 1983).

Game, A., and Pringle, R., *Gender at Work* (Allen & Unwin, London, 1983).

Gamarnikow, E., 'Sexual division of labour: the case of nursing', in *Feminism and Materialism: Women and Modes of Production*, ed. A. Kuhn and A. M. Wolpe (Routledge & Kegan Paul, London, 1978).

Gathorne-Hardy, C. J., *Love, Sex, Marriage and Divorce* (Jonathan Cape, London, 1981).

Gavron, H., *The Captive Wife. Conflicts of Housebound Mothers* (Routledge & Kegan Paul, London/Boston, 1966).

George, V., and Wilding, P., *Motherless Families* (Routledge & Kegan Paul, London, 1972).

Gerzon, M., *A Choice of Heroes: The Changing Faces of American Manhood* (Houghton Mifflin, Boston, 1982).

Goldberg, H., *The Hazards of Being Male: Surviving the Myth of Masculinity* (Nash, Plainview, N.Y., 1976).

Gondolf, E. W., *Men Who Batter: An Integrated Approach for Stopping Wife Abuse* (Learning Publications, Holmes Beach, Fl., 1985).

Gordon, L., 'The politics of birth control, 1920–1940. The impacts of professionals', *International Journal of Health Services*, 5 (1975).

Gough, I., *The Political Economy of the Welfare State* (Macmillan, London, 1983).

Grady, K. E., Brannon, R., and Pleck, J. H., *The Male Sex Role. A Selected and Annotated Bibliography* (US Department of Health, Education and Welfare, Rockville, 1979).

Graham. H., *Women, Health and the Family* (Wheatsheaf, Brighton, 1984).

Gray, E. D., *Patriarchy as a Conceptual Trap* (Roundtable, Wellesley, Mass., 1982).

Green, M., *Goodbye Father* (Routledge & Kegan Paul, London, 1976).

Griffin, S., 'The way of all ideology' in *Feminist Theory. A Critique of Ideology*, ed. N. O. Keohane, M. Z. Rosaldo and B. C. Gelpi (Harvester, Brighton; University of Chicago Press, Chicago, 1982).

Gurden, H., and Hardman, J., 'Sexual politics for men', *Achilles Heel*, 6 and 7 (1982–3).

Hargreaves, J. A. 'The social production of gender through sport', *Theory, Culture & Society*, 3 (1986).

Harne, L., 'Lesbian custody and the new myth of the father', *Trouble and Strife*, 3 (1984).

Harris, J., 'Men & childcare', *Achilles Heel*, 6 and 7 (1982–3).

Harris, M., 'The Dilly boys', *New Society* (6 April 1972).

Harris, O., and Young, K., 'Engendered structures: some problems in the analysis of reproduction', in *The Anthropology of Pre-Capitalist Societies*, ed. J. S. Kahn and J. Llobera (Macmillan, London, 1981).

Harrison, J., 'Men's roles, men's lives', *Signs*, 4 (1978).

Harrison, P., 'Burn your jock straps', *New Society* (15 May 1975).

Hartmann, H., 'The unhappy marriage of Marxism and Feminism: towards a more progressive union', *Capital and Class*, 8 (1979).

Hartsock, N. C. M., *Money, Sex, and Power. Toward a Feminist Historical Materialism* (Longman, New York/London, 1983).

Hearn, J., 'Men's politics and social policy', *Bulletin on Social Policy*, 5 (1980).

——, 'Notes on patriarchy, professionalization and the semi-professions', *Sociology*, 16 (1982a).

——, 'Patriarchy, social policy and men's practice', Paper at Critical Social Policy Annual Conference, Socialist Strategies for Welfare, Sheffield Polytechnic. Mimeo, University of Bradford (April 1982b).

——, 'Radical social work—contradictions, limitations and political possibilities', *Critical Social Policy*, 2 (1982c).

——, 'The implications of patriarchy for men's practice', in *Socialist Action for the 80s. Policies and Practices*, Conference of Socialist Economists (CSE, London, 1982d).

——, 'The professions and the semi-professions: the control of emotions and the construction of masculinity', Paper at British Sociological Association Annual Conference, University of Manchester. Mimeo, University of Bradford (April 1982e).

——, *Birth and Afterbirth: A Materialist Account* (Achilles Heel, London, 1983).

——, 'Birth and afterbirth', *National Childcare Campaign Newsletter* (February/March 1984a).

——, 'Childbirth, men and the problem of fatherhood', *Radical Community Medicine*, 15 (1984b).

——, 'Men's sexuality at work', in *The Sexuality of Men*, ed. A. Metcalf and M. Humphries (London, Pluto, 1985a).

——, 'Patriarchy, professionalization and the semi-professions', in *Women and Social Policy*, ed. C. Ungerson (Macmillan, London, 1985b).

——, 'Changing men's studies: problems, possibilities and promises', Paper at British Sociological Association Annual Conference, Loughborough University. Mimeo, University of Bradford (March 1986a).

——, 'Theorizing Social Planning: Analysis, Critique and Alternatives', Doctoral Thesis, University of Bradford, Bradford (1986b).

——, 'Patriarchy, masculinity and psychoanalysis', Mimeo, University of Bradford, (November 1986c).

——, and Carling, A., 'Studying men', memorandum to Women's Studies Course Team, University of Bradford', (November 1983).

——, Creighton, C., Middleton, C., Morgan, D., Thomas, R., and Pearson, C., 'Changing men's sexist practice in sociology', *Network*, 25 (1983).

——, and Jones, B., 'Radical social work and the problem of management', *Community Care*, 367 (1981).

——, and Parkin P. W., 'Gender and organizations: a selective review and a critique of a neglected area', *Organization Studies*, 4 (1983).

——, and ——, '"Sex" at "Work": methodological and other problems in the study of sexuality in work oganizations', Paper at British Sociological Association Annual Conference, University of Bradford. Mimeo, University of Bradford (April 1984).

——, and ——, 'Women, men and leadership: a critical review of assumptions, practices, and change in the industrialized nations', *International Studies of Management and Organization*, 16 (1986–7).

——, and ——, *'Sex' at 'Work'. The Power and Paradox of Organisation Sexuality* (Wheatsheaf, Brighton, 1987).

Hegel, G. F., *The Logic of Hegel*, trans. by W. Wallace from the *Encyclopaedia of the Philosophical Sciences* (Oxford University Press, Oxford, 2nd rev edn, 1931).

Hester, M., 'Anti-sexist men: a case of cloak-and-dagger chauvinism', *Women's Studies International Forum*, 7 (1984).

Hill, T., 'Rape and marital violence in the maintenance of male power', in *On the Problem of Men*, ed. S. Friedman and E. Sarah (The Women's Press, London, 1982).

HMSO, *Census 1981. Economic Activity Great Britain* (HMSO, London, 1984a).

——, *Census 1981. Household and Family Composition England and Wales* (HMSO, London,1984b).

Hocquenghem, G., *Homosexual Desire* (Allison & Busby, London, 1978).

Hollway, W., 'Heterosexual sex: power and desire for the Other' in *Sex & Love. New Thoughts on Old Contradictions*, ed. S. Cartledge and J. Ryan (The Women's Press, London, 1983).

hooks, b., *Feminist Theory: From Margin to Center* (South, End, Boston, 1984).

Holter, H., ed. *Patriarchy in a Welfare Society* (Universitetsforlaget, Oslo, 1984).

Hornacek, P. C. 'Anti-sexist consciousness-raising groups for men', in *A Book of Readings for Men Against Sexism*, ed. J. Snodgrass

(Times Change, Albion, Ca., 1977).

Howell, M., 'Can we be feminists and professionals?', *Women's Studies International Quarterly*, 2 (1979).

Hughes, M., Mayall, B., Moss, P., Perry, J., Petrie, P., and Pinkerton, G., *Nurseries Now. A Fair Deal for Parents and Children* (Penguin, Harmondsworth, 1980).

Hunt, P., *Gender and Class Consciousness* (Macmillan, London, 1980).

Irigaray, L., 'That sex which is not one' trans. R. Albury and P. Foss from *Ce sexe qui n'en est pas un* (Les Editions de Minuit, Paris, 1977), in *Language, Sexuality and Subversion* ed. P. Foss and M. Morris (Feral, Darlington, Australia, 1978).

Jaggar, A. M., and McBride, W. L., ' "Reproduction" as male ideology', *Women's Studies International Forum*, 8 (1985).

Johnson, D., 'Labour party bans men', *The Guardian* (6 June 1986).

Jones, G. S., *Outcast London* (Clarendon Press, London, 1971).

Jones, T., 'A Small step on—men against male violence', *Revolutionary Socialism*, 9 (1982).

Jung, C. G., *Jung: Selected Writings* introduced by A. Storr (Fontana, 1983).

Jungk, P., *The Nuclear State* (Calder, London, 1979). First pub. in German, 1978.

Kadushin, A., 'Men in a women's profession', *Social Work*, 21 (1976).

Kapp, Y., *Eleanor Marx Vols. 1 and 2* (Pantheon, New York, 1977).

Keat, R., and Urry, J., *Social Theory as Science* (Routledge & Kegan, London/Boston, 2nd edn, 1982).

Kimmel, M. S., 'The "crisis" of masculinity in historical perspective', in *The Making of Masculinities*, ed. H. Brod (Allen & Unwin, Boston, 1987).

Kitzinger, S., *The Experience of Childbirth* (Penguin, Harmondsworth, 1972).

——, *Giving Birth: The Parent's Emotions in Childbirth* (Gollancz, London, 1973).

Knight, C., *My Sex Life* (Women and Labour Collective, London, 1980).

Koestler, A., *The Ghost in the Machine* (Hutchinson, London, 1967).

Kovalesky, M. M., *Tableau des Origines et de L'Evolution de la Famille et de la Propriété* (Stockholm, 1890) cited in F. Engels *The Origin of the Family, Private Property and the State* (Lawrence & Wishart, London, 1972).

Kravetz, D., 'Sexism in a women's profession', *Social Work*, 21 (1976).

Kuhn, A., 'Structures of patriarchy and capital in the family', in

Feminism and Materialism, ed. A. Kuhn and A. M. Wolpe (Routledge & Kegan Paul, London/Boston, 1978).

Lakoff, R., *Language and Woman's Place* (Harper & Row, New York, 1975).

Lamm, B., 'Men's movement hype', in *A Book of Readings For Men Against Sexism*, ed. J. Snodgrass (Times Change, Albion, Ca., 1977).

Land, H., *Parity Begins at Home* (EOC/SSRC, Manchester, 1981).

Lange, L., 'The function of equal education in Plato's *Republic* and *Laws*', in *The Sexism of Social and Political Theory*, ed. M. G. Clark and L. Lange (University of Toronto, Toronto, 1979).

Lasch, C., *The Minimal Self: Psychic Survival in Troubled Times* (Pan, London; Norton, New York, 1984).

Laurin-Frenette, N., 'The women's movement, anarchism and the state', *Our Generation*, 15 (1982).

Leclerc, A., 'Woman's word', in *New French Feminisms*, ed. E. Marks and I. de Courtivron (Harvester, Brighton, 1981; University of Massachusetts, Amherst, Mass., 1980; first pub. 1974).

Lenin, V. I., 'On the question of dialectics', in *Collected Works. Volume 38. Philosophical Notebooks* (Foreign Language Publishing House, Moscow; Lawrence & Wishart, London, 1961).

——, *Imperialism, the Highest Stage of Capitalism* (Lawrence & Wishart, London, 1964).

Leonard, D., 'The origin of the family, private property, and Marxist Feminism', *Trouble and Strife*, 3 (1984).

Lewin, E., 'Feminist ideology and the meaning of work: the case of nursing', *Catalyst*, 10–11 (1977).

Lewis, C., 'A feeling you can't scratch? The effect of pregnancy and birth on married men', in *Fathers, Psychological Perspectives*, ed. N. Beail and J. McGuire (Junction, London, 1982).

McDonough, R., and Harrison, R., 'Patriarchy and the relations of production', in *Feminism and Materialism*, ed. A. Kuhn and A. M. Wolpe (Routledge & Kegan Paul, London/Boston, 1978).

McIntosh, M., 'The state and the oppression of women', in *Feminism and Materialism*, ed. A. Kuhn and A. M. Wolpe, (Routledge & Kegan Paul, London/Boston, 1978).

McKee, L., and Bell, C., 'Marital and family relations in times of male unemployment', in *New Approaches to Economic Life*, ed. B. Roberts, R. Finnegan, D. Gallie (Manchester University, Manchester, 1985).

——, and ——, 'His unemployment: her problem. The domestic and marital consequences of male unemployment', in *The Experience of Unemployment*, ed. S. Allen, K. Purcell, A. Waton, S. Wood (Macmillan, London, 1986).

216   *The Gender of Oppression*

Mackie, L., and Pattullo, P., *Women at Work* (Tavistock, London, 1977).

MacKinnon, C. A., 'Feminism, Marxism, method and the State: an agenda for theory', in *Feminist Theory. A Critique of Ideology*, ed. N. O. Keohane, M. Z. Rosaldo and B. C. Gelpi (Harvester, Brighton; University of Chicago, Chicago, 1982).

Mackintosh, M., 'Reproduction and patriarchy: a critique of Meillassoux, *Femmes, Greniers et Capitaux*', *Capital and Class*, 2 (1977).

Manton, J., *Elizabeth Garrett Anderson* (Dutton, New York, 1965).

Marx, J., et al., *The Daughters of Karl Marx: Family Correspondence 1866–98*, trans. F. Evans (Deutsch, London; Harcourt, Brace, Jovanovich, 1982).

Marx, K., *Early Writings* (Penguin, Harmondsworth, 1975).

——, *Capital. Volume One* (Lawrence & Wishart, London, 1977a).

——, *Capital. Volume Three* (Lawrence & Wishart, London, 1977b).

——, 'Results of the immediate process of production', in *Karl Marx: Selected Writings*, ed. D. McClellan (Oxford University Press, Oxford, 1977c).

——, and Engels, F., *The German Ideology* (Lawrence & Wishart, London, 1970).

Mason, J., 'Gender inequality in long term marriage: the negotiation and renegotiation of domestic and social organisation of married couples aged 50–70', Paper at British Sociological Association Annual Conference, Loughborough University. Mimeo, University of Kent (March 1986).

Mason, S., 'Bristol on the move', *Men's Antisexist Newsletter*, 23 (1986).

Massachusetts Institute of Technology Humanities Library, *Men's Studies Bibliography* (MIT, 4th edn, Cambridge, Mass., 1979).

Meillassoux, C., *Maidens, Meal and Money* (Cambridge University Press, Cambridge, 1981). First pub. in French, 1975.

Mennerick, A. L., 'Organizational structuring of sex roles in a non-stereotyped industry', *Administrative Science Quarterly*, 20 (1975).

Menzies, I., 'A case study in the functioning of social systems as a defence against anxiety', *Human Relations*, 13 (1960).

Metcalf, A., 'A dissenting view', *Achilles Heel*, 1 (1978).

——, 'Introduction', in *The Sexuality of Men*, ed. A. Metcalf and M. Humphries (Pluto, London, 1985).

——, and Humphries, M., ed., *The Sexuality of Men* (Pluto, London, 1985).

Middleton, C., 'Peasants, patriarchy and the feudal mode of production in England: a Marxist appraisal' (2 parts), *Sociological Review*, 29 (1981).

Mieli, M., *Homosexuality and Liberation. Elements of a Gay Critique*, trans. D. Fernback (Gay Men's Press, London, 1980). First pub. in Italian, 1977.

Miller, C., and Swift, K., *The Handbook of Non-Sexist Writing for Writers, Editors and Speakers* (The Women's Press, London, 1981).

Millett, K., *Sexual Politics* (Sphere, London, 1971; Doubleday, New York, 1970).

Mitchell, J., 'The longest revolution', *New Left Review*, 40 (1966).

——, *Psychoanalysis and Feminism* (Penguin, Harmondsworth, 1975).

Morgan, D., 'Men, masculinity and the process of sociological enquiry', in *Doing Feminist Research*, ed. H. Roberts, (Routledge & Kegan Paul, London, 1981).

Morris, L. D., 'Renegotiation of the domestic division of labour in the context of male redundancy', in *New Approaches to Economic Life*, ed. B. Roberts, R. Finnegan, D. Gallie (Manchester University Press, Manchester, 1985).

Morrison, P., 'Our common ground ...', *Anti-Sexist Men's Newsletter*, 10 (1980).

Mort, F., 'Silent about sex', *New Socialist* (July 1985).

Moss, P., 'Parents at work', in *Work and the Family*, ed. P. Moss and N. Fonda (Temple Smith, London, 1980).

Motherson, K. (P), 'Wider we. Towards an anarchist politics', in M. J. Sjoo—K. Motherson, *Women are the real left* (Matri/anarchy, Manchester, 1979).

——, 'Sex and gender', *Greenline* (May 1984).

——, *Cracks in the Shell* (Keith Motherson, Fishguard, n.d.(a)).

——, *Sleep Well, Father Marx* (unpub. ms., Fishguard, n.d.(b)).

NCOPF (National Council for One Parent Families), *One Parent Families 1982* (NCOPF, London, 1982).

newmanifesto, *Men's Antisexist Newsletter*, 22 (1985).

Nichols, J., *Men's Liberation* (Penguin, New York, 1975).

Nixon, J., *Fatherless Families on Family Income Supplement* (DHSS, London, 1979).

Oakley, A., *Sex, Gender and Society* (Temple Smith, London, 1972).

O'Brien, M., 'The dialectics of reproduction', *Women's Studies International Quarterly*, 1 (1978).

——, 'Reproducing Marxist man', in *The Sexism of Social and Political Thought*, ed. L. Clark and L. Lange (University of Toronto Press; Toronto, 1979).

——, *The Politics of Reproduction* (Routledge & Kegan Paul, London/Boston, 1981).

O'Connor, J., *The Fiscal Crisis of the State* (St Martin's, New York,

1974).

Ortner, S., 'Is female to male as nature is to culture?', in *Women, Culture and Society*, ed. M. Z. Rosaldo and L. Lamphere (Stanford University Press, Stanford, 1974).

Pahl, J., and Quine, L., *Families with Mentally Handicapped Children: A Study of Stress and of Service Provision* (Health Services Research Unit, University of Kent, 2nd ed., 1985).

Parke, R., *Fathering* (Fontana, London, 1981).

Parkin, P. W., and Hearn, J., 'Frauen, Männer und Führung', in *Handwörtbuch der Führung*, ed. A. Kieser, G. Reber and R. Wunderer (C. E. Poeschel, Stuttgart, 1987).

Parry, N., and Parry, J., *The Rise of the Medical Profession* (Croom Helm, London, 1976).

——, and ——, 'Social work, professionalism and the state', in *Social Work, Welfare and the State*, ed. N. Parry, M. Rustin and C. Satyamurti (Edward Arnold, London, 1979).

Pearson, C., 'Some problems in talking about men', in *Looking Back*, ed. S. Wise and C. Pearson (Studies in Sexual Politics, University of Manchester, 1984).

'Personal politics', *Revolutionary Socialism*, 9 (1982).

Petchesky, R., 'Dissolving the hyphen: a report on Marxist-feminist groups 1–5', in *Capitalist Patriarchy and the Case for Socialist Feminism*, ed. Z. Eisenstein (Monthly Review Press, New York, 1979).

Phillips, A., 'Sex and class', *Revolutionary Socialism*, 6 (1980–1).

——, and Taylor, B., 'Sex and skill: Notes towards a feminist economics', *Feminist Review*, 6 (1980).

Phillips, J., 'Men and childcare', *National Childcare Campaign Newsletter*, (February/March 1984).

Plato, *The Republic* (Penguin, Harmondsworth, 1955).

Playgroup Pamphlet Group, *Out of the Pumpkin Shell, Running a Women's Liberation Playgroup* (PPG, Birmingham, 1975).

Plaza, M., ' "Phallomorphic power" and the psychology of "women": a patriarchal chain', *Ideology and Consciousness*, IV (1978).

Please Can I Stop Being a Tree Soon? How a group of men looked after 200 children at the 1977 WLM Conference creche (Men's Free Press, London, 1977).

Popplestone, R., 'Top jobs for women: are the cards stacked against them?', *Social Work Today*, 12 (1980).

Radley, A., 'From courtesy to strategy: some old developments in social skills training', *Bulletin of the British Psychological Society*, 38 (1985).

Reader, W. J., *Professional Men: The Rise of the Professional Classes in Nineteenth Century England* (Weidenfeld & Nicholson, London, 1966).

Redstockings Manifesto (1969) quoted in *Sweet Freedom. The Struggle for Women's Liberation*, A. Coote and B. Campbell (Picador, London, 1982).

Reid, G. D., *Childbirth Without Fear* (Heinemann, London, 1934).

Remy, V., 'Brotherhood of terror', *Green Line* 47 (1986).

Renvoize, J., *Going Solo. Single Mothers by Choice* (Routledge & Kegan Paul, London/Boston, 1985).

Reynaud, E., *Holy Virility. The Social Construction of Masculinity* (Pluto, London, 1983). First pub. in French, 1981.

Rich, A., *Of Woman Born: Motherhood as Experience and Institution* (Virago, London, 1977; Norton, New York, 1976).

——, 'Compulsory heterosexuality and lesbian existence', *Signs*, 5 (1980).

Richman, J., 'Men's experiences of pregnancy and childbirth', in *The Father Figure*, ed. L. McKee and M. O'Brien (Tavistock, London, 1982).

Rights of Women, *Lesbian Mothers on Trial. A Report on Lesbian Mothers & Child Custody* (Rights of Women, London, 1984).

Rosenblatt, A., Turner, E. M., Patterson, A. R., and Rollosson, C. K., 'Predominance of male authors in social work publications' *Social Casework*, 51 (1970).

Rowan, J., 'The wound', *Self and Society*, 14 (1986).

Rowbotham, S., *Hidden From History* (Pluto, London, 1973).

——, 'The trouble with patriarchy', *New Statesman*, 98 (1979).

Rubin, G., 'Thinking sex: notes for a radical theory of the politics of sexuality', in *Pleasure and Danger: Exploring Female Sexuality*, ed. C. S. Vance (Routledge & Kegan Paul, London/Boston, 1984).

Russell, G., *The Changing Role of Fathers* (University of Queensland, St Lucia, 1983).

Sacks, K., 'Engels revisited', in *Towards an Anthropology of Women*, ed. R. R. Reiter (Monthly Review Press, New York, 1975).

'Schneller Schlag', *Der Spiegel* (17 February 1986).

Schochet, G. J., *Patriarchalism and Political Thought* (Basil Blackwell, Oxford, 1975).

Scobie, W., '$18m bid for a brothel', *The Observer* (15 September 1985).

Scotch, C. B., 'Sex status in social work—grist for women's lib', *Social Work*, 16 (1971).

Sebestyen, A., 'Sexual assumptions in the Women's Movement', in *On the Problem of Men*, ed. S. Friedman and E. Sarah (The Women's Press, London, 1982).

Segal, L., 'Sensual uncertainty, or why the clitoris is not enough', in

Sex & Love. New Thoughts on Old Contradictions, ed. S. Cartledge and J. Ryan (The Women's Press, London, 1983).

Sève, L., *Man in Marxist Theory and the Psychology of Personality* (Harvester, Hassocks, 1978). First pub. in French, 1974.

Slocum, S., 'Woman the gatherer: male bias in anthropology', in *Towards an Anthropology of Women*, ed. R. R. Reiter (Monthly Review Press, New York, 1975).

Smith, J., 'Top jobs in the social services', in *The Year Book of Social Policy in Britain 1971*, ed. K. Jones (Routledge & Kegan Paul, London, 1972).

Smith, P., 'Domestic labour and Marx's theory of value', in *Feminism and Materialism*, ed. A. Kuhn and A. M. Wolpe, (Routledge & Kegan Paul, London/Boston, 1978).

Snodgrass, J., ed., *A Book of Readings for Men and Against Sexism* (Times Change, Albion, Ca., 1977).

Solanas, V., *SCUM (Society for Cutting Up Men) Manifesto* (Olympia, New York, 1967; London, 1971).

Sørensen, B. A., 'The organizational woman and the Trojan-horse effect', in *Patriarchy in a Welfare Society*, ed. H. Holter (Universitetsforlaget, Oslo, 1984).

Spender, D., *Man Made Language* (Routledge & Kegan Paul, London, 1980).

——, ed., *Men's Studies Modified* (Pergamon, Oxford, 1981).

Stacey, M., 'Masculine or feminine power? Action in the public domain', Paper at International Sociological Association Annual Conference, Mexico. Mimeo, University of Warwick (August 1982).

——, and Davies, C., *Division of Labour in Child Health Care: Final Report to the SSRC* Mimeo. (University of Warwick, Coventry, 1983).

——, 'The application of feminist theory to a study of the retention of male power: the case of researching the General Medical Council', Paper at British Sociological Association Theory Group, Leeds. Mimeo, University of Warwick (September 1986).

——, and Price, M., *Women, Power and Politics* (Tavistock, London, 1981).

Stanley, L., and Wise, S., 'Feminist research, feminist consciousness and experiences of sexism', *Women's Studies International Quarterly*, 2 (1979).

——, and ——, *Breaking Out. Feminist Consciousness and Feminist Research* (Routledge & Kegan Paul, London, 1983).

Stone, L., *The Family, Sex and Marriage in England 1500–1800* (Weidenfeld & Nicholson, London, 1977).

Stout, B., 'From politically gay to publicly bisexual to personally

celibate', *Against Patriarchy*, 1 (1984).
Strange, P., *It'll Make a Man of You ... A feminist view of the arms race* (Mushroom, Nottingham 1983).
Strauss, S., *Traitors to the Masculine Cause: The Men's Campaign for Women's Rights* (Greenwood, Westwood, Conn. 1983).
Tatchell, P., *Democratic Defence. A Non-Nuclear Alternative* (GMP, London, 1985).
Taylor, L., 'The sex picket line', *New Society*, 35 (1976).
Theodore, A., ed., *The Professional Woman* (Schenkman, Cambridge, Mass., 1971).
Timms, N., *Psychiatric Social Work in Great Britain 1939–1962* (Routledge & Kegan Paul, London, 1964).
Tolson, A., *The Limits of Masculinity* (Tavistock, London, 1977).
Tribe, K., *Land, Labour and Economic Discourse* (Routledge & Kegan Paul, London/Boston, 1978).
TUC, *TUC Charter on Facilities for the Under-Fives* (Trades Union Congress, London, 1978).
Turner, B. S., *The Body and Society. Explorations in Social Theory* (Basil Blackwell, Oxford/New York, 1984).
Ungerson, C., *Women and Social Policy. A Reader* (Macmillan, London, 1985).
Versluysen, M., 'Old wives' tales? Women healers in English history', in *Rewriting Nursing History*, ed. C. Davies (Croom Helm, London; Barnes and Noble, Totowa, N.J., 1980).
——, 'Midwives, medical men and "poor women labouring of child": lying-in hospitals in eighteenth century England', in *Women, Health and Reproduction*, ed. H. Roberts (Routledge & Kegan Paul, London, 1981).
Vogel, L., *Marxism and the Oppression of Women. Toward a Unitary Theory* (Pluto, London, 1983).
Wagner, S. R., 'On gentle men', *Changing Men*, 14 (1985).
Walton, R., *Women in Social Work* (Routledge & Kegan Paul, London, 1975).
Weber, M., *Economy and Society. An Outline of Interpretive Sociology. Volume Three* ed. and trans. G. Roth and C. Wittich (Bedminster, New York, 1968).
Weeks, J., *Coming Out: Homosexual Politics in Britain from the Nineteenth Century to the Present* (Quartet, London, 1977).
Weinbaum, B., *The Curious Courtship of Women's Liberation and Socialism* (South End, Boston, 1978).
Weisberg, L., 'Curriculum raising consciousness on campus', *Advertizing Age* (4 October 1984).
Wilensky, H., *The Welfare State and Equality* (University of California, Berkeley, 1975).

Wise, S., and Stanley, L., 'Sexual sexual politics—an editorial introduction', *Women's Studies Internation Forum*, 7 (1984).

Women, Summary Report of the International Women's Conference of the Re-evaluation Counselling Communities held in The Netherlands, 12–17 October 1984 (Rational Island, Seattle, 1985).

Woollett, A., White, D., and Lyon, L., 'Observations of fathers at birth', in *Fathers. Psychological Perspectives*, ed. N. Beail and J. McGuire (Junction, London, 1982).

Zita, J. N., 'Historical amnesia and the lesbian continuum', in *Feminist Theory. A Critique of Ideology*, ed. N. O. Keohane, M. Z. Rosaldo and B. C. Gelpi (Harvester, Brighton; University of Chicago, Chicago, 1982).

Author Index

Aaby, P.   37, 192n
Achilles Heel   28, 168, 172,
    191n, 200–1n
Achilles Heel
    Collective   ix–x, 171
Adams, C.   153
Adams, P.   37, 192n
Adkins, G.   179, 202n
Al-Hibri, A.   50–2
Allen, J. G.   137
Althusser, L.   51
Anderson, P.   93
Anon.   173
Arcana, J.   113
Ardener, S.   145
Armstrong, A. J.   145
Atkinson, P.   41
August, E. R.   178–9, 201n

Balbus, I.   12, 190n
Barker, D. L.   37, 52, 192n
    (*see* Leonard, D.)
Barker, J.   41
Barrett, M.   39–40
Barry, K.   91
Beail, N.   156
Beechey, V.   40
Bell, C.   19, 112, 151, 190n
Beuret, K.   19, 190n
Bevson, J.   82, 196n
Bland, L.   33–4, 141

Bliss, S.   17, 179
Bolin, W. D. W.   126
Borchorst, A.   43
Bouchier, D.   180
Bowen, J.   178
Brackx, A.   28
Bradley, M.   25
Bradshaw, J.   29
Brager, G.   130
Brannon, R.   179, 201n
Brittan, A.   xiii, 188n
Brown, B.   37, 192n
Brown, C.   43, 50
Brunsdon, C.   141
Bullough, B.   142
Burnham, L.   40, 52, 54
Burstyn, V.   94, 108, 110,
    115–16

Campbell, B.   29, 163, 200n
Carling, A.   xiii–xiv, 181–2,
    188–9n
Carpenter, M.   128, 132
Carrigan, T. J.   26–7, 112,
    191n
Castells, M.   51
Chafetz, J. S.   130
Charvet, J.   180
Chesler, P.   123
Chodorow, N.   38, 56, 113
Cixous, H.   90

223

Subject Index